FIRST CHAPTERS IN
RELIGIOUS PHILOSOPHY

BOOKS BY VERGILIUS FERM

THE CRISIS IN AMERICAN LUTHERAN THEOLOGY

WHAT IS LUTHERANISM?

CONTEMPORARY AMERICAN THEOLOGY
In Two Volumes

FIRST ADVENTURES IN PHILOSOPHY

First Chapters

IN

Religious Philosophy

BY

VERGILIUS FERM

Professor of Philosophy in The College of Wooster

ROUND TABLE PRESS, INC.

NEW YORK, 1937

PRINTED IN THE UNITED STATES OF AMERICA
BY SELECT PRINTING COMPANY, NEW YORK

I Dedicate this Volume

to

Four Intimate Companions

Through the Years

MY MOTHER   MY WIFE

JULIUS WILLIAM FERM, D.D.S.

LILLIAN STRANDBERG FERM

CONTENTS

PAGE

Preface _____ ix

PART I.

CHAPTER

WHAT IS RELIGION?

I. Entangled Religious Expressions_____ 3

II. Mistaken Notions _____ 33

III. Definitions _____ 55

PART II.

SOME TYPICAL THEMES IN RELIGIOUS PHILOSOPHY

IV. Traditional Arguments for Belief in
God _____ 75

V. Contemporary Arguments for Belief
in God _____ 94

VI. Current Theories of Value _____ 127

VII. Evil, Theodicy, and Pessimism _____ 145

VIII. The Soul in Ancient and Medieval
Thought _____ 184

IX. Human Freedom and the World of
Reality _____ 207

X. Reconsidering Prayer _____ 247

XI. Human Immortality _____ 255

APPENDIX

A Selected List of Readings _____ 295

Index _____ 307

PREFACE

THIS BOOK falls into two divisions. The first part treats of the nature of religion; the second part is given to a consideration of some typical themes involved in any study of religious philosophy.

In regard to the first part. An interpretative treatment is necessarily implicit in any discussion of a theory of religion. I have openly exposed myself to the risks of criticism in espousing a very definite position with reference to what religion and the religious response are. For a number of years I have been interested in the problem of defining religion, and I have undertaken to acquaint myself with both classic and non-classic statements on the subject. In my files scores upon scores of classified definitions and interpretative statements have been collected, including confessions by eminent writers of their despair of any such undertaking; for some it is an unprofitable and unnecessary undertaking. Not one of these definitions has seemed adequate or defensible and the reasons are stated. It has not seemed necessary nor fit to list such definitions. Only those are presented which seem best to illustrate typical errors in interpretation.

No problem in religious philosophy, it seems to me, is of greater importance than that of defining what religion and the religious attitude are; the implications of any definition and even of no definition are so significant that, paraphrasing a remark of William James on the philosophical problem of ontology, it could be said: Tell me what your notion of religion is and I can predict what you must say on many relevant questions, providing the decorum of logic is observed.

Readers of the first chapter are warned that there is a subtle purpose in it. That purpose very frankly is to turn the mind away from the widespread prejudice that the subject-matter of "religion" is confined to the so-called "great religions of the world." To prepare him for the thesis that the religious mind is found in most unsuspected places and is given to the widest types of expression, it becomes necessary to pick out random examples which furnish the data for the interpretations which follow.

In regard to the second part. It has seemed best to present some of the typical themes of religious philosophy in an expository manner rather than allowing one's own interpretations to intrude and thus prejudice the unwary reader to take sides before he has exposed himself to the major representative views on those questions. Whatever intrusion of myself I have here allowed, has been that involved in compiling and classifying the various types of views and arguments. In any religious philosophy a consideration of certain topics seems indispensable. There is the problem of the existence and character of God discussed in a great historic tradition; there is that same problem restated and reconsidered in contemporary thought; there is the question of what is value, so basic in religion and so vital in contemporary philosophy; there is that perennial problem of evil which casts its ghostly shadow upon every picture depicting the goodness of the universe and, with it, the strong invitation to pessimism; there is that deposit in modern thought from ancient and medieval interpreters of the notion of "soul," a concept which though dead for many contemporary psychologists and philosophers lives on in art, in literature, in music, and in important theological systems, a concept with a history that needs to be retold; there is the knotty problem of human freedom and its setting in the world of Reality, with all of the many implications; there is the question of prayer, the efficacy and value of which this age has serious doubts; and, there is the age-old question of human immortality which is crisp and fresh to every age and about which no philosopher can refuse to give an opinion, if only that of hope.

This book purports in no sense to be a statement of systematic belief. I have not endeavored to present "my philosophy of religion." I have taught a course in this subject for a number of years, and the method of this teaching is laid bare in the manner in which these chapters are put together: first, a survey of the great variety of religious experiences and expressions with an interpretation of their nature; and, secondly, an exposition and classification of some of the major statements of belief upon important religious themes which are found in philosophical literature, leaving the matter of judgment and opinion to the reader who, if he is to be a philosopher, must acknowledge the responsibility of constructing his own religious philosophy.

There will be some satisfaction of having put this material in book form if it helps those students, professional or otherwise, who, in pursuing their reading of contemporary religious discussions and controversies, feel a sense of bewilderment in interpreting and evaluating such discussions. Many such students will probably confess that they find themselves in this confused state of mind very largely because in their formal training or in their general reading they did not get in on the ground floor of the philosophical approach to religion and religious questions. There is a sort of preliminary background presupposed in the reading of much of contemporary religious literature. It is becoming increasingly recognized that the philosophical approach to religion is indispensable; it will be increasingly so in the future. This book, it is hoped, will provide a place for those who feel this gap in their preparation. College and seminary students may feel the propriety of calling it "A First Book" or "Introductory Text" in the philosophy of religion.

VERGILIUS FERM

The College of Wooster
November, 1936

PART I

WHAT IS RELIGION?

CHAPTER I

ENTANGLED RELIGIOUS EXPRESSIONS

The Conflict of Interests and Moods

Man is a creature of a thousand interests and moods
and the creator of a countless variety of performances
which give expression to them. His individual life-
history is a crazy-quilt of cross-currents, and the story
of the human adventure collectively is that of a long
conflict of cross-purposes. Certainly, in many respects
modern man appears to be far removed from his dimly
known human ancestors of the forest primeval; and yet,
the differences are quite largely surface appearances;
underneath lie fundamental kinships. We may choose
to say who shall be our friends, but nature has written
indelibly in the blood who are our relatives. Elements
which go to make up the drama of life are still much
the same as ever; human nature has changed little (if
any). There continues the struggle to get on with oneself, to take care of the thousand interests and moods
which compete for supremacy only to find the competi-
tion thwarted by other potent interests and moods;
there continues the struggle to get on with a world in
which events are far from gentle and smooth; cross-
currents within and cross-currents without.

Time and space and what is vaguely known as "culture" separate modern man from his ancestors and contemporaries, but the same moods, fundamental interests,
and the variety of their expressions hold sway. Man
must eat and sleep; he must find shelter and protection
from wind and rain and cold; he must have air and sunlight; he must exercise and rest; he will seek out companions and shun them; the laughter, the tears, the

3

crushed hopes, the pains and woes, remain all unchanged; there are children to come after, and there are sacrifices to be made; apprehensions of unfavorable circumstances of wind and weather necessitate laying by stores, be they meat, fruit, or vegetables in the cave or life insurance papers in the bank's vault. There is a time for joyful music and a time for wailing; the ghost of death still stalks about and cannot be conquered; there is work and there is play; there is quiet meditation and there is boisterous activity; there are regrets over mistakes and there is stoical apathy. Imaginations still make of men heroes or fools; there are periods of elevation and those of depression; a time for cautious reflection and a time for fearless action; there is fear and there is courage. The world holds out both reality and illusion.

The Dominant Interest

Now all such rhythmic alterations do not come isolated; they come in complexes. Not all is work, and not all is play; not all is unmitigated sorrow, and not all unadulterated joy. Whatever be the interest at the moment that interest though paramount is fed by countless tributaries. Physical needs are always basic, and no extra-physical interest is without that touchstone, however pure we may take art or scientific interest to be. Whatever a man thinks or does there are a host of accompanying influences which surround his thinking and activity. The old faculty psychology with its separate faculties is a theoretical anachronism; the man about whom it spoke is an academic artificiality.

We should call an activity or an interest by its *dominant* or focal emphasis. If a man is engaged in social activity we think of him in company with others, physically present or present in thought. By that we do not mean that he is completely lost in others; we mean only

4

that what he is doing is *dominated* by an interest in and
for others. If a man is engaged in play we think of him
as sporting about dealing in the fanciful, employing
symbols of the real, circumscribing his activity with defined ends; we do not mean that such activity is without labor or without social significance; we mean only
that the activity is *dominated* by a given interest at the
moment. If a man is at work he need not necessarily
not be at play. If one is alone in meditation he is not
necessarily in solitary confinement. If he is eating he
is not necessarily without meditation or without hilarity.
One may laugh amid tears. One may worry and not be
afraid. One may, with the clown, laugh and be sorrow-
ful. No activity represents a single mood. An activity
is characterized by the dominant mood.

The Religious Expression: Not Purely Religious

In what is called religious activity there is, again,
no isolated interest or mood. When Billy Sunday
preached, the religious element was mixed with a great
deal of bizarre entertainment—bizarre to some. In
the temple of the Maid of Angelus there is enacted a
drama of whatever degree of art mixed with the
religious appeal. Some revivalistic programs stand as
classic rivals of the showmanship of Barnum. Sermons
can lay no claim to the purely religious; they may be
alleged works of literary art and admired or condemned
as such, ethical discourses or intellectual acrobatics.
Are those people who drive long distances to attend the
summer services conducted by Professor William Lyon
Phelps of Yale motivated only or wholly by a religious
mood, or is there a strong desire to be entertained by
the literary charm of his popular discourses? Is the
typical service merely an expression of the religious
mood? Are Deacon Jones's ecclesiastical errands motivated solely by a devoutly religious experience or is

there the lurking *motif* of self-display? Does the church treasurer take over the responsibility of paying the preacher's salary because of a predominantly religious interest or is there the unhallowed feeling of self-aggrandizement and power in signing the name to the monthly checks? Does the savage dance his religious dance merely for the sake of expressing an enthusiastic religious mood or is there here a bursting expression of physiological, chemical, and glandular factors initiating and motivating the song in his heart? What is a church without its "sociable," or a ladies aid society without its tea or coffee, or a ministerial meeting without its cigars or funny stories, or a church convention without the meeting of the members of the class of '98? Is the sacred solo an expression of religious feeling or an indication of how far one has come in musical art, or both?

All of which amounts to suggesting that religious activity no more than play activity does not come unmixed. The religious response does not appear naked; to single it out as wholly separate from other moods and interests is to misunderstand it. It comes mixed with a thousand different contexts; with some the mixture is of one brand, with others it is of another—depending, in turn, upon fundamental characteristics of human nature, biological, psychological, and social.

Misinterpretations of the Religious Expression

When some interpreters tell us what is meant by religious activity or the religious mood they see it only in association with one or certain other interests. They tell us it is a form of social activity, a flowering of the sex impulses, a corollary of food-getting, or whatever the physical or social value or need; or that it is the way of loneliness, or the expression of fear, of the woes of pain and of crushed hopes, a fantasy image, or a degenerate form of magic (where magic no longer works to control a given situation); and so on. Such interpreters are both right and wrong. They are wrong for the fact of the matter is that the religious mood and activity is or may be associated with any group of interests and moods; they are right for the truth is that a certain interest or mood may be *dominant* at a given time and circumstance thereby giving a certain emphasis to that activity and mood. Those who study one phase of religious phenomena are tempted to mistake the part for the whole; there is evidence of such a fallacy, for example, among those who have studied the characteristic activities of the primitive group. The student of anthropology and the student of mysticism may claim their own interested approach to reveal the one and only characteristic expression of religious phenomena. Specialists are always thrown open to the temptation of committing the fallacy of exclusive particularity; they fail to note "the varieties of religious experience."

Case Studies Revealing the Unreality of the Naked Religious Expression

The thesis is being defended here, *viz.*, that there is no naked religious interest but that such an interest like all interests is always clothed with and in a setting of others. That no man is purely religious nor a religion wholly religious may be seen by the following concrete expressions taken at random from a variety of sources.

St. Patrick's Purgatory

Consider, first, the beliefs and practices surrounding what is known as "St. Patrick's Purgatory." It is of no immediate concern to attempt to distinguish facts from legends concerning this patron saint of Ireland.

(*Ca.* 389-461.) The record of St. Patrick's fame says that he was a pious man, a follower of Jesus Christ, one who was greatly moved to perform missionary service. Desirous of convincing unbelievers (tradition has it) he prayed for a visible sign by which he could make others see the reality which he saw. The prayer was answered in a number of ways; one such answer directed him to a lonely spot on an island in Lough Derg in the southern part of Donegal County. The voice of Christ spoke to him the promise that anyone who would enter into a certain cave and remain steadfast in his faith a day and a night would behold marvels and would be spared further purgatories. An abbey was built at the spot and an iron door placed at the mouth of the cave; the key to that door was given to the prior. The fame of this shrine spread throughout Europe.

St. Patrick, according to tradition, kept a record of the experiences of those who entered that cave; some never returned and some came back only to relate unspeakable joys and torments. Ceremonies arose about the cave: permission must be granted for the pilgrimage; the perils of the undertaking were laid bare; if the penitent still insisted upon going in, he was given a letter of introduction to the prior of the abbey who repeatedly warned him. Fifteen days of fasting and praying were then ordered after which holy communion was celebrated, holy water was sprinkled, and mass said; a procession was formed and the penitent led to the entrance of purgatory. A final attempt to dissuade the individual from entering was made; if he still persisted a benediction was pronounced and the sign of the cross given; the door was opened and the penitent locked within. The following morning, if the penitent was still there and alive, he was led out amidst rejoicing; after fifteen days of further prayers the penitent was finally dismissed with the promise of special benediction envisaged to St. Patrick. If, however, he did

not survive the ordeal the door was again locked and
no further mention of his name was made.

The classic legend of Sir Owayne Miles's visit to the
place is preserved in a poem by that name. A literature
sprang up about St. Patrick's cave in Italy, Spain, and
France. In 1497, Pope Alexander VI ordered the destruction of the shrine. During Queen Elizabeth's reign,
Irish lord justices ordered the complete destruction of
the cave, prohibiting the continuance of a convent on
the island. Today, the Irish still pay pilgrimages to
Lough Derg.

Here we have a kind of human behavior which reveals a number of interests and moods. The dominant
one may well be the religious. One may say that for
some, very likely the motivating impulse is the religious; the pilgrimage then is a religious act; the beliefs
in a place of purification, the ideas of self surrender and
endurance, and the promise of peace of heart are religious; the shrine itself is a religious edifice, the cave a
religious object, the ceremonies, religious institutions,
the priests, the prayers, the rituals, religious performances. And yet, these behaviors and ideas, the whole
scene and drama itself, are not wholly religious. The
priest guarding the cave may not be without secular
guile; possibly, there is in the key to the door the
symbol of man's lust for power over others (writ large
in the history of religious institutionalism); possibly,
there is in the rigorous ceremonies the same symbol of
dominion over self and others; possibly, there is in the
earnest quest on the part of the penitent a mood of
humiliation—without any religious significance—over
some grievous misdeed for which conscience alone cannot atone; possibly, there is not lacking a spirit of adventure, of curiosity, the spirit of heroism; there is,
perhaps, the hope that somehow a hero will be born
and generous acclaim given; possibly, there is that old
human love for the mysterious; there even may be the

desire of committing suicide in an approved way, if the pilgrim be tired of life.

The historian will tell us that the *motif* of the whole legend and drama can be traced through a social institution long forgotten but practiced by reason of habit rather than by reason of reason. It is highly probable that the beliefs surrounding St. Patrick's Lough Derg were relics of a pre-Christian legend and practice. The practice of going to mountains and caves to do penance was performed by Chinese and Japanese Buddhists. D. A. Mackenzie argues that the practices performed at St. Patrick's shrine date back to Buddhist teachers and pilgrims who, searching for a Western Paradise, carried with them ancient modes of behavior which later were incorporated into a supposedly Christian custom.[1] In other words, the religious custom is not wholly religious; it is shot through with traditional, social, and cultural practices. In making the pilgrimage one is not motivated *merely* by a religious mood; one is doing the thing that has been done by generations; one is unconsciously imitating the past; the imitation itself may be quite far removed from any religious significance.

The Kentucky Revival

About 1800 occurred what is called the Kentucky Revival. This widely known event is classified as religious. That the revival was not wholly a religious phenomenon has been pointed out sufficiently by the hounding psychologists. A great deal of it consisted in sport and physical exercise. When men rolled about the ground with head and feet together, through mud and over rocks, they may have suffered some pain and the cost of a tailored suit, but there was not lacking the call of the primitive and the thrill of being children once

---

[1] See his *Buddhism in Pre-Christian Britain* (1928).

again. When men and women barked like dogs in a supposedly religious frenzy there is something quite akin to the phenomenon of a college professor who shouts like mad on a volley-ball floor. The jerks and twists which are the outward signs of an inward apprehension are not without the pleasing effect which accompanies all rhythmic motion. There is even subtle satisfaction in becoming fatigued. The scars one has won by such disporting are symbols of heroism.

No one can live on the level of the socially conventional at all times; a religion which allows conventions to be blown to the winds on occasion is not without psychological and physical appeal. When one "got religion" in such a revival one got not only religion but exercise, fun, play; one was in others company, one won social approval, one worked up an appetite (of one kind or another). The Kentucky Revival is only another instance of the strange mixtures of interests where the religious is supposed somehow to have been dominant. It is another case of religious entanglements.[2]

A Sinner's Religious Apology

F. M. Davenport vouches for the truth of the following incident. In a little Tennessee town a collection was being taken in behalf of the colored minister. A brother in the church volunteered to make the rounds to gather groceries, clothing, and whatever else goes into such a ministerial surprise. With a borrowed cart and a pair of steers loaned for the purpose by an old colored lady he skipped to Chattanooga and sold the entire donation including the cart and the steers; he then went on a lark. When, some time later, the rascal turned up in town it was determined that there should

---

[2] See *The Kentucky Revival: or A Short History of the Late Extraordinary Outpouring of the Spirit of God in Western States of America* (reprint, 1846), R. M'Nemar.

be a church trial before there was any legal action. The trial opened with a large crowd of indignant townsfolk. The defendant sat on the platform with the preacher; asked to state what he had to say for himself, the following is the testimony:

> "I ain't got nuffin to say fo' myself," he began in a penitent voice, "I'se a po' mis'able sinner. But, bredren, so is we all mis'able sinners. An' de good book says we must fergib. How many times, bredren? Till seven times? No, till seventy times seven. An' I ain't sinned no seventy times seven, and I'm jes' go' to sugges' dat we turn dis into a fergibness meetin', an' eberybody in dis great comp'ny dat is willin' to fergib me, come up now, while we sing one of our deah ole hymns, and shake ma hand." And he started one of the powerful revival tunes, and they began to come, first those who hadn't given anything to the donation and were not much interested in the matter anyway, then those who hadn't lost much, and then the others. Finally they had all passed before him except one, and she stuck to her seat. And he said, "Dar's one po' mis'able sinner still lef', dat won't fergib, she won't fergib." (She was the old lady who lost the steers.) "Now I sugges' that we hab a season ob prayer, an' gib dis po' ole sinner one mo' chance." And after they had prayed and sung a hymn, the old lady came up, too! [3]

The recorder of this incident sets this down as an example of hypnotism with no "spiritual" element; he interprets it as a case of naked suggestion. No doubt, the incident furnishes a fine illustration of the power of suggestion for the psychologist, but this is not to say that there is in it no religious element. The fact may well be that the religious *motif* is there, but it may be, quite obviously, less dominant in its unhallowed setting. The meeting is a religious one, the concepts are religious, and so are the ways of behavior. But, the sublime is mixed with the ridiculous (there is ofttimes but a shade between them), the serious with the humorous,

---

[3] *Primitive Traits in Religious Revivals* (Macmillan, 1910), p. 51ff.

the awkward with the clever, the humble with the ego-
tistical, and so on.

The Toda-Dairy Priests

Some years ago Dr. W. H. R. Rivers investigated a
strange people who had retired from the rest of the
world and set up a community in the Nilgiri hills in
southern India, numbering some less than a thousand.
The religion of these Todas revolves about their interest in the supplies for physical sustenance. Their staple
diet consists of butter and buttermilk. The milk supply
comes from the buffalos. A certain number of these
are held to be sacred and their milk must not be drunk;
the Todas themselves know not why this is so. It is
a part of a tradition where the wherefores are forgotten.
If the milk of the sacred animal is partaken of without
certain formalities one will suffer certain penalties.

The church and the priests have as their function to
make safe the preparation of buffalo milk. The church
is a dairy and the ministers are dairymen. There are
two compartments in the dairy, the one sacred and the
other secular. In the first compartment there are preserved special vessels into which the milk is poured and
in which it is turned to butter and buttermilk. In the
second there are special containers which receive the
butter and the buttermilk taken from the first compartment; midway between the two compartments are intermediary containers into which the food supply is to be
poured and from these into the non-sacred containers.
A ritual accompanies the transfer. Thus, by the help of
priests and ceremony the sacred is made available to the
profane and the taboos overcome.

The priest dairyman is consecrated to his task; he
must remain celibate; he must not come into contact
with the dead; his own diet is of a certain kind and must
be attended to with certain rituals of precaution; he

remains inaccessible to ordinary people except on certain occasions; he wears a garb of a certain kind; he never cuts his hair; his nails must not be manicured. The investigator reports that he found the dairymen priests performing their work without really knowing why they were doing it; they performed perfunctorily and slovenly. He found that the profession was not a desirable one since the regulations were so strict. Many of the priests were young men and not always so careful about the taboos. Ways of circumventing rules were practiced; a kind of technique for pretense and deceit was set up so that the life of the priest would be less severe.

Here the mixture of the religious and other interests is too evident to mention. Here are traditional practices quite without significant meaning; concern over the food supply; the element of magic is there; there is emotional excitement. The names of certain deities are mentioned, but appear to perform no real function in the present practices. The chief interest is the dinner and the customary way in which it is to be prepared. The thing is done on the level of the habitual.[4]

The Cult of Magna Mater

Take the case of the religious practices of the so-called mystery cults which flourished in the Graeco-Roman world. Here we have a curious combination of religious interests mixed with others. As an example consider the cult of the *Magna Mater*. This cult dates back beyond the sixth century B.C., and had its home in central Asia Minor. The cult centered about giving homage to a feminine deity and her lover, Attis. Both of these gods were conceived to typify natural phenomena: the winds, the sea, the earth; the Magna Mater especially typified the wilder aspects of nature while the hero-lover

---

[4] *The Todas* (1906), W. H. R. Rivers.

symbolized vegetation and the seasons. Even as the seasons come and go so Attis is born and reborn. There is a time for wailing and a time for rejoicing.

The cult celebrated an annual festivity on the Ides of March. A tree was brought in from the woods and ceremoniously placed in the temple. The tree is the symbol of vegetation. The god Attis had died under a pine tree, according to the legend. A funeral service was held, followed by a day of fasting. Vegetables were forbidden and, likewise, fruit. Meat, however, was eaten. The fast probably began the fifteenth of March and was climaxed about the twenty-fourth with the "day of blood." The great Mother was supposed then to inspire her devotees to endure the sorrows in mourning for the dead Attis. The ritual was that of frenzied dancing, the clashing of cymbals, the lacerating of the flesh, the whirling of the bodies, howling, sprinkling of blood from self inflicted wounds upon the sacred tree; the flow of blood was the sign that there was a genuine participation in the sorrow of the Mother. Those who would excel, who would really prove that they had entered upon the spirit of the occasion, performed revolting operations upon themselves, ran naked and wild in the city streets. Men, who had thus lacerated themselves, were considered fit to become priests, the consecrated bridegrooms of the great Mother. No longer men among men, they wore feminine garbs and their hair long. They were now themselves on their way to become gods.

The next day the suffering is turned to joy. The resurrection of Attis is celebrated. Salvation of men became the theme. On the twenty-fifth of March the celebration of frenzied jubilation began, a day called *Hilaria*, in which there was to be no mourning. There was no limit to pleasures; it was a day when morality was on a vacation. Then followed a day of rest. The grand finale came with the ritual of washing the goddess in the Almo; post-nuptial purification ceremonies were enacted; her statue was conducted with great solemnity to the river; and then the springtime was ushered in with flowers and all that goes with spring festivals.

Many more and complicated customs grew up around the great Mother, *e.g.*, the sacrifice of a bull in both public and private ceremonies in which priests literally bathed themselves in blood, marriage ceremonies of men with the goddess, the eating of sacred food, a communion service in which somehow the god was eaten, etc.[5]

Here we have the religious interest mixed with the sensuous, the occult, the satisfactions which attend a frenzied emotionalism; a mixture of fears, hopes, joys, pains, ecstasies, social and physical indulgences, drinking, eating, sleeping, dancing, release from strains of life, expressions of primitive impulses—what, indeed, is lacking?

The Peyote Cult

A certain John Rave is credited with having introduced the practice of eating an herb called peyote among the Winnebago Indians. Let us follow this story as it culminates in a striking religious practice. Rave was himself an Indian, a member of the Bear clan, who had participated in the customs of the Winnebago. He had a bad reputation; a roamer and a good-for-nothing. He had married many times. He had been a heavy drinker. He had joined a cheap circus. In one of his wanderings he came across a group which had the peculiar custom of eating a certain medicinal herb, and he joined in a quiet celebration by eating it, too. This was in Oklahoma and it was remembered by him as the turning point in

---

[5] *Pagan Regeneration* (1929), H. R. Willoughby. Chap. V. On the religious practice of eating the god in a communal meal see *A Short History of Christian Theophagy* (1922), Preserved Smith.

his life. Whereas before he had been a murderer, a good-for-nothing, as he himself admitted, he became a new man. The medicine had worked wonders.

It was in the middle of the night, he relates, with a group of Oklahoma Indians that he began to eat the stuff. Immediately, strangely overwhelming experiences possessed him. He tried to vomit and could not. Everything went round and round. Something was moving in his stomach. He thought he had committed suicide. It was a terrible night. The following night he was persuaded again to eat and he ate seven peyote. This eating produced visions. He saw snakes. He jumped to dodge them. He saw men with horns and long claws reaching for him; they seemed to be throwing spears. Then it occurred to him that the peyote was doing this to him. He cried out to the medicine man for help. According to his own story, help came; his suffering ceased. Again, he ate more peyote. Again he had visions. And in the middle of the night there came to him a vision of God. He prayed aloud for help. He addressed the medicine man as a holy one who had come to save him. He saw visions of the good, and the beautiful. He felt good. The feeling of holiness crept upon him. He felt himself becoming dedicated to a missionary enterprise. His wife appeared to him in a vision and there was a serenity about the experience he had never before known. He surrendered his life to God. Never before, he said, had he realized the holy; now he had; and he must go and tell it to his tribe, the Winnebago.

The peyote is described as a medicine plant acting powerfully as a stimulant when enough of it is eaten; the nervous system is brought to a high state of tension; the pupils of the eyes become dilated; the eyes become glazed in appearance; the limbs become rigid; it produces first a choking sensation and sometimes prolongs sleep; visions are frequent. Visions may be of various

17

kinds, as *e.g.*, seeing snakes, lions, flags, hideous looking men, eagles, and what not. Its effects produce new insights, changes, conversion. What it did for the Oklahoma tribe and for Rave it did for the Winnebago; once introduced, it was made a part of their religious practices. Tobacco, we are told, was a sacred weed to the Winnebago—smoking is stimulating; it had an elevated place as a religious object. And now, another weed, the peyote, was made sacred and became the center of a religious cult among that tribe.

"It is now twenty-three years since I first ate peyote," Rave testifies, "and I am still doing it (1912). Before that my heart was filled with murderous thoughts. I wanted to kill my brother and my sister. It seemed to me that my heart would not feel good until I killed one of them. All my thoughts were fixed on the warpath. This is all I thought of. Now I know that it was because the evil spirit possessed me that I felt that way. I was suffering from a disease. I even desired to kill myself; I did not care to live. That feeling, too, was caused by this evil spirit living within me. Then I ate this medicine and everything changed. The brother and sister I wanted to kill before I became attached to and I wanted them to live. The medicine had accomplished this." [6]

Here, again, the religious interest and expression are all mixed up with other interests and expressions. The influence of drugs and stimulants of one kind or another upon an individual, producing strange and striking visions, reveals the interrelation of the physiological

---

[6] *37th Annual Report of the American Bureau of Ethnology*, pp. 393-394 and quoted in *An Approach to the Psychology of Religion* (Harcourt, Brace, 1927), J. C. Flower, Chap. IV. The psychological analysis of Rave's experiences as given in this book will furnish rewarding reading. It fits beautifully in with that author's highly workable and significant thesis that a "religious experience" of the first-hand type consists always of an apprehension of something strange and mysterious with which existing mechanisms of adjustment are not adequate to cope.

with the psychological, thus complicating the material that is involved in the religious frame of mind. The extreme mystics with their practices of self-intoxication are examples in one form or another of the same type of entanglement. The religious mood may well be induced by narcotics, by a general feeling tone or by some form of ecstasy. If normal human living cannot furnish it for some people stimulants may set it going. And once going, all sorts of moods, reactions, practices, and interpretations follow, depending upon time and place and circumstance. The religious interest is not of itself.

A Pioneer Baptist Preacher

The following excerpts taken from the autobiography of an early American Baptist preacher may be useful to underline the theme with which we are concerned. Professor W. W. Sweet says of the author of this autobiography that he may be taken as a "representative of the average frontier Baptist preacher." Jacob Bower who was born in 1786 in Pennsylvania writes thus about himself:

> My parents belonged to the denomination of christians called Tunkers, as early as I can recollect, my Father kept up regular morning and eavning worship in the family . . . We were instructed in such lessons as we were able to understand, such as this. Be good children, all good children when they die will go to a good place, wher Jesus is, and many pretty Angels, and they would be happy forever. Bad children when they die will go to a bad place, where there is a great fire, and the Devil and his Angels tormenting the wicked forever. These instructions were ingraven on my mind . . . and were a means of continual restraint from being wicked. In January after I was six years old, the Lord took my good Mother home to Heaven, and I wished very much to go withe her to the good place she had gon to. I was yet unconcious of sin in myself, and my anxiety to die and go to the good place wher Mother was, greatly increased.

Sometime in July following, my Father brought home a step Mother, and it was not long before my anxiety to die increased more & more. Often I would steal out and sit down by myself and weep with anxiety to die and go to the place where Mother was. Thus it continued with me till one morning in the month of May after I was seven years old. About the breake of day, my Father, as his custom had been, was offering up his mornin thanksgiving to God. And while he was praying, I desired that I mite die and be wher Mother was. But suddenly a thought came into my mind, that if I died I could not go to the good place, and I would never see Mother again, for she was good and had gon the good place, But I was bad, and if I died I must go to the bad place, and be tormented forever as Father had been telling me! This thought made me weep aloud as though I had been shiped; when Father ended his prayer, he asked, "What ailes you?" I said, I dont know. From that time I date my first awakening. I mention this because of some who are sceptical in relation to a child so young becoming concious of sin & punishment. Oh the great responsibility which rests upon parents with respect to the early education & training of their children. This kind of teaching . . . made a lasting impression, and had a powerful influence on my conduct in future life, so that . . . I was quite a moral youth. I was kept from immoral practices. I lived a farasee, trusting in my good name, and innocence, till I was in my nineteenth year.

. . . I distinctly recollect a scene which transpired one afternoon at a baptizing, after the preacher came out of the water he gave a most thrilling exortation—I was situated on the oposite bank of the stream with some other youths, but even I was aware I found myself overwhelmed in a flood of tears, and I could not help it . . . When the congregation was dismissed, I wrung the tears out of my handkerchif.

. . . My Father had . . . emigrated to Shelby county K-y . . . About the first of October. 1811. I and my wife paid them a visit.

. . . But when the time arived that we must lieve for hom, I felt unusually solemn. My Father accompanied us about four miles to a large creek, and now the time came that we must take the parting hand. I put on as chearful a countiance as posible, and said, Well Father,

come let us take a parting *dram*, perhaps it may be the
last we shall ever drink together. I dont want to drink
a drop, said he, I have somthing to say to you, Jacob, Well
Father, said I, what is it? "I want you to promise me,'
said he, 'that you will serve God & keep out of bad company." Well Father I will, said I, Farewell, Farewell.
I started to go accross the creek, which was about thirty
yards accross, and as my horse steped out of the water to
rise the bank, instantly my promise staired me in the face.
Although he had given me the same council, and in the
same words, perhaps an hundred times before, Yet it never
produced such an impression on my mind as now. To
serve God and keep out of bad company wrung in my ears
all day long, I had promised my Father, and God heard
it, that I would do it, but alas how can I, and he expects
that I will do it. I began to feal in a way quite different
from what I had ever done before . . .

By the direction of my Father we stoped with a verry
pious, good old Baptist . . . put up with him for the night,
I was restless—walking about—eat no super, often the
deep sigh—my face in my hands &tc . . . The good old
man soon discovered what the matter was with me. Began
most earnestly to exhort, and direct me to trust in the
saviour. At the same time quoting many passages of scrip-
ture for my encouragement . . . I slept but little all night.

Early the next morning before it was quite light, we
were on the road . . . Soon we met large companies of
Negro-s . . . at length we met an old man walking by
himself, I stoped him, and enquired of him, where they
were all going so early this morning. The old negro said,
"we are all going to Beards Town to see a fellow servent
hung to day for killing his fellow servent." I started on
with this thought, how does that man feal, knowing that
he must die to day. Suddenly, as if some one had asked
me. And how do you feal? You dont know but that
you may die before he does. All of a sudden, (ah I shall
never forget it) as if a book had been opened to me, the
inside of which I had never seen: I got a sight of the
wretchedness of my heart—a cage of every unclean and
hateful thing. (ah thought I. here lies the root of bitterness, the fountain from whence all my sinful actions have
flowed. My mind & heart have always been enmity
against God, who is so holy that he cannot allow of no
sin . . . How can I ever be admitted into Heaven with such

a heart? it is uterly imposible. Lost, lost forever lost
. . . I could see no way of escaping eternal punishment.

This day passed . . . four days brought us to my own
house . . . My sister . . . met us at the gate and said,
"why, Jacob, you look verry pale, have you been sick
since you left home? . . .

. . . But the ever memerable morning of the 17th day
of December 1811. About 2 oclock A.M. when most
people were in their beds sound asleep. There was an
Earthquake, verry violent indeed. I and my wife both
awoke about the same time, she spoke first, and said, Lord
have mercy upon us, what is it shaking the house so?
From a discription given of an Earthquake in Germany
by a Tunkard preacher in a sermon when I was about ten
years old, I immediately recognized it, and replied, it is
an Earthquake. The Lord have mercy upon us, we shall
all be sunk & lost, and I am not prepared. O God have
mercy upon us all. I expected immediate distruction, had
no hope of seeing the dawn of another day. Eternity, oh
Eternity was just at hand, and all of us unprepared . . .
Many families ran together and grasped each other in
their arms. One instance near to where I lived, the woman
& five children, all gathered around her husband, crying
O my husband pray for me, The children crying, Father,
pray for me, O. pray for me, for the day of Judgment
is come, and we are unprepared! The people relinquished
all kinds of labour for a time, except feeding stock, and
eat only enough to support nature a fiew days. Visiting
from house to house, going to meeting Singing—praying,
exoting, and once in a while ketch a sermon from a
travelling Minister. Men, Women and children, everywhere were heard enquiering what they must do to be
saved. This shaking continued more or less for near two
years, sometimes just percievable . . . But now it appeared
to me, that surely no one was as great a sinner as I, none
had such a wicked heart, and such vile thoughts . . . I
became resolved to press forward, I would pray & serve
God though he send me to hell, yet I will lye at his feet
and beg for mercy as long as I am out of hell. Sin now
appeared exceeding sinful to me, I strove to shun it all.
Holiness appeared & of all things the most desierable but I
could not attain to it. I often tryed to pray in the woods,
but I felt not better, I could find no relief for my
troubled conscience.

... My toung never can till, nor my pen discribe, the strugglings & anxities I passed through about this time.

All nature appeared to be dressed in mourning, and the god of nature frowning, oh what a time of melencholy.

Well, on the afternoon of the 8th day of February 1812 ... I said to my wife ... suppose we go to your Fathers and spend the night ... and we went; ... almost the first news we heard was. "Your cousin Billy has professed to get religion and is as happy a man as I have ever seen." Joy filled my heart for only a moment, and dispair seized upon my mind. Ah, thought I; God has mercy in story for everybody, and everybody can be saved but me ... Gods mercy toards me is clean gon forever ... Before the sun rises again I shall be dead and in hell. I ran away behind the barn and tried to pray ... The more I tryed to pray, the less hope I had of being saved. Just about midnight, I was sittin a chair ... Suddenly my thoughts turned to the sufferings of Christ, and what he endured on the cross ... The next thought that passed through my mind was. If it was done for sinners, it was done for me. I believed it. The storm calmed off, my troubled My troubled soul was easy. I felt as light as a fether, and all was quiet—pieceful—tranquil and serene. This transpired about midnight, and I had not slept for several nights previous, for fear that if I went to sleep, I would awake in hell. I thought of lying down. I first walked out of doors, and everything I could see, appeared intierly new. The trees (I thought) lifted their hands up toards Heaven as if they were praising God. I ... beheld the bright twinkling stars shining to their makers praise ... Glory to God. Thank God. Bless the Lord O my soul. ...[7]

And so the story goes on and on. A better illustration of the relation of the religious frame of mind with the emotion of fear could hardly be had.

Fear has everywhere played a dominant rôle in the history of religious feeling. And with fear is hidden a set of beliefs or practices which motivate it. A theology or mythology of a God filled with consuming

---

[7] *Religion on the Frontier: The Baptists 1783-1830* (Holt, 1931), W. W. Sweet. Chap. VII.

wrath and threatening endless punishment to those who stand outside his favor is abundantly illustrated in religious autobiography. The feeling that one is outside this favor, that one is lost, is a tremendous provocative of religious feeling. The incubations of such a doctrine and practice dating almost from the earliest of childhood impressions are something that can hardly be overcome, unless, indeed, a powerful counter-conversion sets in. It is a case of doctrine and practice set up as a norm and a violent effort to translate that doctrine and practice into an individual's own experience.

New England Puritanism

The case of Bower is typical of what was held to be a normative Christian experience among grown-ups and children in Puritan New England. The whip of an alleged sanctified code of conduct and of theology was waved over the heads of those under the authority of well-intentioned religious leaders.

One whole day and a part of another were given each week to religious meditation and instruction. The Sabbath day began three o'clock Saturday afternoon when catechization began. Any infringement of the rules of Sabbath observance was punished by a fine or by whipping. One infractor is recorded to have been given the choice of a whipping or a fine of ten shillings for carrying a grist from the mill on the Lord's Day. A youth's conscience became troubled because it was recalled that on the Sabbath day some whittling had been done behind a door. A public trial took place to pass sentence upon a certain culprit who had absented himself from public worship; in spite of his plea that he had fallen into the water on the previous day and that his one "go-to-meeting suit" was too wet to wear to church he was whipped. Two lovers who sat under an apple tree in an orchard on a Sunday afternoon were brought before an ecclesiastical court for having profaned the Lord's day.[8] A child who asked what heaven is like is told that it is an eternal Sabbath; to which the child asks what she had done to merit going to such an awful place.[9]

Misbehavior at church was common, especially among boys; and it was no light offense. One is not permitted to engage in "larfing" nor even in smiling nor playing with the hands. No one is too little to go to hell for however minor the infraction. Children are children of wrath. Whitefield likened children to rattlesnakes and alligators; Edwards called them vipers.[10] To be small is not to be beautiful. The young are agents for hell, ripe for damnation; even little snakes are poisonous. Children are directed to see that hell is yawning at them unless they become converted; it is a state a thousand times worse than a whipping; and hell is a place where there is an everlasting burning. The child who goes to bed without praying has the devil for a bed partner.[11] Children hear sermons directed to adults but which apply to them. "You have often seen a spider or some other noisome insect when thrown into the midst of a fierce fire, and have observed how immediately it yields to the force of the flames. There is no long struggle, no fighting against the fire, no strength exerted to oppose the heat or to fly from it. Here is a little image of what you will be in hell, except you repent and fly to Christ." This is the famous Jonathan Edwards preaching.[12]

Mere youngsters were directed to confirm in religious feeling the theology and ethics held to be normative for all Christians. They held their own prayer

---

[8] See *Children and Puritanism* (1933), S. Fleming. Chap. II.
[9] *Ibid.*, p. 63.
[10] *Ibid.*, p. 69.
[11] *Ibid.*, p. 90.
[12] *Works*, Vol. VI, p. 103.

and testimony meetings; they even reproved their elders for sin. A girl fifteen years old thus warned her father that she could see the devil in his face and that he was plunging headlong into hell, that all the prayers he ever made in the home were but abominations in the sight of the Lord; and that her mother was no better off.[13]

Religious Humanism

In contrast to such fearful expressions, the following expression may be set down. Here we find the critical mind blatantly opposing traditional heritages and at the same time maintaining the religious frame of mind. The Rev. Mr. Earl F. Cook relates how, after tramping all day with three companions, he spent the night in Glacier National Park. He set down in his diary the record of what is taken to be a first-hand "religious experience":

> There was no sound except the crackling of the fire and the occasional slow movements of one of us putting another hunk of wood on the embers. The sparks went scurrying upward in the canyon of trees. The forest was silent; now and then a slight wind coming down from the valley from the glaciers above us audibly caressed the tops of the trees. There was a tremendous loneliness. The woods crowded upon us and the trees seemed to protest our presence as "they invisibly sucked life from the dead forests beneath them." Inky blackness was beyond the trees at the stream's edge. The fire made dancing and fantastic shadows in its circle of light. The forest was a weird, ominous, and terrible thing of beauty that night. It seemed to watch us, waiting to subdue and capture us. The fire alone seemed strong enough to protect us from it. No wonder man has had gods of fire and worshiped the flaming sun. The wilderness crushed the spirit into a strange and expectant peace. The stars through the crevice between the trees sparkled and made

---

[13] Fleming, *op. cit.,* pp. 179-180.

one lying on his back on the boughs itch with wonder,
although the body was dead from exertion.

This itching with wonder over the great expanse,
the utter darkness, and the lonely silence is made to
be the key to religious feeling. It is a basic *motif*
running throughout genuinely religious expressions of
mankind. The sense of mystery encompasses us. What
shall we do about it? Men have tried to set up metaphysical and theological explanations to no avail. Each
attempt to explain the mysterious universe has turned
out to be but another myth: comforting and reassuring
as long as it lasts. Men's imaginations have conjured
all sorts of explanations which have solidified into
dogmas. Even as the snowball in the wet snow gains in
size with each turn, so theory piles upon theory until
mighty systems of thought are built—only to be melted
away by the sun of a more adequate understanding.
Today we see the melting away of hosts of such age-
old explanations. The modern sciences have little com-
fort to give man as he continues to wonder about himself
and his place in the scheme of things. We are but
specks upon the earth and the earth is but an out-of-
the-way place in a galaxy among possibly greater galax-
ies. How unkind nature is with its earthquakes, storms,
tempests, and poison-bearing germs. Only a little while
are we permitted to do this wondering and then—silence.
There is no special dispensation for such inquirers. Like
the beasts of the field man is ignorant of ultimate meanings and his own fate. How insecure he is under such
a cold canopy. The old refrain "God's in his heaven
and all's right with the world" is a familiar tune of a
yesterday, but it sounds queer to modern ears. "When
one first realizes what the scientific view means, when
one first becomes conscious of this brute power against
which we futilely struggle with no chance of ultimate
victory, then the thrill of life departs and existence

seems worthless. I know when the significance of science dawned upon me, my house of thought tumbled down like a house of cards and I felt as though I were gripped by a deathly illness. Months passed before the taste of life became sweet again.

"But then it came to me as it has come to other men —that it is part of religion and true humanhood to turn from vain regrets. It is part of religion to stay and to conquer, not to flee from our gravest and sorest troubles. This is no easy task, and if man would be man and not a traitor to human divineness there is no other road out of the sombre wilderness of science. Even though nature cares not for us, we must care for ourselves and make life magnificent." And the clergyman goes on:

> I recall poor Friedrich Nietzsche. He, too, had seen what science means when it speaks about the universe. He saw that the whole universal process goes on and on without ceasing or turning a hand for mankind. Is it all worth while, he pondered? One day, broken-hearted and dismayed, he was walking in the forest of the Harz Mountains and lay down to rest. He fell asleep. When he awoke, the sun was going down, making long slender shadows among the trees, the birds were piping their songs, the sky was a blaze of gold and purple. Feeling all this, Nietzsche reflected: Ah! even if life gives no more than this brief moment of beauty, then life is infinitely worth while and precious. It was this single touch of beauty that gave him energy again to go on his sad and stormy road.

Does all this mean utter futility? Only a narrow-visioned man would say yes. Nature furnishes us an expanse of desert sands, but here and there is found an oasis. Here and there are flashes of glory. Or, changing the figure: "There are times, as it were, when I feel the old earth swing under my feet as she sails on her aimless voyage through the cosmic sea to the port of nowhere. I know there is no meaning in it for us of the earth, for we may be wrecked tomorrow and sink down into the impenetrable depths of space, but meanwhile there is a glory, a mystery, an enchantment in knowing that we are part of this amazing voyage and adventure . . . Nature, although she may strike me down, has blessed me with a sense of wonder and has made me a citizen not of today but of yesterday and tomorrow. She may curse me, yet she can cheer me. She may not care for me or my fellows, but we can wring from her a few pearls of beauty and joy."

We can no longer, with Job, trust God though he slay us, hoping that somehow righteousness and kindness will ultimately prevail. Nor can we with Emerson love the wind that bends us as willows in the wilderness. The only Nature we know is the Nature that gave us the Black Death and threatens us with tuberculosis, cancer, syphilis, and a thousand equally bad scourges. Such nightmares are not our friends even though Nature would minimize them by occasional respites in us of joy and laughter. What then can we do in such a world, if we cannot love it and hold our hopes unbounded? We can create and sustain and enjoy whatever makes out of life a bit of joy and laughter. "Although the universe cares not particularly about our morality and our ideals, we must care for them. Upon our shoulders is being carried the ark of life through the wilderness. All the virtues, all there is of goodness, kindliness, courtesy is of our own creation and we must sustain them, otherwise they will go out of existence into darkness, as a star goes out. Apart from us, they are not. They are children born to humanity in its climb out of the valley of brutality, and we humans must give them color and zest." This is the unbridled truth in the teachings of "modern science." There is no use trying to conceal the lies handed down to us by our fathers who saw in an unfounded hope only the optimism they desired.

And yet—the preacher continues: "Somehow there is an impelling voice in us that calls us to be more delicate in conduct than we are, to be more generous in speech. Although the natural outcome of the evolutionary processes of creative synthesis, this voice may be called divine. It once slept in the rock, then it dreamed of language in the animal, and in man it awoke and became vocal. . . . It says that, even though we all are being marched toward an abyss which swallows everything, we must somehow while it is still day put beauty in the place of ugliness, laughter in the place of tears; that we should make our brief stretch in eternity a stretch of time to a better social order; that we should dispel ignorance with knowledge, hatred with love; put reason above prejudice and science above tradition."

Thus, though there is no God, no hope that reaches beyond this present existence, a nature none too kind, we may cultivate those little respites between prolonged pains and frustrations and make the most of them. There is still something to do for ourselves and our fellowmen though nature may be quite against us. We can still itch with wonder; we can make the most of our laughter; we should still strive to create beauty and satisfactions; we must still uphold our moral sensibilities for these are for our ultimate contentment. Though casting away the philosophies and theologies of our "myth-creating ancestors" we can move and have our being with a light in our eye amid the blackness, the quietness, and the infinite stretches of that expanse which encompasses us round about. That is for us religious experience; and it is worth something when it comes home to us.[14]

---

[14] Quotations from "The Universe of Humanism," by Earl F. Cook in *Humanist Sermons* (Open Court, 1927), edited by C. W. Reese, pp. 117 ff.

Devil Worship

An interesting development of religious expression is the reaction of the Araucanian Indians to the teaching of the early church fathers in Southern Chile. Clarence Allis, a son of a Presbyterian missionary, relates the story in the following way: When Almagro, a Spanish Conquistador, proceeded down into the most southernly parts of Chile, on his tour of conquest, he not only went fully armed but he also had in mind the spiritual welfare of the vanquished. Among his followers were the padres of the Catholic Church.

In due time the padres brought to the natives the story of Christ crucified. The teaching of God the Father, the Son, and the Holy Ghost was given them; as well as the story of the Garden of Eden and the fall of man. Good and Evil were introduced to them in terms of the struggle between God and the Devil. God was defined as an almighty Father, good, beneficent, merciful; the Devil was pictured as the Prince of Hell, the instigator of all that is evil. Punishment came from the Devil. Hell yawned for its prey.

As time passed on, the communities were left to their own development. The scarcity of padres made it impossible to have a spiritual adviser in each community, so an arrangement was effected so that, at stated intervals, itinerant priests visited the settlements from time to time. Many times these regular visits had to be postponed inasmuch as the conquering army was getting farther and farther away.

Now the story goes that once when a padre returned he found that the pictures of the Blessed Virgin and that of Christ had been taken from the altars by the native converts and the picture of the Devil was found to occupy the most prominent place. Horrified, the priests asked the natives why they had done this terrible thing. The answer came: If God is so good and merciful as you have said he does not need our worship nor our offerings; the Devil, you have said, is bad and we are concerned more about him!

Religious feeling, it would appear, is not necessarily tied up with a concern over a god conceived to be good; it may encompass a god conceived to be bad. Infinite is the variety of religious expressions.[15]

---

[15] A Selected List of Readings will be found in the Appendix to this book, arranged according to the chapter topics.

CHAPTER II

MISTAKEN NOTIONS

The Cult of the Vague

The random examples of religious expressions which we have cited plainly reveal that they are never purely religious. Just why these expressions should be called religious has not been stated; thus far we seem to have been begging the question. Why are certain human moods and activities—mixed as they all are, more or less, with other moods and interests—to be called religious? When is a mood or an activity religious? Certain defensible criteria must be sought or otherwise our terms are arbitrary. This leads us directly into the matter of definitions.

A student once turned in an examination paper in which he defined certain philosophical terms in such a way that the professor could hardly judge whether or not he actually knew what they meant. Not an uncommon occurrence, indeed. He was called into account for what he had written and at the same time notified that he had failed to meet the requirements of the examination. His apology for setting down vague answers to the questions was something like this: From high school, he said, he had been a student of the fine art of rhetoric. He had learned both in theory and by practice that the way to get oneself across is to put one's ideas in such a way that those who listen can take them as they choose and be pleased. In this way there is no offense and the speaker or writer is thus on the side of the favorable edge especially in matters of dispute and doubt. The written answers to the questions, accordingly, were so phrased as to give the reader

33

no occasion for offense and the writer the advantage or benefit of any possible doubt!

This student may not be heralded as a high-priest in the art of expression either by professors of rhetoric or by a discriminating public, but he surely was a priest after the order of Melchisedek in sophomoric art. The truth of the matter was that he really did not know; so, he wrote his answers in a way that they might be regarded as either right or wrong, or perhaps neither, trusting that his examiner was a gentle reader who was given to that disposition described by the apostle which "beareth all things, believeth all things, hopeth all things, and endureth all things."

The vagueness of some ministers of religion is hardly less than that of the sophomore, when they glibly suggest that what the world needs above everything else is religion and who fail to get across what is meant. Or, if defined, they frequently confuse it with a special brand of theology or philosophy or of some particular ecclesiastical theory and practice. We may well take some of their enthusiasm and suggest that what is needed in our contemporary confusion is an adequate conception of the nature and function of religion. The latter question is surely prior to the former in both order and importance. Whether or not the world needs any or more religion depends very vitally upon our conception of the religious mood and practice.

There is a growing intolerance today against the cult of the vague. The student who thinks he can get along with general answers dubiously put is quite out of step with the marching of his generation. The minister who shouts for a return to religion without clearly and definitely showing the validity and reasonableness of his plea is a pathetic figure who attracts to himself only those whose thinking moves in an age of yesterday; at the same time he repels that increasing circle of discriminate people of this generation. The anathema against the vague has come from respected quarters. It is a part of the scientific spirit—the great hope for progress in understanding and wisdom—that if one is to come to terms with anything one must see it in focus.

One can never hope to wrestle the secrets of nature if one acquiesces in half-way impressions and blurred concepts. The tools must be kept sharp. There is no virtue in trying to hit the bull's eye with a sponge. And not only is it a folly but, positively, it is a vice. Among the philosophers it is the logician whose blood-pressure is increased when he finds loose and dangling concepts paraded as if they meant something. One of the most recent developments in contemporary philosophy is that now flourishing under the name of mathematical logic which shies at conventional language because words have a way of preventing sharp and clean and precise meaning. To understand anything, the modern symbolist insists, one must say definitely what one means. Thus does he explain, in part, his own use of the precise symbols of mathematics. Whole systems of thought totter and fall by pointing out ill-defined concepts. The Achilles' heel in many of the major philosophical systems is to be found in dubious concepts underlying major ideas. Readers of the Platonic dialogues are familiar with Socrates's insistence that those who search for truth and understanding must watch their terms; analysis is an important highway to progressive and intelligent interpretation of the ideas and behavior of men.

Mistaken Notions

Now, in the history of the subject of definition of what is to be understood by the religious mood and activity, there appear certain more or less formal notions and interpretations which are quite at fault when subjected to certain tests and criticisms. We shall consider such "mistaken notions" briefly in order that we may profit by them.

The Inadequacy of the Etymological Approach

The meaning of some terms becomes clear when one traces their etymology. The term "philosophy," for example, is illuminated by a reference to its root in the Greek where it signifies a love of wisdom. Unfortunately, however, not all terms are made clear by this approach. In the course of time a word persists though it bears a changed meaning; the Oxford English Dictionary is full of such cases of changed meanings. One would not think, for example, of defining "evolution" by appealing merely to its Latin origin; the concept today is far removed from the idea of unrolling which is implied in the original roots; an epigeneticist would regard himself as an evolutionist though in no sense in accord with the etymological significance of that term. The word "science" which is supposed to mean knowledge is surely much more definite than its etymology implies. If we were to take the word "religion" and trace it to its Latin source we would find ourselves compelled to define it either as "being bound" (*religare*) or "gathering together" (*relegere*) according to whichever scholarly opinion we followed. Very obviously, the etymological approach here is most unsatisfactory; the root ideas are much too broad to be of any consequence. If we are to find an adequate definition of "religion" we must search for other ways of approach.

Confusion in Words

When many speakers and writers discuss "religion" they commonly fail to make a distinction between a person who is religious, a person who is considered to be religious, a religion as a body of doctrine and of practice, and objects, events, institutions, behaviors which are referred to as religious. There is patently a difference between an object that is a religious object and a person who is religious and these together over against religion—and yet the interchangeable uses of terms fail to show such differences. Surely a religious object or event is not religious *in the same sense* as a person who is religious. And what is more, a person who is performing a religious act *may* not be religious *in the same sense* as a person who *is* religious. One need not be accused of tautology if one were to suggest that a religion is not always and in all respects religious; or, in other words, there may be non-religious elements in a given religion. Furthermore, religion-in-general is not necessarily synonymous with religion-in-particular.

The point we here attempt to make is this: there is a confusion in the terms "religion" and "religious" (not to speak of the adverb "religiously") which because they are *used* interchangeably are taken to *be* synonymous. The words themselves hide real distinctions in meaning. When we are told that what the world needs is religion we may wonder what is meant: whether, a body of beliefs and practices, a certain frame of mind, a particular brand, "a religion in general," certain types of practice or ways of conduct, a theology, or a philosophy? This loose play of words belongs to the cult of the vague and has no place in the matter of defining other than to reveal a type of mistaken notions.

We shall find that popular usage is so grounded in this confusion that we shall be compelled to employ the terms indiscriminately when considering the views of writers on this general subject. Any adequate definition, we shall also find, will necessitate the limitation of the words "religion," "a religion," "religious" to certain particular meanings. Clarity demands parting company with a host of writers as well as with popular usage. Before making any such distinctions it is well to consider further inadequate conceptions.

The So-Called "Psychological Errors" in Definition

The older psychology tended to treat the mind as though consisting of wholly separate departments or faculties. Like Gaul, the mind was divided into three parts: thinking, feeling, and willing. The error of this approach did not consist in stressing certain characteristic phases of mental life but in setting up such clean-cut lines of demarcation as to lead to abstractionism and psychological artificiality. The danger of all analysis of dynamic processes lies in distorting the real into something unreal and remote from actuality. In general, the psychological errors consisted in treating aspects of the mental life as though they were separate entities. Many definitions of "religion" reflect the kind of mistaken notions characteristic of the older type of faculty psychology. We shall, under the next following headings, consider examples of each of these so-called "psychological errors."

"Religion" As the Expression of Intellect

Some people would seem to maintain that "religion" is a matter of belief. One is religious, it would appear, if one believed something. What this belief consists of may find many expressions; the main characteristic, however, is that it is a belief. If one subscribes to a creed, a set of creeds, certain theological doctrines, or a philosophical interpretation of the universe, one is thereby religious. Many people would seem to think that "religion" consists in an intellectual affirmation that there is a Deity, however conceived.

Two random examples of formal definitions may

here be cited. James Martineau has defined religion as "the belief in an ever living God, that is, in a Divine Mind and Will ruling the Universe and holding moral relations with mankind." The well-known definition of Hegel runs as follows: religion is "the knowledge possessed by the finite mind of its nature as absolute mind." According to Hegel, it would seem, if one possessed the rational insight that one is a part of rational totality, a drop in the ocean of rational being, one is religious. To be religious, it would appear, one must be wearing a certain kind of intellectual spectacles. Of course, this definition cannot be taken out of the framework of the Hegelian philosophy. For him the world reveals a logical process: the working of the dialectic process of thesis, antithesis, and synthesis; the real is the rational and the rational is the real. It would appear to follow, accordingly, that to be religious is to be an Hegelian! Most obviously, this conception is narrow on more than one score. It typifies the mistaken notion among both intellectuals and *hoi polloi* that "religion" consists of an intellectual subscription to some doctrine or dogma or metaphysical system.

It may well be asked whether "religion" is merely a matter of belief; *e.g.*, may one not on intellectual grounds alone believe any of these things, in a God, in an ultimate purpose, in the Hegelian rational order, in the Westminster confession, and at the same time be non-religious and even irreligious?

"Religion" As the Expression of Feeling

The second type of the so-called psychological error is to say that "religion" is merely a matter of an indiscriminate feeling. When one feels, one is religious. It is not so much a matter of belief or a matter of behavior as it is that one merely feels. A convert at a New York camp meeting undoubtedly is attempting to express what "religion" is to him when he is supposed to have exclaimed: "Brethren, brethren, I feel—I feel—I feel —I feel—I feel—I can't tell you how I feel, but O I feel! I feel!"[1]

Of course, the question immediately raised is: is any kind of feeling religious? We should not expect a reputable writer who attempts to define the religious attitude or the religious feeling to say that it is mere feeling-in-general. We should rather expect of him to define it in some limited sense. Though there are passages in Schleiermacher's writings which would seem to indicate that "religion" for him consisted of the vaguest kind of feeling, Schleiermacher did come to make the discrimination in his famous definition that it is "the feeling of absolute dependence." For him the characteristic thing about religion is not a belief nor a behavior but a feeling state. Confronted in his day with a church membership active only on paper, a membership whose indifference to the things of religion was confessedly due to agnosticism and atheism, and becoming tired of preaching to empty pews and lonesome in his professional ministrations, Schleiermacher did what every good minister ought to do: he went out to find out what the trouble was. His people were having intellectual difficulties; they couldn't believe what they thought they should believe and hence lost interest in what they considered to be religion. Schleiermacher who evidently had difficulties of his own and was honest enough to affirm them, began to reconsider the whole question of the nature of the thing he was trying to do. He came to the conclusion that "religion," after all, was not a matter of articles of faith nor a theory of the universe; rather, it was an emotional experience which could be had, and in a vital way, devoid of the ministrations and perplexities of the intellect. He told his people

---

[1] From a quotation in *The Religious Consciousness* (Macmillan, 1920), J. B. Pratt, p. 184.

that their conception of "religion" was all wrong; that they could believe or disbelieve what they wished; that, after all, the genuine earmark of a genuine religious interest is to be had in one's feeling—a feeling of absolute dependence.

Upon what, it may be asked, should one feel one's dependence? The answer came forthwith that the "What" is secondary to the experience; that the "What" does not make one religious but the feeling state itself. The whole subjectivistic movement in modern religious theory, which has been increasingly prominent since his day, minimizing the value and function of credal statements, has its roots in Schleiermacher's vigorous defense of this notion.

We still hear it said that it does not make any difference what one believes, that creeds may be taken or left, and that "religion" is a matter merely of an emotional experience. The cry "away with the creeds" is symptomatic of this development. Stand out under the starry sky or remain in the quiet of your own chamber, let yourself go in rapturous feeling of utter dependence, and you will "understand" what it means to be religious. So much so was the feeling element stressed by Schleiermacher that Hegel, the rationalist, is supposed to have made the very unkind remark that Schleiermacher's dog, accordingly, must have been very religious. In fairness to Schleiermacher it must be added, however, that he refers, on occasion, to the "What" as the Infinite, the Universe, and as God; the emphasis, notwithstanding, was placed upon the feeling of finiteness, however the Infinite may be conceived.

A recent expression of the nature of "religion" bordering along the same line is the well-known view of Rudolph Otto who would identify "religion" as a feeling of aching helplessness, a feeling of the *mysterium tremendum*. Schleiermacher's notion of the feeling of absolute dependence is given a critical analysis; Otto would have it that such feeling of dependence implies a "creature feeling" in which something "numinous" is felt. Concepts can only suggest and indicate what this numinous feeling is; they are inadequate to describe it. We may indicate the feeling that is religious by such expressions as "aweful," "overpowering," "urgent," "holy," "*mysterium*," "terrible," "fascinating," "spooky." There is something *sui generis* in religious feeling.

Otto's view, however, is classified under another heading, that of *a priorism*, which we shall presently discuss. He himself uses the word "feeling" so frequently in his analyses that it seems appropriate to give his view passing mention in connection with "religion" as the expression of feeling.

Three criticisms occur when we are confronted with this emphasis upon feeling. First, it is said that there is no such thing as pure feeling apart from other phases of mental life. Secondly, it is pointed out that feeling is always coupled with a feeling *about* something cognitively recognized. Schleiermacher is supposed to have sensed this latter difficulty by his introduction of the category of the Infinite, Universe, a God as the object about which a certain kind of feeling plays. And thirdly, religious feeling must be a certain character of feeling; otherwise there is no point in calling a feeling religious.

"Religion" as the Expression of the Will

Views which belong in this class in general emphasize "religion" as activity of one kind or another. It is not a matter of emotion nor of intellectual belief but a matter of doing. The religious man is the behaving man.

The saying of St. James is often quoted as giving the essence of "religion." "Pure religion and undefiled before our God and Father is this, to visit the fatherless and widows in their affliction, and to keep oneself unspotted from the world." (James I:27.) Plainly, there is no attempt here to give a formal definition; moreover, the author is interested in what a religion ought to consist of rather than what it is. If one were to ask a typical "lodge" member what his conception of "religion" is one would probably hear him define it somewhat after the fashion of this biblical quotation. Quoting this isolated passage from the Bible as authority, he would probably hold that all "religion" consists of (even according to the Bible!) is doing well by one's fellow-men. This type of error will be further considered under a heading which comes later in a discussion dealing with the confusion of ethics with religion.

A classic formulation of this general type of definition has been given by Immanuel Kant when he spoke of "religion" as "the recognition of all our duties as divine commands." The definition may not fully come under the classification we here make since there is in it the element of "recognition" and that of "divinity." Nevertheless a casual acquaintance with Kant's very fascinating philosophical viewpoint will reveal that for him the life of the practical reason (which is his formula for activity) assumes the constructive place in his scheme of things. You cannot know *Das Ding an Sich* (the world of Reality), says Kant, but you ought to act as if. There is in all of us a moral imperative which is categorical; this moral imperative comes to us as a thundering ought, a part of our mental being; this ought compels us to make assertions about the world of reality even though we cannot know it. The essence of "religion" is to be had in the fulfilment of that which is implied by our moral nature; it is not a matter of emotion or faith or belief but it is of the essence of the will, the practical reason.

The general fault with this type of definition is, first, a tendency to set up an artificial psychology where the practical man overshadows the emotional and theoretical man; secondly, there is a tendency to identify "religion" with ethical conduct; and, thirdly, there is a tendency toward inconsistency where such definitions aiming to emphasize man's motivations smuggle in other sides of his mental make-up (*e.g.*, Kant).

Further Psychological Errors

It was the fashion among older writers to simplify the whole matter of man's religious nature by referring to a "religious instinct." Not always defining clearly what is meant by a "religious instinct" such writers have thrown little or no light upon the subject; we still have to distinguish a religious instinct from any other instinct. It is now considered by modern psychologists a dubious practice to employ the term "instinct"; not much is gained by it and a great deal of confusion has come of it. If we refer to "religion" as something instinctive we still have on our hands the necessity of describing that which is distinctly religious. Professor Starbuck has made the attempt to describe the religious instinct as the "cosmo-esthetic sense" and the "teleo-esthetic sense," and, more specifically, as "a delicate sense of proportion or relation or fitness or harmony that directs consciousness and determines at each point the particular advantageous response or emphasis." [2] One may still wonder what distinction there is between "religion" and "cosmo-esthetic" and "teleo-esthetic." An instinct, we are now cautioned by modern psychologists, is but a name for a more complex type of unlearned behavior; if this is so, no light is thrown upon the problem by referring it to unlearned behavior; to set up special explanations for special cases is to violate a sacred principle in all scientific procedure, *viz.*, that

---

[2] "The Instinctive Basis of Religion," an abstract of which appears in the *Psychological Bulletin*, VIII, pp. 52-53.

of the law of parsimony. We may as well, then, talk about the nature and origin of play, or of music, or of art, as so many unique expressions of a unique "play instinct" or a unique "music instinct" or a unique "art instinct"—which plainly invites further darkness and confusion.

The law of parsimony commands of us that we must not multiply entities beyond necessity. If this law cautions us against speaking of a special religious instinct it also forbids our appealing to what some recent writers are terming the *"religious a priori."* According to this type of view there is in the rational make-up of man a unique way of dealing with his ideas, a peculiar kind of innate pattern into which framework he sets his ideas and experiences. In general, the view may be stated as follows: The mind has certain peculiar ways of dealing with sense material and ideas; it gives these a frame of reference. For example, Kant held that these ways of handling mental material were themselves not so much ideas as ways or modes; one *relates* sense-material and ideas, one *substantializes* them, one *numbers* them, and so on; these ways or modes or categories are innate; they are *a priori*; we are built that way. Now, it is asked, may there not be a way of relating ideas which is of the essence of "religion," a way that is *a priori*, innate, related to man's mental make-up in a way similar to those categories set up and marked by Kant? May there not be in the very warp and woof of man's rational nature a special category which may be called "religious," a category which presents in a simply apprehended presence the Divine in the soul? "Religion," according to Ernst Troeltsch, is rooted in man's mental framework as a special category or form resulting in an apprehension, however dim, of the presence of the Superhuman and the Infinite.

Criticisms of the "religious *a priori*" follow those already cited against a special "religious instinct." Such an explanation is obscure; it violates the law of parsimony; the psychology implied is antiquated; there is a tendency to regard mental nature as consisting of "states" or forms rather than that which it is, an ongoing dynamic process; its analysis is accordingly, artificial and abstract; little light is thrown upon the fundamental nature of "religion." Why, it may well be asked, may one then not speak of a "philosophical *a priori*" or an "esthetic *a priori*," a "scientific *a priori*," a "moral *a priori*"—indeed, where shall one stop? One might as well take literally the popular reference to a "religious sense" as meaning that there actually is such a special sense; thus, one sees something of the danger in the appeal to a special organ or way or mode of apprehending, implied by *a priorism*.

"Narrow Conceptions"

When some people think of "religion" they think of some particular form or expression of it. They generally think of their own particular "religion." If one were to define "religion," say in terms of Christianity, this would be a case in point. One would then have to say that non-Christians are outside the pale of the definition. What shall we then say of Buddhism, Mohammedanism, Confucianism, Judaism, Zoroastrianism, Jainism, Taoism, and the so-called "great religions" of the world. It should be very obvious that the term "religion" carries far wider connotations than any particular form thereof. This fallacy of particularism is found to characterize the undisciplined mind.

"When I mention religion," says Parson Thwackum, "I mean the Christian religion, and not only the Christian religion but the Protestant religion, and not only the Protestant religion but the Church of England." [3]

---

[3] A quotation given in *The Religions of Mankind* (Abingdon, 1921), E. D. Soper, p. 18.

One hears it said, again, that "religion" consists in going to church, honoring the Virgin Mary, believing that Christ died for one's sins, believing in a personal God, and in personal immortality. Certainly not all religious beliefs and practices consist in attending a formal church service, in believing in Jesus as the Messiah or as a second person of the Trinity, or even in the belief in the existence of a personal and benevolent Deity. Certainly, one may live the life of a solitary mystic and be religious. As we have seen in our first chapter, a wide variety of beliefs and practices may well be subsumed under the heading of "religion." To define the general term "religion" in terms of its highest reaches and expressions is obviously too narrow.

Even Hegel commits this error in defining "religion" in terms of what amounts to Hegel's own philosophy. It is clear that a definition must be broad enough to include the widest variety of beliefs and practices.

"Broad Conceptions"

Another type of mistaken notion is in the direction of the opposite extreme. If one feels the necessity of overcoming the criticism of a too narrow conception there lurks the danger of defining one's terms so broadly as to lose the *differentia* which one seeks. A lowest common denominator must be sought, but it must not outrun significant meaning. For example, if one should say that "religion" is wonder or a feeling of awe or reverence, this surely is not stating the *differentia*. One may surely wonder and be fearful and even be reverent without being religious or having anything to do with "religion." Should one say that "religion" is love? But surely one may love and be in love without being religious or having anything to do with "religion." Or again, should one say that "religion" consists in being loyal to the best? But surely one can be loyal to the very best that one knows and not necessarily be religious or have anything to do with "religion."

The Confusion of "Religion" with Ethics

We have already indicated this type of error. It is rather typical of what may be a certain type of religion, *e.g.*, "lodge religion," "humanism," and the like.

"The heart of religion," writes A. Eustace Haydon, "the quest of the ages, is the outreach of man, the social animal, for the values of the satisfying life."[4] The satisfying is the good, however conceived. The quest for the good life, accordingly, is of the essence of "religion." Haydon's view, thus, illustrates the very wide tendency in recent religious theory to identify "religion" with ethics. The widely quoted definition of E. S. Ames would appear to be another example of this type of error. "Religion" according to him consists of "the consciousness of the highest social values." He limits religious behavior to social activity and frankly follows the logic of his definition by admitting that little children who have not reached the level of personality (*i.e.*, babes who approximate more nearly the level of animal life), defectives, idiots, imbeciles, the insane, criminals, in short non-social beings, are non-religious. He limits his definition not only to social activity but to social activity at the highest level consonant with a particular group. This would seem to imply the criterion of the good, however conceived, as belonging to the highest. It would be difficult to maintain this as a descriptive definition since "religion" has been associated with the lowest type of ethics, both individual and social. If one were to confine the definition to such a norm as the highest values one would have to rule out a good many chapters in the history of what is popularly known as "religion." For example, were

---

[4] *The Quest of The Ages* (Harpers, 1929), p. 68.

one to grant that the cases cited in our first chapter are instances of the religious spirit, Ames's definition would fall short with reference to some of them.

Let us put it this way: is it not possible to be religious without acting in an ethically approved manner; may one not be religious and at the same time behave immorally or *a*-morally? And again, may one not behave according to the highest moral standards and satisfactions, however conceived, and not necessarily be religious? Rudolph Otto, in his study of primitive religious expressions, would insist that the earliest expressions were *a*-moral in character: the sense of eeriness or the feeling of the holy was, he thinks, beyond the category of the good in the primitive consciousness.

It is highly doubtful that the criterion of a socially defensible ethics is satisfactory as a descriptive concept here. It rather smacks of what "religion" ought to be, which plainly is not the question at this point. Such descriptive material from religious history as is contained in the two notable volumes *A History of the Warfare of Science with Theology* by Andrew D. White and in the essay entitled "The Dark Side of Religion" by Morris R. Cohen [5] is sufficiently forbidding to identify "religion" and ethics.

If "religion" is to be identified with moral conduct then it would be necessary to drop either term. Again the law of parsimony compels us to pare down our entities; too many entities lead to confusion.

The Confusion of Normative and Descriptive Definitions

Many definitions of "religion" are at fault in a confusion of the normative with the descriptive approaches; they define what a "religion" ought or ought not be rather than what it is. A few samples, beyond those

---

[5] *Religion Today* (1933), edited by A. L. Swift, pp. 75 ff.

already noted in other connections, will reveal this type of error.

S. Reinach sets forth the amazing definition: "I propose to define religion as: A sum of scruples which impede the free exercise of our faculties." [6] After criticizing a number of definitions Dr. Soper, in a popularly useful book on comparative religions, gives a formal definition as follows: "It is a relationship of conscious dependence on higher powers; it makes a demand on the whole of man's life, intellect, emotion, and will; it is both individual and social; it is worship, yet it is more than worship; and it conserves all the values which give worth and meaning to human life." [7] This definition plainly is formal; there is an attempt to formulate an inclusive picture which will not be marred by certain common mistaken notions; and yet, the very last clause reveals the normative rather than the descriptive approach. Frankly we should ask: does all religion conserve "all the values which give worth and meaning to human life?" Perhaps "religion" should effect this result; but, historically speaking, has it done so? The answer plainly is in the negative. It has often fostered evil, superstition, error, and a thousand human woes. Take another recent and formal definition: "Religion we then understand as an expression of confidence on the part of human beings, individually or collectively, in the goodness of the real universe, which leads to communion with the power or powers believed to control it." [8] Such a definition excludes extreme humanists or any who have yet not attained to some metaphysical view of the world; it omits those who lack such a positive confidence in the goodness of reality; it would include only those who claim some relation to higher powers as suggested by some form of worship.

---

[6] Quoted in Soper, *op. cit.,* pp. 18-19.
[7] Soper, *op. cit.,* p. 25.
[8] *The Religious Response* (Harpers, 1929), H. W. Wright, p. 14.

Case after case could be cited in which this definition would not apply (the first chapter will furnish some examples); the problem then would remain as to how certain behaviors and attitudes of man ought to be classified if not under "religion." In short, this formal definition seems to have smuggled in what a "religion" ought to be in the most fundamental terms; it is hardly sufficiently descriptive. Let us cite another case where a normative interest appears to have entered into a description of what religion is. William Adams Brown says informally "that in religion we have first-hand contact with superhuman reality. Most definitions of religion are at fault in that they restrict the area of this contact too narrowly. They make a part do duty for the whole: dependence as with Schleiermacher, responsibility as with Kant, enfranchisement as with Ritschl. Religion is all this and more. It is submission to the will of a greater; gratitude for the experience of deliverance; loyalty to the call of the unseen; adoration of the supreme excellence. . . . Religions differ not only in the elements they include but in their capacity for self-reformation and renewal. . . ." [9] Is all "religion" submission, gratitude, adoration, involving a "first-hand contact" with superhuman reality? How about the extreme humanists with their affirmed lack of interest in metaphysical reality? This expression on the part of Professor Brown, like so many other expressions about religion, wears the air of the sermonic and the hortatory.

"Religion" Defined in Terms of God

Many writers insist that any adequate definition must have in it a reference to a god or gods. Take the following definition. "Religious experience is an aware-

---

[9] *Contemporary American Theology* (Round Table, 1933), edited by Vergilius Ferm, Vol. II, p. 87.

ness of God giving assurance as the self seeks harmonious relations with Him." [10]   This appears to be an easy way to set up a line of demarcation; but it turns out to be far from so simple a solution.   There are two points to be considered.   First, if one is to define "religion" in terms of a belief in or an attitude toward or a behavior having reference to a god, one has upon one's hands the problem of defining god.   This turns out to be far from easy.   If one were to define god broadly enough to include the great variety of conceptions, the term "god" apparently loses its supposed *differentia*.   To allow the definition to rest with a vague notion of god may be an unavowed failure in the avowed attempt to be explicit; such a type of definition plays the trick of seeming to have defined where one really has not succeeded.   Secondly, to define "religion" in terms of god, say in the theistic sense, is to leave out many examples and instances of what on other grounds appears to come under the classification of religious phenomena.   For example, how then should we classify certain attitudes and behaviors of the Australian bushmen (investigated by Spencer and Gillen), the Todas (as described in our first chapter), the Jains,[11] the early Buddhists, the extreme humanists, extreme pantheists and mystics, *supra*-theists (those who view god as more than personal), and even the recent atheistic cults?   If we rule out the term "religion" in such cases we have another and perhaps a more serious problem on our hand, *viz.*, how then shall such attitudes and behaviors be classified?   We are thus faced with the dilemma of omission and a narrow definition on the one hand and inclusion and a broad definition on the other; this dilemma seems resolved by

---

[10] *Religious Experience,* The Methodist Fundamental (Holborn, 1928), W. R. Wilkinson, p. 76.

[11] Jainism began by denying outright any supreme being.   Mahavira, its founder (died 527 B.C.) condemned the practice of praying to or even talking about any deity.   See *The World's Living Religions* (1924), R. E. Hume, p. 48.

choosing the lesser difficulty in the matter of classification, *i.e.*, by broadening the concept "religion" to include certain attitudes and behaviors not necessarily involving a god concept (after the usual pattern and certainly not in the more rigid theistic sense).[12]

William James once wrestled with this problem of definition. Finding it necessary in a formal definition to include a reference to the divine [13] he felt prompted to make an apology for this reference. He was quite unwilling to omit such cases as early Buddhism and the transcendentalism of Emerson (where there was lacking a Deity *in concreto*) from the category of "religion." And so he broadened his conception of divinity. "We must, therefore, from the experiential point of view, call these godless or quasi-godless creeds 'religious'; and accordingly when in our definition of religion we speak of the individual's relation to 'what he considers the divine,' we must interpret the term 'divine' very broadly, as denoting any object that is god*like*, whether it be a concrete deity or not." [14]

Fearfully conscious of the dubious term "godlike," James goes on at length to indicate what presumably is meant by the term. When he is all through with his discussion it would appear that he might well have omitted the term altogether; in his hands a supposedly specific term turned out to be vague. The better wisdom, it would seem, would have been to have left out

---

[12] If the reader has some doubt as to the vagueness of the god concept, let him read such a book as *My Idea of God* (1927), edited by Joseph Fort Newton. He will there find Jew and Gentile, Catholic and Protestant, Modernist and Fundamentalist, Christian Scientist, Quaker, Ethical Culturist, Humanist, Empiricist, and Mystic—leaders in contemporary religious thought—speaking of god as if in a confusion of tongues. The editor of this book confesses that he finds it "difficult to find unity in such variety."

[13] "Religion" meant for him *the feelings, acts, and experiences of individual men in their solitude, so far as they apprehend themselves to stand in relation to whatever they may consider the divine.* The *Varieties of Religious Experience* (Longmans, Green, 1902, impression of 1919), p. 31.

[14] *Op. cit.*, p. 34.

the concept of divinity or deity and to have made the definition more general. A further quotation will show how conscious James was of his difficulty. "But the term 'godlike,' if thus treated as a floating general quality, becomes exceedingly vague, for many gods have flourished in religious history, and their attributes have been discrepant enough. What then is that essentially godlike quality—be it embodied in a concrete deity or not—our relation to which determines our character as religious men? . . . For one thing, gods are conceived to be first things in the way of being and power. They overarch and envelop, and from them there is no escape. What relates to them is the first and last word in the way of truth. Whatever then were most primal and enveloping and deeply true might at this rate be treated as godlike, and a man's religion might thus be identified with his attitude, whatever it might be, toward what he felt to be the primal truth." [15]

---

[15] *Ibid.*, p. 34. James, however, was quite unwilling to give up the defining concept of the divine, however vague, even though he seems to admit, in the same context, that the term "religion" may well have broader significance. However carefully his definition was framed, it appears that the normative approach asserted itself strongly in his own interpretation of his definition.

CHAPTER III

DEFINITIONS

Criteria for Defensible Definitions

This business of defining "religion" thus turns out to be a highly complex affair. Because a task is difficult one need not necessarily despair; certainly this is no sign that it is impossible. The case is either for no definition with attending vagueness in discussion or a definition, however defensible, with certain logical implications. One must make his choice for the one or the other. The choice that is here made is to face the difficulty resolutely, attempt a careful definition, or set of definitions and follow through the implications.

In the immediately preceding chapter there emerges in the discussion certain criteria which may well serve as tools in the framing of a defensible viewpoint. As a summary, we set down the following points: (1) etymology is of little help; (2) since the words "religion" and "religious" do not carry the same meaning, certain distinctions should be made, *e.g.*, a religious man is to be distinguished from a man's religion, a cow as a religious animal is not religious in the same sense as a person who is religious; (3) the psychological errors warn us of the psychological artificiality of taking one phase of mental life as the expression of the whole and of appealing to some abstracted and unilluminating terms as "instinct" and "*a priorisms*"; (4) the conception must not be narrow but must be inclusive; (5) it must be inclusive but not colorless; (6) a distinction should be made in respect to ethics, some *differentia* should here be noted; (7) the conception must be descriptive and not normative; and, (8) the difficulties with reference to a god-concept must be recognized.

If we have pointed out the common errors, this is not to say that none of the views may not have something to contribute for a constructive viewpoint. It will be our contention, *e.g.*, that even though one must be careful not to identify "religion" with feeling, feeling may be basic to man's religious response. How this is so will be shown as the discussion moves on.

The Terms "Religion," "A Religion," and "Religious" Distinguished

Up to this point we have been employing the concept "religion" in a spongy way—even as it is used in popular language and in formal expression. We shall now part company with that concept as thus vaguely employed, and mark out three distinct meanings and the corollaries that follow. For us the adjective "religious," the generic noun "religion" and the specific noun "a religion" will each carry a specific meaning. It is our contention that no satisfactory conception of the whole question is possible without making these three distinctions. As an introduction to the formal definitions which follow we shall set the reader to meditate upon certain general considerations.

It is conceivable—is it not?—that a person may behave in a religious manner without himself being religious; and, conversely it is conceivable—is it not?—that a person may be religious without behaving in a manner which would be recognized as religious. A person, at a service of worship, may conceivably sing "Onward Christian Soldiers" or some other hymn with a great deal of gusto and thus behave in a manner that may be considered religious; and still in the very midst of such religious behavior he himself may conceivably not be religious. He may be trying out his voice on himself and others; he may be just feeling exuberantly good; he may like to sing. The choir may behave according to the decorum of the sanctuary and sing the words of the psalmist or whatever else is set to music and thus behave in what may be regarded a religious manner; but this is not to say that the choir members are themselves religious.

This writer carries the memory from college days of college boys joining the choir of a certain church and doing their very best as participants in religious services, whose interests and actions were prompted and fed by the *motif* of a hopeful outcome of an intense courtship. One may genuflect in the religious manner and at the same time be intensely engrossed upon the present market value of "American Tobacco." In such a case, one is behaving in a religious manner without being religious. Speaking from the converse side, one might be religious without anyone recognizing it. An individual may never take part in any public religious exercise (and be put down by some as non-or ir-religious) and yet be intensely religious. One may do the unconventional thing and yet be religious; one may be terribly quiet and go the lonely path and still be religious; one may stand outside of any church organization or social formalities and still be intensely religious.

It is said of Josiah Royce that he rarely went to church and preferred symphony concerts to conventional organized efforts of religious expressions. Of course, he was classified by many whose criterion of the religious spirit was intolerably narrow as being non-or ir-religious. No one who reads far into Royce's great philosophical works and tries to enter into the spirit of his thought will deny that America's distinguished philosophical idealist was a deeply religious man. One may readily appreciate why Royce behaved as he did; one may sympathize with that sense of loneliness which he must have felt whenever his mind, soaring into lofty realms, soaked in metaphysical speculations and rigorously disciplined in the niceties of logical thinking, came into contact with forms of religious exercise and expressions cribbed and confined by some public leader and interpreter of life's meaning who excelled in passion at the expense of insight. A symphony concert may well become the stimulus to and the outlet for the religious mood for such minds as Royce's. The point is: a religious man may be very lonely; he may not act in the conventional religious manner and fit into the expected social frame but he goes his way, has his reasons, and holds his peace. His reasons may be more valid than is evident to those who are screwed down to conventional heritages.

It may sound paradoxical to say that a religious man is not religious; this, however, may not be a paradox. It may well be that the man who is considered religious by certain social standards is really not religious. It may seem paradoxical to say that a non-religious man is religious; but, this too, may not be a paradox. The apparent difficulty here lies in the use of the adjective "religious" which may be used in two senses. A religious man who really *is not* religious may be said to be a religious man only by reference to the *possibility* of his being religious though he may not at the given moment *be* religious. In this case, the man is religious by proxy and not genuinely religious. In other words, the basic term here is the adjective "religious" associated with the verb *to be*.

We may, perhaps, see this double-usage of the term more clearly in terms of objects, or circumstances. It hardly needs to be pointed out that the term "religious" may conceivably be applied to all forms of behavior, circumstances, and things. All sorts of objects, events, and circumstances have historically become religious objects, events, and circumstances; *e.g.*, a Roman cross, locks of hair, milk, cows, blood, bones, wine, gowns, candles, incense, altars, collection plates, murders, anniversaries, shouting, silence, hopping, totems, fish, beads, washing, eating, drinking, carousing, fasting, bowing, crawling, singing, teasing, dirtiness, head hunting, marrying, sacrificing, initiating, barbering, clashing of cymbals, harps—there is no limit. Even laughing has had a religious significance. In one of the festivals of the so-called Shinto religion when offerings are brought in procession before the shrine, the chief calls loudly: "According to our annual custom, let us laugh." [1]

What, it may be asked, makes any object, event, or circumstance religious? Surely these are not religious *per se*; or, in other words, these are not religious in the same sense that a person *is* religious. Their status is the same as that of a religious man who is not religious (as above indicated). If this be so they are religious by proxy, by a reference to some person(s) who is (are) religious. Any object, event, circumstance, or man may be described as religious only if there is a reference to the possibility of some individual(s) who is (are) religious. This may appear to be somewhat verbose; but unless these distinctions are made and understood the search for the satisfactory definition of terms seems hopeless. If the reader has not caught the significance of these statements he may understand their meaning in the subsequent analysis of terms.

We may best introduce the discussion of the term "religion" by pointing out a parallel. One may have a philosophy without being philosophical. One may, for example, affirm that one's philosophy of life is described as some form of Christian theism and yet, one may be quite unphilosophical about it. One may have reached this conclusion as a matter of custom and tradition, never giving it the kind of concern that a

---

[1] *An Anthology of Recent Philosophy* (Crowell, 1929), D. S. Robinson, essay by E. S. Ames, p. 540.

typically philosophical approach would demand. One may then ask: Why, if a philosophy may be held without one's being philosophical, call it a philosophy? The answer is that a system of thought is a philosophy only by reference to people who *are* or *were* philosophical. If there be no such reference, such a "philosophy" would be something else; it would, perhaps, then be a system of dogma, or "dogmatic" doctrines.

What is true here of the noun "philosophy" and the adjective "philosophical" is true of "religion" and "religious." One may have a religion without being religious. It may sound as a paradox to say that one has a religion even though one is not religious. But this is no paradox. Suppose, for example, someone should ask, "What is your religion?" You reply, "My religion is *familias* Christianity, *genus* Protestantism, and *species* Methodism." That may merely mean that I have been born and raised into this classification and division and that I am recognized as belonging to a certain category. I may act in a way that it would seem that I was religious. I may even attend church. But, for all that I may not be religious. Why then call this classification "religion?" The answer is the same as above. A religion is what it is only by reference to people who *are* (or *were*) religious. If people no longer were religious the term religion would be a misnomer; it may be a philosophy, a social practice, some form of conventionality, or what not.

Furthermore, when I speak of "a religion" I do not mean all "religion." Religion in general is not synonymous with religion in particular. As a matter of fact there is no such thing in the world of flesh as religion in general; there are religions in particular. It is a notorious fallacy to speak of religion doing something, saying so and so, achieving this or that, promising one thing or another. This fallacy goes by the name of *the re-ification of abstractions.* There is quite a difference between the abstract generic noun "religion" and the particular noun "a religion." Religion in general always has reference to particular religions. The upshot of the matter may be stated thus: even as there would be no particular religion apart from a reference to people who *are* (or *were*) religious so there would be no meaning to the abstract term religion-in-general apart from particular religions. Hence religion in general also has reference ultimately to individuals who are religious.

We thus come to the view that of the three terms, "being religious" is basic. The approach we are here making may be called the positivistic, nominalistic, individualistic, humanistic, and naturalistic; the word "naturalistic" may well serve as a summary description of this approach.

What Does It Mean to Be Religious?

We are now ready to give a formal definition of the basic term. *To be religious is to effect in some way and in some measure a vital adjustment (however tentative and incomplete) to w(W)hatever is reacted to or regarded implicitly or explicitly as worthy of serious and ulterior concern.* This definition, we would hold, does no violence to any of the serious errors listed and discussed in the preceding chapter. One's being religious is not a matter of *mere* believing, *mere* indiscriminate feeling, *mere* doing, nor is it the outcropping of some mysterious instinct or *a priori*. The definition, we hold, is inclusive, that is to say, it does not exclude such attitudes and behaviors on the part of man that ought to be included. This definition does not confuse the subject with ethics. This definition takes care of the god-concept in the only way that seems permissible;

it is not committed to theism, supra-theism, pantheism, nor atheism. Furthermore, it can hardly be charged with being too narrow and exclusive.

According to the above definition a person may be religious without doing anything at all after the manner of what is regarded as religious according to certain religious patterns. On the other hand, were he to subscribe to certain religious creeds and submit himself to conventional behaviors and ideas of a given religion, and did not effect in some way a vital adjustment (however incomplete) to something of more than passing and serious concern, he would not *be* religious.

Some brief explanation may be set down with regard to certain words in the formal definition. By "vital adjustment" is meant that there is something that matters; that that something makes a difference. Whatever emotional stress is involved, whether of fear, surprise, love, hate, and so forth, is of secondary significance in the inclusive and descriptive definition. In other words, various people will find that what concerns them involves various types of reaction under various circumstances. The adjustment involved need not be final, satisfactory, or complete. Furthermore, the adjustment involves the whole person.

The "whatever" in the definition is confessedly a terribly broad term. It is necessary to use such an inclusive concept inasmuch as people have regarded *that something* toward which they react religiously in such a variety of ways. The "whatever" may be merely apprehended, not comprehended. There may be an awareness which, in its initial stage, lies below the threshold of conceptual formulation. I may, for example, react to a "whatever" coming through the door while I am engaged in lecturing before a class. I may be terribly aware of that something; that it is making a change in the present atmosphere of the classroom; but I do not know in any concise way what it is. In other words, people may react with concern to something dimly apprehended but not conceptualized. One can hardly call this "whatever" a "god" *necessarily*, in an inclusive and descriptive definition. There is the danger of being too specific in such a definition. We have already indicated, moreover, that such attempts to insist upon a god-concept in an inclusive and descriptive definition are not as successful as they have appeared. If, however, we could construct a satisfactorily inclusive definition of "god," then, perhaps, it may well be that some people who are religious, possess, in the apprehension of that "whatever" toward which they react, *what may turn into a god-concept*. Plainly, it is not the god-concept *per se* that makes a person religious; there may well be, as we have said, a religious disposition which lacks such a concept. To put this in other words, there is for the religious mind a *that*; the *what* of the *that* may not be clear; it surely is not *necessarily* a *thou*.

A word about the terms "implicitly" and "explicitly." These terms merely mean that there is a *that* either dimly apprehended as a *that*, or, comprehended as a *what*. The religious mind, we hold with James, is always serious; something matters.

The word "ulterior" requires some special consideration. A student critic once raised the seemingly embarrassing question: may not a professional pugilist as such be religious according to this definition? Does not the prize-fighter effect in some way a significant adjustment to what seems to him to be of serious concern? The answer here is very simple. Psychologically, the professional prize-fighter may have certain of the very definite marks of being a religious individual as implied by the definition. One says, for example, in popular language, that a person takes his profession as a religion; there is a great deal of partial truth in such a statement. The religious individual is deeply concerned; there is something that really matters. It may well be that a religious individual has more in common with the professional pugilist than he has with a person who merely has a religion; the person who has a religion may have something which really does not matter a great deal.

There still remains the question, however, whether or not the seriously concerned professional pugilist should be called "religious." If no *differentia* are set up in this matter, then, indeed, we shall have seemed to have committed the error of a too broad conception. A lover then would be religious. The *differentium* suggested in the formal definition is contained in the word "ulterior." By "ulterior" we do not mean ultimate; the term "ultimate" is entirely too strong, having the implication of finality. By "ulterior" it is meant that there is something which matters beyond one's immediate everyday horizon; there is involved the reach out toward those hinterlands which surround all of us. Now, in this sense, a professional pugilist surely does not regard his profession as any *such* hinterland. And we can say this for two reasons.

In the first place, man has the capacity to react to something that lies beyond his immediate, everyday, and commonplace experiences. The very possibility of reacting toward the long-range-future is an instance of this capacity. The whole realm of imagination reveals that man is not circumscribed by the limits of the here and now. Even the rankest positivist will have to admit man's capacity to react to hinterlands; these may not be final nor absolute nor ultimate; rather, they are surrounding shadows; and shadows may be terribly real. In other words, man is so constituted that there are matters of ulterior nature toward which he can and does react. The religious man is thus close to the artist.

In the second place, the world holds out for all of

us a hinterland, something ulterior, something of a shadow, somethings that are near but far, and overwhelming. Beyond the visible and the tangible hills there is always the possibility of more—even the invisible and the intangible. We shall never in our finite existence get rid of mystery. There is "wind and weather," a thousand frustrations; man may get the feeling *ad interim* of confidence, but never the persisting feeling of sufficient confidence. A finite existence always implies a hinterland. These two considerations, the capacity to react toward a hinterland, and the fact that there are such hinterlands, are always involved in the mind which is religious. Now, if the professional pugilist should react to his profession in this manner he is, by definition, religious; though this is theoretically possible it is highly improbable. No matter how much a person may be concerned over his immediate interests which extend into the vague tomorrows, it is unlikely that any such interests will fall into the same category as that implied here by the word "ulterior."

If some quip should interject the remark which Hegel is supposed to have made against Schleiermacher, that a dog would by the above formal definition be religious, no further answer than that above indicated need be given. A dog, it would then be implied, will be considered to have reached that level of discrimination of the ulterior of which man is found capable—a challenge which thus becomes a boomerang!

What Is "A Religion?"

"A religion" may be defined as a set of meanings and behaviors having reference to individuals who are religious. In other words, "a religion" is a body of theory and practice which has relevance to people who are themselves religious. This reference may be actual or it may be potential; it may be implicit or it may be explicit; the point is, the reference is always there.

Without this reference "a religion" ceases to be a religion; it may be a philosophy or some form of social practice.

If we were to turn back the pages of known human history we should expect to find that people were religious before they had "a religion." Having what has been described as the religious attitude or mood it was but a natural step that there should follow an expression of it in some crystallized manner. There is here involved the psychological principle of overt action; one must *do* something, go and tell some one else; one must frame one's deepest feelings in more satisfactory conceptual terms. The framing of meanings and the setting up of behavior-patterns with reference to the religious attitudes and responses are the original way in which "a religion" was formed, viewed from the perspective of human history.

It would, further, be natural to expect that in the setting-up of meanings and behavior-patterns material should be drawn from non-religious sources. "A religion," therefore, will reflect to a very great extent (how much we shall discuss later) the ideational patterns and the mores of the group. Each religion, accordingly, will reflect a non-religious context, a cultural level, and a social pattern.

What may well be called the inverse process begins early. By an inverse process is meant a reversal of the above order. Instead of the order being that of first becoming religious and then setting up a particular religion, for the great majority the order becomes that of getting "a religion" and then attempting to become religious. This inverse process becomes the usual routine of the masses in the operation of the socio-psychological laws of suggestion and imitation. "A religion" can be taught, but not so the religious frame of mind; the latter is caught on the wing, always, however, implicitly if not explicitly sustaining the former. In this

66

sense, many people may enter into the practices of the accepted religion and yet pass from the scene without themselves becoming religious.

Consider a halty analogy. It is presumable that people would never have skates if they were not (potentially if not actually) skatish. Suppose people hopped; skates would never have been invented as we now know them. Suppose that all people should begin hopping and suppose we should still have such things as skates. Would these skates be skates? The answer: these skates would be skates only so long as there is a reference to skatish people. But suppose there no longer were any such references even in memory. Then, though the skates would be called skates (words do somehow carry over) they would be something other than what they were. They would, perhaps, then be doorstops, weapons, parlor ornaments, or what not. Their being skates depends, in other words, upon the reference to people who are (or were) skatish. It is this point that we are attempting to make in reference to the term "religion." "A religion" would no longer be such if there were no religious people. If all people should cease to *be* religious then "a religion" in the course of time would cease to be what it was. This does not mean that *all* people would have to be religious in order to have "a religion" remain "a religion," no more than it would mean that all people must be skatish in order that skates remain skates. It only means that some of the people are religious and others potentially so.

For the so-called religious genius, the religious frame of mind is of deeper significance than any given religion. The religious genius, of course, may employ the symbols and practices of the particular religion into which he is born; often however, because for him the religious frame of mind is so real, he feels ready and free and compelled to revise that religion in a way that will best suit his frame of mind. Most of us, however, belong

67

to the masses. We get our religion first and then we are supposed to get religious about it—whether we succeed or not. It is evident that frequently a religion will stand in the way for some people in their endeavor to become religious.

Under social pressure a religion gets standardized. Thus is formed a so-called "great religion." Conceivably, however, there may be as many particular religions as there are individuals. That there are certain outstanding religions is due to mass conformity. A person's religion often acts as a proxy for the religious spirit.

What is "Religion?"

The term "religion" is a generic term; a class name for all conceivable religions, formal or informal. It refers to all those meanings, articulations, crystallizations, behaviors, which collectively refer to particular religions. Religion-in-general is not only a term covering those classical expressions known as the great religions of the world but also the innumerable particular and private religions unknown or unrecognized by mankind.

It is plain, accordingly, that there is no such thing as religion-in-general unless, of course, we are followers of some such metaphysical realism as that of Plato. We have already indicated the particular bias, if you will, of this approach in the matter of definitions, *viz.,* naturalism.[2] The world has never known a universal religion; it is presumable that it shall never achieve a collective religion-in-general. Men being what they are with a great variety of cultural backgrounds will make religions, but not "religion." The term, however, is useful in the sense in which all abstract nouns are useful. It is a gross error to employ the term in any concrete sense. Accordingly, it becomes a jar upon

[2] *Ante,* p. 61.

one's ears to hear such expressions as: "what the world needs is religion," or "religion teaches," or "religion promises." Religion-in-general does not exist; at most, it subsists.

A Religion's Theology and Philosophy

A theology and a philosophy may have nothing to do with a religion. There may be no reference whatsoever in a theology or a philosophy to the religious spirit. A theologian or a philosopher is not necessarily religious any more than a religious person is necessarily a theologian or a philosopher. When, accordingly, we speak of a religion's theology and its philosophy we are speaking only of an aspect of the field of theology and philosophy or of an aspect of a given religion.

As we have defined our terms, a religion need not necessarily include a theology nor a philosophy. This point must be made clear.

A theology is a discussion (systematic or unsystematic) concerning a god (or gods) and god's relation to the world and to human experience. Whether or not a religion has something in it which may be termed a god-concept (and, accordingly, whether or not it may have a theology) will depend upon a satisfactory definition of the god-concept. Now, "god" may be defined either from the religious or the non-religious viewpoint. The so-called classical discussions concerning god and god's possible existence have, in the main, followed the non-religious approach. This approach we shall consider in other chapters. A different turn in the definition will occur whenever we approach the problem from the religious angle.

Religiously considered, the term "god," in the minimum sense, denotes or points to *that* in the whatever of serious and ulterior concern which is taken to be of supreme significance or worth. If, as is possible, a religious frame of mind recognizes either implicitly or explicitly nothing in that whatever which stands out in distinction to other phases which appear to matter greatly, then, by definition, there is no god involved in that frame of mind. Conceivably, a person may be religious, according to the definition, and not possess anything corresponding to what may be appropriately called a god; he may react to some strange phenomenon or phenomena, to a set of principles (however poorly formulated), to a vague mass of indefinite material, to a "cause," or to what not. The point here is: in the "religious experience" of individuals, a god-concept or anything which may appropriately be called such, is not *necessarily* involved. If a god is involved in that "experience," "god" is *that* which stands out as supremely focal in what is taken to be of ulterior concern. The "whatever" is the larger area in which the focal point, if any, is god.

The above is not a typically theological definition, to be sure. It is the minimum definition—or as much as can be said in an inclusive sense—considered from the viewpoint of "being religious." What, the further question is suggested, is "god" from the viewpoint of a given religion? The reply is: "god" is conceptualized in so many ways by the great variety of personal religions that only a minimum characterization can be given; in this minimum sense, "god" is *in essence* the *that*, however further pictured or symbolized, which is of supreme significance in any interpretation of the world. This "god" however, though it may be the god of a given religion, *is not necessarily the god implicit in the religious attitude itself*; in the one case, "god" may be related to the religious attitude only potentially, in the second case, the relation is actual. In other words, I may have a religion which involves a god and not be at the same time religious. The god of a given religion is not necessarily synonymous with the god involved in the religious frame of mind.

This latter distinction is important. If, as we have maintained, religions are crystallizations, *i.e.*, conceptualizations, formulations, and behavior-patterns, there is present a large mass of material incorporated from non-religious sources. Among such material which enters into the body of a given religion are ideas and behavior-patterns which affect the god-idea. If, for example, an expressed Christian religion characteristically possesses the father-concept as symbolic of god, such a concept may well have entered into the body of that religion by way of secular borrowings taken from Hebrew family life. Such a non-religious idea becomes a part of religion and becomes a religious idea. It is questionable that such an idea came out of the religious attitude itself; rather, the father-concept seemed to articulate and describe the *that* in the religious feeling of the Founder. It came to symbolize that which mattered supremely.

A religion's theology, thus, is by and large a borrowing from social contexts. The present vogue of applying the socio-historical method has thrown much light upon religious ideas and behaviors for the simple reason that such ideas and behaviors reveal themselves to be just such borrowings. A theology becomes religious only by a reference to people who may be or have been religious. It is no more intrinsically religious than is a cross or an altar. Theologies and philosophies become religious theologies and philosophies only by proxy as do any objects, events, or circumstances. There is thus nothing *uniquely* true about them or nothing supernormal or abnormal about them. They are as true as anything else in the life of man may be said to be true, and by the same token, natural and normal.

PART II

SOME TYPICAL THEMES IN RELIGIOUS
PHILOSOPHY

CHAPTER IV

TRADITIONAL ARGUMENTS FOR BELIEF IN GOD

The question of the existence of God is intimately related (as are other questions) to one's general metaphysical position; how one has voted already in regard to the nature of reality will determine, for example, whether or not one may or must logically be a pantheist, theist, atheist, or agnostic.[1]

In Western Christian thought, in which stream belief in a personal God (theism) has been dominant, it is somewhat curious to note that early thinkers did not attempt to demonstrate God's existence but, on the whole, assumed such a belief. It is no less curious (and perhaps significant) that not only is a well-reasoned and rounded-out argument for the existence of Deity conspicuously absent in the great religious and moral traditions and literature of the Hebrews as well as of later Judaism but that the recorded utterances (in this regard) of Jesus and those of his "inspired" interpreters rest also upon unquestioned assumptions. Arguments appear, of course, in the development of Christian theology, but these take shape largely under the influence of and by the assimilation of Greek thought (especially by way of Platonism, Aristotelianism, and Stoicism) and through a developed theory of religious knowledge and faith (especially by way of Oriental mysticism, Neo-Platonism, and a developed ecclesiastical doctrine of revelation).

Since this development is not only interesting but

---

[1] For a discussion of the various types of metaphysical views *see* my *First Adventures in Philosophy,* Chaps. V-XIII.

informing in reference to a long period of tradition let us pause and take a hasty glance before gathering together the so-called classical theistic arguments.

Plato's "Proof"

Aristotle (384-322 B.C.) took over much from Plato (427-347 B.C.) including Plato's argument for the existence of God, and the church helped itself generously to Aristotle. Plato was one of the very first in Western thought to state a so-called "proof." In the famous tenth book of his *Laws* (his "swan song") he argued in characteristic fashion for the primacy of the soul or mind over body; soul, he asserted, initiates, orders, and inhabits all things that move and it is only reasonable to assert that such processes as we see in nature, though external to us, are initiated, ordered, and inhabited by a similar cause, a Supreme Soul. Consider, he suggests, the movements of the stars, how they go about in perfect circular order; are not these concrete evidences of an ordering Mind, a Soul that is Supreme and Good? [2] Here we have in embryo what later developed into what is now known as the *cosmological* (appeal to a First Cause for an explanation of nature) and the *teleological* (purpose) arguments.

St. Thomas Aquinas and the "Medieval Synthesis"

Important in this general development of Christian theology and fundamental to an understanding of the whole medieval tradition, particularly of the reasoned grounds for the belief in God, is a theory of religious

---

[2] There is considerable debate in the matter of interpretation of Plato's notion of God (gods) and his doctrine of Ideas. For an elementary exposition of Platonic idealism and realism, and Neo-Platonism, *see* my *First Adventures in Philosophy*, pp. 150 ff. A bibliography of Plato is given in the Appendix to *op. cit.*, Chap. VII.

knowledge and faith that culminated in what is known as the "Medieval Synthesis." To understand this development we must go back for a running start.

From Greek tradition the church inherited a theory of knowledge which it adopted into its orthodoxy, *viz.*, that we have two channels by which we come to know the world: sense and intellect. Through the senses we apprehend the fleeting, changing world of sense, a faculty which flows out to sensible objects and identifies one with that object; through the intellect we become acquainted with the stable and permanent in experience, such as principles and laws, which principles and laws shape and govern the world of sense. To illustrate: one can through the faculty of sense become aware of an object falling to the ground, but one cannot through sense, but only through "reason," understand the principle underlying such behavior, *e.g.*, the law of gravitation involved. One apprehends the world thus through both faculties.

Following Aristotle, who emphasized the world of Nature, Greek thought made much of these modes of apprehension. However, when Greek thought came into contact with Oriental thought (especially at Alexandria where west met east) a new faculty was introduced into western tradition by the adoption of the eastern insistence upon its own unique mode of knowing, *viz.*, by what came to be called by a number of terms, ἔκστασις, πίστις, rapture, faith, intuition. This introduction of a mystical theory of knowledge made for three faculties, and to the third, however interpreted, was given the special rôle of an acquaintance with the supernatural world. Neo-Platonism developed this emphasis upon intuitionism.

As subsequent Christian theology took shape, to these three ways of knowing was added a fourth, *viz.*, the growing body of sacred tradition (oral and written).

Gradually it came to be emphasized that religious knowledge had a way of its own, the validity of which was dependent upon nothing else than itself. This fourth way came to be linked with the third (since, as the reader will see, intuitionism standing by itself becomes embarrassing to tradition) in what came to be called revelation and faith.

It was the Aristotelian, St. Thomas Aquinas (1225-74)[3] who wove together these threads and gave to Catholic theology (and to later Protestant orthodoxy) a systematized theory of knowledge which had direct bearing upon what came to be the accepted traditional mode of stating the case for the existence and character of God. Briefly, the "Medieval Synthesis" as drawn up by the systematic theologian, Aquinas, was as follows: What is belief?—asks Aquinas. Answer: belief is thinking with assent (not a mere act of trust or confidence). We believe anything when we give our assent to anything. Now, assent comes in two ways, by logical or intellectual necessity and by a voluntary act of faith. In the first instance, we are compelled to believe certain things (*e.g.*, that a straight line is the shortest distance between two points). This is knowledge. But knowledge does not stand alone upon reason; it is linked up with sense. In fact, our senses prod our intellect and together these constitute knowledge. This knowledge is of the world of nature and is limited to that sphere. It cannot give us "supernatural knowledge;" for instance, we cannot see God with our eyes, nor hear God with our ears, nor touch God with our hands;—and yet, we do have, through knowledge, certain limited evidences *that* God exists (as well as of certain other simple doctrines of the Christian creed) though we cannot give, by this same channel, any *adequate* picture of *what* God

---

[3] On the philosophy of Aristotle, Thomism and its contemporary expressions in Catholicism, see *First Adventures,* etc., pp. 277 ff.

is.[4] The second way in which we give our assent is by a voluntary act of faith. Here we enter the realm of the supernatural, not by intellectual compulsion but by an act of will. In this instance, our intellect is motivated by our will (even as in the other case our intellect was motivated by sense). But, it may be further asked, how, in turn, is the will itself motivated? Answer: our will has a way of its own; it is stirred to activity through being motivated by sheer desire for certain things and it is stirred to activity through being motivated by the tremendous power embodied in the Christian revelation and tradition. In this latter way our intellect gains entrance into the higher realm where not only is the *that* of God (given in knowledge) confirmed but the *what* of the *that* is made clear and certain. It is the realm of faith and it is a realm that moves in its own right, confirming and supplementing what knowledge *per se* cannot give (nor take away!).[5]

Thus, in the thought of Aquinas, was a synthesis (of sense, reason, will, intuition, faith, revelation, tradition) effected, the influence of which extends to our modern day where orthodoxy still obtains—a synthesis that forms the background to an orthodox statement (Catholic and Protestant) of the case for the existence and character of God.

The Three Classical Arguments and the Kantian Criticisms

We turn now to a critical consideration of the traditional arguments for the existence of a personal God—

---

[4] The kind of evidence of the existence of God that is here meant, it needs hardly to be pointed out, is that which we have already mentioned, *viz.*, the Aristotelian-Platonic, cosmological, and teleological evidence.

[5] What Aquinas held as to the character of God need not detain us; except, perhaps, to say that he made much of the transcendental idea (Unmoved Mover) of Aristotle, adding the Trinitarian doctrine and a Christology (concerning the nature of Christ) after the pattern of St. Augustine.

the *ontological,* the *cosmological,* and the *teleological*—
as these were gathered together by the apologist, the
famous rationalistic thinker, Christian Wolff (1679-
1754) who set them up only to have them torn down
by the terrific bombardment of that *desperado* of
modern critical thought, Immanuel Kant (1724-1804).

The *ontological argument* was stated clearly by
Anselm (1033-1109), the famous archbishop of Can-
terbury, who desired to combat a fluttering skepticism
of his day. This argument, it is worthy to note, was
rejected by Aquinas as unworthy of a place in Catholic
theory. (Aquinas, the Aristotelian, held that the only
way—apart from revelation—that God can be known
to exist is the way of induction from sensibly perceived
facts; Anselm's appeal to the existence of God through
the nature of thought itself, he felt to be too precarious
a foundation.) Anselm reasoned thus: I have an idea
of a Being than which nothing greater can be conceived:
this idea is that of the most perfect, the most complete,
the infinite, the greatest conceivable; now an idea which
exists in reality (*in re*) is greater than one which exists
only in conception (*in intellectu*); hence, if my idea
is the greatest, it must exist in reality. Accordingly,
God exists! Descartes (1596-1650) formulated this
kind of an argument in another way: I have an idea of
a Being who is infinite and perfect; how can I, a finite
and imperfect being have such an idea which is beyond
my experience? I surely could not have concocted such
an idea all by myself. Where then did I get such an
idea? It came from the outside, from God. Hence,
the presence of such an idea proves the existence of
such a Being! [6]

Anselm's argument has been attacked in a number of
different ways. A contemporary monk, Gaunilo, replied
that according to such an argument if we should conceive

---

[6] For a brief exposition of Descartes on this point, see *First Adventures,* etc., pp. 458 ff.

of a fabled island as the most exquisite we should be compelled to infer its existence; to which Anselm retorted: Gaunilo's illustration belongs to the category of arbitrary notions and not, as in the case of the notion of a perfect being, to the class of necessity. In other words, says Anselm, the perfect-Being-notion is unique; it is one which is indispensable! Kant's criticism was similar: adding the idea of existence to the idea of the perfect (an attribute supposedly implied in the idea of the perfect) does not make the perfect thereby to exist; adding the idea of existence to the idea of a hundred dollars does not (unfortunately) make a hundred real dollars. Conceived existence and real existence are falsely made synonymous in the ontological argument. Moreover, according to Kant, concepts without percepts are empty; on this basis, since God cannot be perceived in the realm of sense-perception and since this perfect idea (ideal) belongs to the conceptual merely, this idea is empty. Start with an idea and you end with an idea. As to both Anselm's and Descartes's arguments one may ask if one actually does have such a positive idea of the perfect; whatever approach we make to such an idea, does it not move along the way of negations?

The weakness of the ontological argument in its traditional form has long been recognized. Besides the criticisms above given there is the very obvious fallacy of begging the question enmeshed in it. If one could accept the (Platonic) realism underlying Anselm's general argument—for example, that the most real is the most perfect ideal (universal) and that finite-perfection (particular) is real only by virtue of its participation in the perfect ideal (universal) thus embedding the idea of the finite-perfect (particular) in the very warp and woof of the universal, the perfect ideal which is the most real—such an argument takes on greater significance. The *reality* of God, the most perfect ideal (universal), accordingly, is involved in the *idea* of God, the finite-perfect (particular). At any rate, the argument is fascinating though it is convincing only to those who are already convinced and hardly so for those who lack such a conviction.

The *cosmological argument* for the existence of God (appearing in certain aspects of Anselm's statements and implied in Descartes's formulation) in general argues on the basis of the causal series back to an Uncaused Cause or First Cause. Here in this world is a series of causes including the world itself. Now, what caused these causes, what caused the world? Answer: there must be *the* Cause of all causes, the necessary ground of all that is; it is God. This argument is very common in traditional thought; it is employed by Plato in the *Timæus* and the *Laws* (as before mentioned); it is embedded in the notion of the Unmoved Mover in Aristotle's philosophy; and it is implied generally in the notion of a Creator. Kant's criticism involves two steps: first, how do you know when you come to a First Cause by tracing out the causal series? Why stop where you do? Is there not a cause back of the alleged first-cause? Is there not, after all, an endless chain, an infinite regress in the causal series? Is it not purely a dogmatic gesture to stop where conceivably you might go still farther? Might there conceivably not be a plurality of first-causes? But, secondly, suppose you do stop with an alleged First Cause, how do you know that this is God? As the argument stands, may not such a "First" Cause be a Devil or Demiurge? To say it is God is to smuggle in the ontological argument (a perfect being, etc.) which, as we have shown (says Kant) will not hold. The cosmological argument assumes a starting-point, but says nothing further *per se* about the nature of that starting-point. Surely it can hardly argue for theism. And if this is not a sufficient refutation of the general argument, adds the critic, let us raise the serious question concerning the use of the category of cause implied in the argument. So far as human experience is concerned we know of no such ultimate cause; is it not too, an empty concept, barren of perceptual experience?

The *teleological argument* runs somewhat as follows: I find myself in a world which is not chaotic; but a world of order. How does it come that things fit so well together? Am I not compelled to say that such a world is the work of a skilled designer? And is not this designer God? This argument has been a fascinating one; Plato used it; Bacon appealed to it; Christian theologians have favored it all along. It may be said to be a species of the cosmological.

A notable expression of this argument was given by the English theologian and Christian apologist, Paley (1745-1805), in his famous *Natural Theology* (published in 1802), a book which was one of the standard texts in denominational colleges a generation ago. Unmindful (or unaware) of the criticisms of Kant, Paley set forth an argument from analogy somewhat as follows: Consider a watch discovered by some "savage" on a desert island; now, what must such a person say of such a thing; surely, this is evidence of some intelligence; such a complex mechanism as a watch with its various wheels fitting in with each other, clicking away in a marvelous and orderly fashion, surely could not have just happened, by chance; the only reasonable explanation is that it gives evidence of design, of purpose, which in turn reflects a designer, a purposer, an intelligent being. Back of that watch is purpose and back of purpose is a Purposer.

Now, Paley's analogy is clear: consider this world; how complex and wonderful it is; do we not behold a mechanism truly as remarkable as the watch, a grand drama of order and sequence, purposes and designs in nature; how can these things be unless they point to a supreme Designer, Purposer, God? To show this character of nature Paley gathered together an astonishing array of interesting data about animals to impress his readers with the evidence of design in Nature.

It has been pointed out that such an analogy limps. It may be that some kinds of complex mechanisms, like the watch, are made by intelligent beings; but this is not to say that other kinds of complex mechanisms, like plants and animals, *therefore* came into existence in the same way! In other words, the underlying assumption here is that, granted there is order in nature and that there are adaptations, conscious design is the only explanation. Moreover, it may be asked, how could Paley argue on the basis of this analogy for the purposive character of human beings as a part of the general design of a Designer? Is, in other words, the human being a part of the Designer's design? The analogy of the watch does not seem to take care of this factor (assuming that human beings are not wholly mechanical) since the analogy appeals to mechanical features only. If the human being is to be included as a part of the general design of a Designer, does not the analogy by implication run the argument into a dilemma: either the human being must itself be included among the mechanisms, a part of the mechanistic order, a cog in the wheels (an embarrassing conclusion for such teleologists), or, if the human being is free, spontaneous, unpredictable, and at least in some measure unlike the mechanistic order (as, undoubtedly, the analogy purports), then it lies outside the implications of the analogy, and, accordingly, outside this argument for purpose (also an embarrassing conclusion for such teleologists). The analogy, accordingly, does not take care of non-mechanistic features of the world and, presumably, of human beings; strictly, only mechanical systems, accordingly, are designed. The analogy thus halts at an important point.

This "watch-maker" or "carpenter theory" of the

world-process (as it has been called) has been greatly weakened by the explanations set up by the natural sciences, especially by the theory of Natural Selection, by purely mechanistic explanations, by the emphasis on the part of contemporary teleologists on an immanent rather than an external and supernatural teleology, and by the counter-argument of dysteleology (evils in nature).[7]

Kant, however, held that, of the three arguments, the teleological carried the most weight. Yet, the very most one can argue for on the basis of this argument, said Kant, is an Architect, an Arranger, and not a creative, supreme, and omnipotent God. For, as the argument stands, it appeals to the analogy of a human designer who, though he manipulates his material, does not create it. The teleological argument *as such* does not present a first-class God. To make more out of the argument (as those who employ this argument seem wont to do), said Kant, one has to appeal to the cosmological (for a creative First Cause) and this in turn to the ontological (for the kind of God which theism presupposes); but, by such an implicit appeal, one is thrown back on the difficulties encountered in the first two arguments; in other words, one is back where one started!

Kant's Constructive View of God

The Kantian criticisms of the three classical arguments in their traditional form are widely accepted as valid. It is interesting to note that Kant favored what may be termed a special form of the *moral argument;* and, since he is such an important figure in philosophical criticism, we shall pause to consider his own positive claim for God's existence.

To understand the Kantian "argument" we must

---

[7] On the controversy of mechanists, vitalists, and teleologists, see *First Adventures,* etc., Chaps. XVI-XVII. Especially, see "The Case For and Against Teleology," pp. 363 ff.

digress a little to show its relation to other aspects of his philosophy.[8]   Briefly stated, speculation brings us to an impasse!   We do not get the real (noumenal) world, however we try, either through speculation by itself (since his thesis states that concepts without percepts are empty) or by linking speculation with perception which gives us, at most, only the appearance (phenomenal) world.   But, landed as we are in skepticism (as to that real world), by a critical analysis of our knowledge-claims, we are not without light, said Kant.   For, there is another side to mental life.   We are not only theoretical and speculative beings; we are beings with a practical and moral nature.   Whereas one side of our nature as human spirits leads us to make theoretical assertions which, critically considered, do not give us real Reality, the practical side of our nature which is directed to action rather than to theory expresses itself in a compelling way, issuing in imperatives, and *forces* us to make certain assertions about Reality.   These imperatives are of two "kinds."   Some are *hypothetical*, that is, they are, if you please, "if types."   For instance, our practical nature ("practical reason") issues imperatives of *if musts: if* certain ends are to be attained one then *must* do so-and-so.   But, notice, there is another imperative embedded in this side of mental nature which lacks the hypothetical "if" character; it is *categorical*, unconditional.   It cannot be shaken off.   It comes unsought; it admits of no exceptions or compromise; it weighs us down; we cannot escape it; it thunders at us with a presence of an awful reality.   We do not speculate it into consciousness; it is here independent of our theories.   To express it may be as difficult as it is unnecessary.   We may call it duty, the

---

[8] To appreciate fully Kant's *constructive* position, one should have in mind his *critical* philosophy.   Kant's general theory of knowledge is very fascinating.   For an elementary exposition of it, see *First Adventures,* etc., Chap. XXI, "The Critical Philosophy of Kant."   In this section (as in the preceding) we are paraphrasing his views freely.

moral imperative, "the ought," the "moral consciousness"; but however expressed, it just is! [9]

Now this categorical imperative enables us to go on
and say something about the character of the world of
circumstance; it forces us to make unavoidable judgments. What, then? In the first place, since it is given
to us "to ought," surely we ought to be able to do what
we ought (at least in some measure). The ought implies
not only a "should," a "must" but a "can." Otherwise
the ought is morally meaningless. Would it not be the
height of folly if we ought and could not what we
ought? If "can" is implied in a morally meaningful
"ought," this means that we are *free* to do what we
ought. Our first necessary postulate of the moral
consciousness then is that we are free beings, self-determining. We have shown, on the basis of theoretical
(or pure) reason, says Kant, that the whole phenomenal
world is bound up in the vise of causation, rigid necessity, without a glimmer of freedom. But true as this
is in that phenomenal and mechanistic world, it is hardly
true in the world of moral consciousness; what is true
in one set of circumstances is not true in this other.
We belong to two worlds: the one mechanistic, the
other free. The practical reason compels what the
theoretical reason denies, *viz.*, freedom. You cannot
understand freedom but you can be sure about it. If
you were not free you could not have this categorical
command in your moral consciousness on any morally

---

[9] Kant sought to give theoretical expression to the categorical imperative in different ways (though these expressions have but one
meaning) somewhat as follows: Act always in conformity with that
maxim only which you could will that it should become a universal
law; act always so as to treat all rational beings as ends in themselves;
act always so that you can see in your act the Will in the rôle of the
Universal Law-giver. For a direct acquaintance with Kant *see* the
volume *Kant: Selections* (1929), edited by T. M. Greene. Kant's
argument for the existence of God given in our discussion is contained
in his *Critique of Practical Reason* (1788). The date of publication
of his great, critical, and epoch-making work *Critique of Pure Reason*
was 1781.

meaningful basis. Thou oughtest, therefore thou canst. Freedom, accordingly, is the first postulate demanded by the practical reason.

In the second place, there is a further necessary postulate which arises in the thundering moral consciousness. Consider its nature: it sounds commands which have no finite limit; it is always compelling from more to more toward a flying goal. Like the horizon before us, we may move toward it but we do not reach it—it is always ahead. It sets a limitless task. The insatiable ought moves me from more to more. Now, is it not clear that such a moral command cannot be realized in finite time? Surely, the grave is not its goal. Does not such an infinite task, which it implies, demand infinite time? What, then? We are compelled to say (postulate) on the basis of this ought that we are immortal; otherwise such a command is morally meaningless. Immortality, then, is the second necessary postulate demanded by the practical reason.

In the third place, we are forced to postulate on the basis of the categorical imperative an eventual triumphant outcome or realization of these demands (at least in an increasing and commensurate manner); otherwise, they are, again, morally deficient. If we ought to do the right, ought not this ought to become realizable (at least, increasingly so) and ought not the ought have an appropriate cosmic setting? Consider the folly of such an ought in a world of circumstance which commands it, but at the same time would offer neither sufficient opportunity nor time to realize it, and which, moreover, would furnish for it no adequately sustaining background. That there is such an appearance of folly in the world of experience is surely evident to anyone, without any belabored argument.

A life of four-score-years-and-ten (to say nothing about physical, environmental, mental, and moral handicaps) cuts us off without our being able to give adequate expression to all that we ought to do and become; and during that brief span the accompanying results of our feeble expressions of that ought often bring grief, chagrin, and despair. Ought not this ought, accordingly, to have a setting beyond the short life-span of man and one that is more appropriate than the dismal background which the world of circumstance by itself appears to offer—if this ought is a valid ought? Not only ought there to be further outreaches (personal immortality) but eventually more propitious circumstances. Ought not, for instance, one who attempts to realize that ought, to be happy? (And, conversely, we might ask: ought not the one who does not attempt to realize it to be unhappy?) Is there not an evident implication in the moral command not only that more time be allowed for its adequate realization but a cosmic setting favorable to those who give expression to it?

Surely, says Kant, there is: there is the implication of the *summum bonum*, the highest good, in the categorical ought in which not only is the ought realizable (in more adequate time and circumstance) but crowned with appropriate and commensurable rewards. The *summum bonum* implies duty fulfilled (at least in increasing measure) and desire satisfied, virtue eventually realizable, and happiness commensurably attained. Unless this is so, such a command of the moral consciousness is morally indefensible—it is not, then, the *summum bonum;* not that the moral consciousness rests upon its eventual realization and proper satisfaction but that its realization and commensurate satisfaction are morally bound up with it *as the highest good.*

In this world of mud and tears, how true is it not that the man who attempts to be virtuous, to realize the ought, is often unhappy, and the man who seeks and even attains to what he experiences as happiness is often not virtuous? Surely, such a circumstance affords an unjust background *per se* for the categorical imperative; surely, in this life, as it is, there is no guarantee of the sublime union of virtue and happiness morally embedded in the *summum bonum*. That such a union ought to be eventually consummated remains a necessary implication or demand of our moral consciousness. How, then, can these things be? It is necessary, Kant argues, to postulate the existence of a world-ground which is of a character sufficiently capable and moral to bring about the union of this virtue and happiness. God is required, in other words, not for the sake of eventually making a man happy or virtuous but for making a virtuous man happy. The assurance of the existence of a God rests morally and certainly upon the unconditional demand of a morally meaningful moral consciousness. God is the third necessary postulate demanded by the practical reason.

Are we, then, certain of the existence of such a World-Ground? Theoretically: no; but practically and morally: yes. The existence of God is not a theoretical assertion but a morally certain imperative of our moral nature. Not only ought we to have *faith* that *God ought to be* but we are driven by the categorical drive of our moral nature to a *necessary affirmation* that *God is*. And not only are we morally sure *that* God is but we are as certain in some respects *what* God is; we are certain, for example, that God is "a moral Being" and that God possesses *at least* such a character as is consonant with the demands of our moral consciousness. This does not, we repeat, permit us to set up a metaphysical picture of God on mere theoretical grounds or allow us to speculate *ad libitum;* what we *can* say of God's character is what we *must* say on the grounds of that highest good embedded in our moral nature. This may indeed not be much; but it is something and it is necessary.

An Appraisal of the Kantian View

The critical reader may feel prompted to suggest a number of criticisms of Kant's constructive "argument." He may say that this is hardly an argument; it is rather a dogmatic assertion since it rests not upon an argumentative basis but upon an unconditioned and unarguable position. With this criticism, Kant, in a sense, would have to agree. But then, why argue as he does? Is there not a contradiction of the initial dismissal of all argument (theoretical reason) in the later set of doctrinal statements which, after all, are "arguments" based upon practical reason? Has not Kant lugged in, for example, the cosmological argument in accounting for the moral consciousness—a World-Ground as *the cause* of our moral nature? It would appear that he has and that his constructive position is beset with philosophical argument. But, let us try to be fair with him.

It is evident that a moral Being (God) is brought into the picture in a way that savors strongly of the cosmological argument; but, Kant would perhaps say in reply to the charge of contradiction something to this effect: "I do not *argue* God's existence upon the basis of *mere* argument nor do I rest my case *merely* upon the implications (logical as they are) of the moral consciousness; fundamentally I appeal to the moral consciousness itself which does not reason out such conclusions in the ordinary rational way but commands and compels them. Call it argument if you will, but it is nothing apart from moral necessity."

We may feel disposed to translate all this by the term "experience," or more exactly by "moral experience," or by a sort of intuitive certainty; but we dare not do so, since such terms as "experience" and "intuition" would tend to distort Kant's general metaphysical system and render it wholly self-contradictory. It would be truer, perhaps, to say that we have a moral *a priori* independent of experience or independent of intuition-in-the-sense-of-immediate-experience, and independent of the categories of reason. This moral *a priori* is *sui generis* and it abides in man's will rather than his "reason." As such, its imperatives, its commands (which may be stated in a number of different ways) have the force of arguments, but are not *mere* arguments; their very "rationality" has a color of its own given to it by that moral *a priori*.

If this is so, we may feel disposed to ask further if Kant's psychology is not at fault; in other words, can man's psychological nature be thus cut up into such a separable compartment as is implied by a distinct moral *a priori*? Is there not a psychological artificiality involved here? Would not Kant have to modify his psychology considerably, in the light of modern genetic studies if he were to speak today? Furthermore, granting that the implications of a God are convincing as drawn from the *summum bonum* of the moral consciousness, has not Kant taken a tremendous leap from a kind of rationally vague and originally pure, moral *a priori* to the highly differentiated claims of the *summum bonum*? Can we be so certain of the implications of the *summum bonum* when the *summum bonum* has such a vague setting itself? Again, is it possible (other than in an artificial way) to harmonize Kant's constructive statement about God with the rest of his philosophy?

Other criticisms may (and should, perhaps) occur to the reader. But, laying these aside, what, in general, may be said in Kant's favor? It is quite generally agreed that Kant's notable contribution contained in his constructive view on the question of God lay in his emphasis upon the *moral* approach. It has been the tendency of subsequent thinkers—those who have found genuine difficulties with the traditional arguments, difficulties in certain systems of philosophy which imply the existence of a God but at the expense of a *bona fide* theism, difficulties in an appeal to a shadowy "intuition" or to a vague "religious experience," and who, at the same time, regard a belief in a God as not only permissible but essential to an adequate interpretation of reality—to make much of the moral nature of man as the ground for their belief or faith in the existence of a God. Such a ground, it is argued in general, not only strongly suggests the *existence* of God but points to the *character* of God. A mere argument for *existence* as such, it is plain, is no argument for the *quality* of that existence. Hence, a moral argument (not necessarily the Kantian form) has the merit of a two-edged sword; it not only carves out an argument for existence but an argument, at the same time, for quality. It might, indeed, be easier to argue for existence than for quality (especially in the light of the problem of evil, granting that the quality of good is a necessary attachment to the religiously valid God-concept). The merit of the moral argument lies in its emphasis upon the qualitative character of experience as its starting-point; the quality of God is guaranteed in the very argument itself. This, so it is maintained, is the chief merit of the moral approach since it gives the kind of God (if it gives an argument at all) which is the God of a religiously valid religion and worthy of worship and adoration. Of what encouraging use is the assurance of the existence of a God if that God is a Devil or a Neutral Entity? Hence, many theists today look back upon Kant with gratitude for the direction he has given their thought even though they cannot follow him in goose-step fashion.

CHAPTER V

CONTEMPORARY ARGUMENTS FOR BELIEF IN GOD

We turn, now, to consider some contemporary arguments for theism which follow upon the Kantian criticisms of the traditional arguments. The classification we here follow is quite arbitrary for the simple reason that there is much overlapping in the forms in which present-day arguments are set forth.

The Naïve and Dogmatic "Argument" from "Religious Experience"

Consider, first, the "argument" from "religious experience." This assumes a number of forms and, accordingly, must be judged by the form and manner in which it is presented. There are some who appeal to what they glibly call "religious experience" as giving one assurance of God's existence without giving to others any adequate notion of what is really meant. Such a position may be satisfactory to the one who has the experience, but it is, at best, a "testimony" rather than an argument. Such an appeal slips through the fingers of the philosophical inquirer (for which some take a "thank God" attitude!) and is beyond examination. He may look with respect upon such an appeal or view it with grave suspicion, depending upon whether or not he finds appropriate "fruits" of such an experience.

There have been so many false prophets in the world that it has become legitimate to put any such philosophically-isolated claims under suspicion. It has been remarked that "experience" is a weasel term; it might mean any or everything and perhaps nothing; and "religious experience" may be even a still "weaslier" term—a covering for a subjective wish and a hope rather than a genuinely defensible awareness of an objective f(F)act. Furthermore, to chisel out "religious experience" in too nice a manner from other experience may be to commit the same psychological error as described above in connection with an appeal to a separate "moral *a priori.*" This type of naïve and dogmatic "argument" is as philosophically indefensible as it is irrefutable, and need not detain us further.

The Mystic Claim

Alongside this statement appealing to "religious experience" in a crude and glib manner and its attending objections (at least, warnings) should go the claims of many *extreme* mystics. These people say that they possess "inside information" with reference to the existence and character of God. It is rather characteristic of such extreme mystics to make extravagant claims (such as the unreality of the physical world, of time and space, of individuality, of evil, etc.), and to go the way of pantheism rather than theism and to assert an extreme monistic idealism.

We should, however, hesitate to condemn all mystic claims on the ground that there are strong philosophical objections to their extreme expressions. That there is much to be said for a *mild* type of mystic experience and its claim to an assurance of the existence and character of God, is now being championed by a number of philosophically respectable thinkers. For example, Professor Rufus Jones, a life-long student of mysticism, distinguishes two types of mystic experience: the *via negativa* and the *affirmative.*

According to the first or extreme type the claim is that we can be sure of the existence of God, but we cannot say anything about God, for to say something is to limit what is itself beyond limitations. Hence, all "characteristics" of God are partial, negative, and untrustworthy. This form of mystic experience and utterance has been characteristic of many Roman Catholic mystics, and it is the kind of mysticism found in Plotinus and Neo-Platonism and in Indian thought.[1] However, the more valid form is the affirmative or less extreme type which is expressed in the New Testament by Saint Paul and Saint John and revived by the more humanistic movements of the Renaissance and the Reformation; further classic names of this type are: Hans Denck, Pascal (1623-1662) famous for his *Pensées* (or Thoughts), Thomas Traherne, Jacob Boehme (1575-1624 — who influenced Schelling, Hegel, and Ralph Waldo Emerson), George Fox, (founder of the Quakers) and others. It is characteristic of this type not only to claim an immediate awareness of a Presence but to affirm the character of that Presence in a positive way, *e.g.,* that it is akin to the human spirit (*i.e.,* it is essentially spiritual in character), that it possesses moral qualities, that it is transcendental but yet immediately self-revealing (for those who practice appropriate spiritual exercises), and that (for Christian mystics) it is historically revealed in the great saints and above all in the person of Jesus Christ. This type of mysticism is essentially Christian as Professor Jones has outlined it; it is a sane, wholesome type; for those who have had their candles lit, it is a source of light revealing a worshipful God.[2]

This mild type of mystic experience which claims to have an immediate awareness of the existence and character of God is, from the point of view of other philo-

---

[1] Excerpts from the *Upanishads* and from Plotinus are given in *First Adventures,* etc., pp. 116 ff.

[2] *See* his essay "Why I Enroll with the Mystics" in *Contemporary American Theology* (1932), edited by Vergilius Ferm, Vol. I., pp. 191 ff; especially pp. 199 ff.

sophical considerations (unless one insists upon an extreme monistic ontology) more defensible; but, unless it can be put into the framework of a defensible analysis of the peculiar experience itself, especially as to its knowledge-claim, it is not as convincing as it *philosophically* ought to be; for, if one has the experience and cannot give at least a *reasonable* (not necessarily a completely rational) account of it, one can hardly escape the charge of dogmatism, of error, or illusion. It is rather customary for many such mystics to suffer such charges in acquiescence since they admit their inability to give a satisfactory analysis; they are content in merely affirming their profound conviction of a "revelation" (or in Quaker language "an opening"). A "revelation" standing by itself is, however, at most a testimony; it is hardly an argument. To those who lack it no argument can of itself bring conviction either of God's existence or (what is religiously important) of God's character.

Hocking's Revision of the Ontological Argument

Attempts have, accordingly, been made to give such an alleged immediate awareness of personal Deity a reasonable setting in the scheme of things. When this is done, such a religious mysticism has assumed the character of an ontological argument. It is just this that Professor Hocking of Harvard has sought to do in his well-known book *The Meaning of God in Human Experience* (1912). He recasts the older ontological arguments and gives the newer form (which he regards as highly defensible) a mystical or intuitional setting. The sum and substance of Hocking's view is that instead of trying to deduce the existence of God from an idea of God (*e.g.*, Anselm), we affirm the idea of God from an experience of God. For, consider: are there not some ideas which we would not have if we did not have an experience of the realities which such ideas express? Take such ideas as the self, other-minds, the world; are not these ideas based upon experience (an intuitive feeling)? How does it come that you speak of self (an idea)? Answer: because in intuitive experience such an idea is grounded. How, of other-selves (an idea)? Answer: because you tacitly appeal to a feeling of social *rapport* which sustains such an idea. How, of the world (an idea)? Answer: because not only do you have in sense-experience an immediate awareness of external nature but you have an immediate awareness of that Nature as-a-whole, an Other-Self.

Such ideas, as we have named, rest upon an intuitive awareness of *a whole;* and we should never have them if it were not for *the Whole experience* which they report. Reality-as-a-Whole (Absolute) has its setting in experience; apart from such an experience there could be no such idea. It is *the* idea of ideas, *the* whole of wholes. Now, what characterizes religious mysticism is an intuitional experience of an all-inclusive-Whole, which is to say, God.[3] It is the merit of mystical ex-

---

[3] Intuition and intellect, he maintains, always go together. Some intuitions are original and some acquired. It is characteristic of an intuition to perceive *wholes;* intuitions act as a framework for knowledge which fills out details for these intuitional *wholes.* (*See* his *Types of Philosophy*, 1929, p. 208 ff.)

To underline his insistence upon an immediate awareness of an all-inclusive Whole (*i.e.,* to sustain his revised ontological argument), he sets up a dialectic by and through which this monistic insight is to be interpreted. Briefly, these are the knowledge-details: *Thesis:* An object (world, or whatever you please "out there") is what it is only to a self (me); *Antithesis:* Yet, this object is "out there," independent of *my* self. How can *both* be true? *Synthesis:* (a) Do *we* (you and I) not have experiences of the *same* object (rather than each having his own object)? Answer: we do. How is this possible? Answer: Through our immediate awareness of each other's minds we are aware of the *same* object. Thus, the object is what it is for me (and for you) and yet it is more: it is what it is for *us.* The *synthesis* is thus effected by a resolution of both the *thesis* and *antithesis,* both of which are true. (b) With the "out there" thus joined to *me* and to

perience to give testimony *par excellence* to such an idea; the mystic is the one who has the most comprehensive experience of the Absolute. It is characteristic of the mystic, accordingly, to seek solitude and detachment from all particular things and persons—particular-as-they-appear-on-the-surface—and to enter into that deeper and sacred realm of unity in this Absolute through the awareness of the Whole; and for him this is the very essence of worship. The ontological argument is thus, according to Hocking, brought down from the heights of mere speculation-in-a-realm-of-mere-ideas to an empirical grounding; thus, it becomes respectable in the measure that it is grounded in human experience.

A number of critical questions may occur to the reader. For example: is the God of valid religion the Absolute? Must one pay the price of an ontological idealism to get the realism involved in Hocking's experiential appeal to the Absolute? [4] In other words, must one drink from the cup of an absolute idealism to get the experience of the reality of God? Or, to reverse the order, must one, having the alleged experience of the

---

you and to *us* and we to one another in a common social experience—which is *more* than merely *my* experience or *your* experience or even *our* experience—are we not at once in the presence of a larger Experience which includes the "out there" and you and me and all of us in an all-inclusive Whole—the underlying Reality, the larger Self which creatively binds everything together into a unity of Selfhood? This *final synthesis* then, is God, and it is not only implicit in each step in the dialectic but it is that awareness of *the Whole* given in the typical mystical-religious experience. (Hocking's dialectic is much more elaborate, of course, than here stated.)

[4] It may be well here to point out that Professor Hocking makes much of the knowledge-value of feeling. On this score, the intuitional experiences of the mystic which form the setting of ideas are not to be dismissed as mere dogmatic pronouncements; for, if it be true that such "feeling experiences" can be defended in a reasonable way as issuing in knowledge, the claim at least becomes respectable. For a "reasonable" defence of mysticism or intuitionism *see* the following sections in *First Adventures,* etc., pp. 95 ff; 119; 251 ff; four forms of intuitionism, 494 ff.

reality of God therefore *tout de suite* become an absolute idealist? Are these two indissolubly linked? [5]

The "Religious A Priori" Argument

Very closely allied to the "argument" from "religious experience" is another "argument," *viz.*, the appeal to what may be (and has been) called the "religious *a priori*." [6] According to Ernst Troeltsch (1865-1923) —who follows but modifies the Kantian philosophy— there are bound up with religious experience, certain *a priori* (given) elements of rational insight, certain indisputable certainties, independent of speculation, among which is "the sense of the presence and reality of the Super-human and Infinite." This religious experience which possesses such rational certainty is *sui generis*, that is, it is not to be identified with the moral consciousness as such nor is it (with Kant) to be considered as a deduction (however necessary) from the moral consciousness.

The religious *a priori* is a separate category of the human consciousness, existing in its own right and issuing in certain rational intuitions. The existence of God is assured in the given rational elements which are ushered in by the religious consciousness. Thus, God's existence is guaranteed as an axiomatic truth and certainty, not by mere speculation nor by an ethical consciousness but by an experience which stands on its own

---

[5] The reader should ask such further questions as: What about the character of such an Absolute? Is it concrete enough to be morally significant and worshipful? How about the possibility of error in intuitions? Must not intuitions be subjected to criteria other-than-themselves in order to stand the test of validity (*i.e.*, are intuitions standing-alone sufficiently dependable)? Are we here not in the morass (or should we say "Canaan"?) of pantheism? May not such a mystical experience of the Whole (the Absolute) be a kind of "nature mysticism" without any *necessarily* religious reference? (This latter query is suggested by our previous discussion of the typical religious response.) For a reply to such questions as these, the critical reader must, of course, turn to Hocking's own detailed exposition.

[6] *Ante,* pp. 45 ff.

feet (so to speak) and has its own ways of knowing. Tune in on this experience and you get a rational conviction which is to be gotten only on this wave-length or by this station. No wave-length or station can give you this first-hand assurance other than religious experience itself; and it is not a vague experience attended by probabilities or surmises but it is an experience which gives definite knowledge and overwhelming certainty. It is experience coupled with reason, or rather, it is reason grounded in experience; and it is a definite kind of experience and a definite kind of reason. God is given immediately, is present, is real, is a fact of the religious *a priori*. God, if reached in any other way, says Troeltsch, is not the God of religion.[7]

Brief mention ought to be made of another expression of the religious *a priori* by a celebrated contemporary, viz., Rudolf Otto.[8] In his widely known book *The Idea of the Holy* (rev. ed., 1925), Professor Otto conducts an analysis of the religious *a priori* beyond that of Troeltsch. It is his claim that such an analysis reveals that the *a priori* element in the distinctly religious experience is the awareness of the holy or the sacred. This is not to be understood, he hastens to say, as an awareness of goodness (though it may and does eventuate in such a conception); rather, the holy or the sacred signifies an awareness of something mysterious, terrible, awe-inspiring about Reality, a *mysterium tremendum* which

---

[7] It may be noted that the positions of Troeltsch and others who follow Kant, differ significantly in their analysis of the intuitional "argument." The older intuitionists (preceding Kant), on the whole, held that the mind is endowed with certain ultimate and self-evident axioms. One such axiom is that of the existence of God and that God has certain definite characteristics (*e.g.*, God is eternal, favorably disposed to mankind, etc.). Thus the Stoic Cicero "argued." Many pre-Kantian theologians—*e.g.*, the eighteenth century Deists—held that the evidence of God's existence is axiomatic. Troeltsch and others, however, insist that the *a priori* is more than a rational certainty; it is empirically given; as such they combine the rational with the empirical.

[8] *Ante,* pp 41-42.

in its original non-rational, non-ethical, non-esthetic nature can be called (for lack of a better term) the *numinous*. Whether this *numinous* is to be interpreted as an emotion, a sensation, or as a special "religious sense" is not so evident (on this point there is room for various interpretations); one thing is clear in Professor Otto's meaning, and that is, it is *sui generis* and forms the background for our awareness, our cognition of the Divine. He sets up a convincing case for his "religious *a priori*" in his collection and interpretation of the testimonies found in religious literature, especially primitive expressions and "first-hand" experiences. Before religious men had a clear conception of a God they were aware, through a kind of overwhelming "eeriness," of that Presence; and this unique awareness, though not to be identified with a moral consciousness, furnishes the religious mind with a peculiar susceptibility to such ideas as the unity and the goodness of such a Being, worthy of worship.

Characteristic of this type of "argument," *i.e.*, an appeal to a "religious *a priori*" which we find in the positions of Troeltsch and Otto, is the appeal to a definite kind of knowledge which is furnished by religious experience, a knowledge which is independent of any other avenue. It is an appeal to experience coupled with rational intuition. It departs from Kant's type of argument in that it sets up its own structure independent of the moral consciousness. Some critics, on this basis, hold that such a divorce is costly to a knowledge of the *character* of God necessary to a vital and worthy religion. It goes beyond the usual mystical appeals since it resolutely tries to set forth an analysis.

Whether its psychology is sound is a matter open to serious question; for instance, it might well be asked (as was pointed out concerning the moral *a priori*) whether men have separate sets of categories in certain types of experience and whether such nice distinctions are psychologically permissible? The price of analysis is often paid by the coin of artificiality. Further, we may ask critically, what is meant by the religious experience itself? The answer to this latter question appears uncertain and somewhat circular in the writings of these men. For, the religious experience seems to be bound up with the "religious *a priori*" and the "religious *a priori*" with the experience. And again, it may be asked, whether such an analysis, however credible, is sufficient by itself? Is there not the need, as we have suggested above, of further testing of what is *claimed* to be given immediately in such an *a priori*? If we allow this as another form of the ontological argument may not such an "argument" need supplementation in order to assume a more valid form? This is not to suggest that much may not be said for intuitionism (however differently stated); but only to point out that intuitionism may need something beyond itself if a more valid *argument* for the existence and character of God is to be constructed.

An Idealistic Argument

Consider next the argument for God's existence which modern idealism (historically, at least) has offered. In its rather typical form it runs something to this effect: The world as we know it is known only in relation to a knowing self. We know of no world apart from the knowing self. Well, then, what about the world when the self ceases to know (*e.g.*, the unconscious state or death)? Does this world which appears to have an existence independent of our knowing then evaporate? What about the world before there were human minds? Does my body cease to be when I am not conscious of it? Surely not. What then? Answer: it continues to exist because it is continually being known by a greater-than-I. This greater knowing Self is God, the Divine Knower.[9]

Critics of this type of argument counter with an attack upon this fundamental claim of the earlier modern idealists, *viz.*, that reality because it is known only through idea is therefore essentially idea.[10] What if reality is fundamentally *more* than idea, *e.g.*, in some respects fundamentally *other-than-idea?* Moreover, is this reality which thus holds the world together in or by its Mind, the God of valid religion? Is such a God religiously satisfactory? [11] Is not an argument achieved at a great expense, *viz.*, the necessary adoption of the idealistic philosophy itself? Moreover, some will ask, has not Kant shown that to build up a structure merely upon ideas leads to a speculative emptiness? [12]

The Value-Argument and Ritschlianism

We turn now to a consideration of a widely influential argument, to which (for want of a better term) we shall give the name: the value-argument for God's existence. It assumes a variety of forms and, like so many of the

---

[9] *Cf., e.g.,* the dialectic of Hocking, *ante,* pp. 98-99, foot-note.

[10] *See* the refutations of Berkeleian Subjective Idealism in *First Adventures,* etc., pp. 483 ff. Contemporary idealists tend to soft-pedal this old-time epistemological refrain, preferring to plead the cause of human values as grounded in reality.

[11] This latter charge is directed particularly to the absolute idealists. The reader will here notice the veiled accusation of pantheism again, the implication being that such a God is neither *necessarily* moral nor worshipful. Certain followers of Hegel—notably such idealists as E. Caird, J. Caird, J. H. Stirling, John Watson, W. T. Harris, Josiah Royce—as well as Hegel himself, have been highly conscious of the seriousness of the charge of pantheism in their views and have sought to overcome it by asserting that though nature is not God as commonly understood yet from the higher point of view all Reality is God. Whether or not it is defensible to hold the view that nature is nature from one point of view and yet the manifestation of the Absolute from another point of view (the higher synthesis) is a matter that needs critical examination.

[12] *Cf.* Kant's criticism, *ante,* p. 81. It is only fair to remark that to such a charge certain idealists reply by interpreting Kant's doctrine in favor of idealism.

modern currents of thought, claims its parental source in the critical philosophy of Kant. It is to be distinguished in general by its distrust of both metaphysics and mysticism; it would have nothing to do with *a prioris* or intuitions nor with speculative arguments however seemingly logical. It would appeal rather to human needs and to judgments of worth (value). In the thought of R. H. Lotze (1817-81), there is an inkling of this type of argument, where it is suggested that what ought to be must be, that what has value must also be real. No matter what the sciences may say to the contrary, he suggests, there is something in the feeling of value that furnishes reason with the status of asserting what is. At first glance, this seems to be the Kantian argument all over again; but this is not so. For, in the thought of this general school, though the moral consciousness issues in compelling assertions as to the nature of reality (Kant), judgments of worth (value) may be more than moral judgments; they may even have a character distinctly religious.

No name is perhaps more celebrated in this line of thought than that of Albrecht Ritschl (1822-89), the German theologian whose influence was great enough to inaugurate the most celebrated nineteenth-century school of Christian theology, a school which carries his name. From his predecessors and contemporaries, Ritschl drew his thoughts freely, and against them he reacted violently; we need but mention Kant, Schleiermacher, [13] Hegel, and Lotze. His notable book, *The Christian Doctrine of Justification and Reconciliation* (Eng. tr., 1872), betrays at once a marked bias (which he freely admits), *viz.*, the Christian approach to the problem of the reality and character of God. Like many others of fertile mind, he set forth abundant and rich suggestions which provoked subsequent controversy and rendered his own thought not always self-consistent.

---

[13] *Ante,* pp. 40 ff. Schleiermacher's dates: 1768-1834.

What we are here interested in, however, is his approach to the question of God's existence. Typical of the religious slant on life, he says, is man's practical solution of the enigma of his existence. For, consider: man is subject to a domineering world of nature and yet he is a spiritual being possessing the impulse to assert his independence of nature. It is this practical self-assertion, arising from man's deepest nature and need, of the worth of human personality and its evaluating tendencies, independent of theoretical or practical obstacles, which constitutes the religious spirit. It makes judgments of value which are trustworthy in their own right. There are two kinds of "value-judgments" (a term which through him has become celebrated) which man applies to the world of his experience: first, there are what he calls *concomitant* (dependent) value-judgments—those which operate in our interest in perceived facts, in scientific knowledge, and in theoretical cognition, which are accompanied by an expression of worth; [14] secondly, there are what he calls *independent* value-judgments—those which extend beyond perceived facts out to an ideal order, judgments of worth which make affirmations independent of any claims of theory or so-called scientific fact. The religious spirit moves in this latter realm; it makes judgments of worth independently, even as moral judgments, however close to the religious spirit, move freely in the moral sphere. Now, these independent religious value-judgments express a relation of man to his world; they express man's superiority and yet his higher dependence; they express faith in the existence of a superhuman spiritual power by and through which man's own worth is vindicated and his victory over every obstacle is assured.

---

[14] Even our so-called disinterested scientific knowledge (he says) is not free from this evaluating process; *e.g.,* our awareness of stern facts hardly takes place without an initial interest, and such interest is itself a value-judgment.

God, accordingly, is not reached through speculation, nor by "evidences" in nature, nor in intuition, nor in an *a priori*, nor in a mystical experience; God's existence as well as God's nature are known essentially in the religious value-judgment. This independent value-judgment asserts man's need of such a God and the consequences following upon such an assertion sustain this judgment. Indeed, this is no speculative proof; it is rather a common testimony of those who share in the experience of deliverance from the bonds of Nature and recognize the Divine factor in that deliverance. Call it faith if you will; but it is a faith that is grounded in a judgment of worth which, in turn, promotes satisfaction and practical assurance.[15]

There are a number of strains in this type of thought. There is a subtle appeal to experience, to faith, to moral worth, to social confirmation, to revelation; yet there is a fundamental agnosticism with reference to an appeal to mere experience in the mystic sense, to rational faith-as-such, to the deliverances of the moral consciousness by itself, to metaphysics, and to the deliverances of the sciences. There are marked pragmatic strains (*e.g.*, that such an affirmation of God works!), a Christian bias (if you will) and a note of subjectivity (*i.e.*, no Divine Reality apart from the individual's religious value-judgment) the escape from which is sought by an appeal to history and to religious fellowship. His followers have helped themselves freely to different interpretations, and we need not concern ourselves here with them. The noteworthy factor in the Ritschlian type of argument is the emphasis upon value which in modern philosophical thought has played an increasing rôle; especially is this emphasis to be noted in con-

---

[15] He goes on to show how Christian doctrines are thus to be interpreted independently of any metaphysics or scientific world-view. Let speculation do its worst, he would maintain; the religious man has his own inner assurance of the kind of God which is exhibited in "the Christian Revelation."

temporary theistic belief. The reader will readily note how this type of argument differs from the others which we have considered; he will determine for himself (by a little reflecting) the merits or demerits of such an approach.

The Moral-Religious Faith Argument of Baillie

A type of argument which follows closely upon the one we have just been considering as well as upon the typically Kantian constructive argument, is the moral argument. We have given sufficient consideration to this approach in our exposition of Kant to suggest its general thesis. It needs only to be pointed out, however, that the moral argument in its modern dress need not follow the Kantian form completely. There is considerable room for variation and even of digression.

An example of such a digression coupled with a bit of Ritschlianism and colored by what may be termed "religious faith" is to be had in the thought of Professor John Baillie, formerly of Union Theological Seminary (New York).[16] Let us summarize his view briefly. Beginning with the fact of the moral consciousness, our certitude of duty, which has foundations of its own and in no need of argumentation, Baillie insists that a religious view of the world is inevitable. Moral experience has a logic of its own, original and certain; this logic issues in religious faith, or (to put it differently) creates about it a certain context of beliefs and attitudes (*e.g.*, trust) about the nature of reality, which constitutes the religious point of view. Giving that moral consciousness a deeper meaning and giving significance to the values bound up with it, this is the typically religious expression. One does not reach such meanings outside

---

[16] A very lucid exposition is contained in his *The Interpretation of Religion* (1928).

the inner circle of the moral claim; nor does one argue oneself into it; rather, having it, a religious perspective is an inevitable result. He who stands outside must forever be a stranger. Now, the logic of moral experience gives rise to religious faith which in turn has its own logic.

In other words, certain very definite beliefs and attitudes arise from the religious faith which in turn was prompted by a moral logic. All this is quite independent of any metaphysical speculation or of scientific body of fact; it has a character of its own and depends on itself alone. The only way to appreciate the force and validity of the claims of religious faith is to go down deep and nourish the very tap-roots of the moral consciousness itself; if this is alive all else will follow simply and inevitably. It will be found that, among other certainties, there will come, as naturally and inevitably as the ripened fruit that issues from a healthy fruit-bearing tree whose roots are properly nurtured, the conviction that God exists and that God is the Moral Absolute which is getting expressed in the absolute character of the moral claim.[17] The logic of religious faith, however, compels us to say more. For instance, if we must say, (as we must, according to Baillie) that our environing world exhibits itself to be (in at least an important phase of it) a moral order revealed in our moral consciousness, are we not forced to assert that it is under intelligent control? And is this not to say that God thus assured upon the basis of that moral consciousness must be a Spirit and a Person; for, is not the moral consciousness itself bound up with spirit and with

---

[17] The reader may wonder what is meant by the moral claim. Baillie suggests among other readings the following: the worth of self, the obligation to seek and follow duty, loyalty, love, honor, truthfulness, purity, unselfishness—all of which may give rise to uncertainty as to *how* these are to be realized but which issue in no uncertainty *that* they should get expressed.

personality? Whatever more God may be, is God anything less? [18]

There may be rational difficulties, says Baillie, in this type of "argument." But if there are, we are reminded that the difficulties are not of our own making but somehow inhere in the fact that moral and religious certainties have a way (and validity) of their own and do not submit to coldly impersonal logic; we stir up difficulties which are admittedly insuperable as soon as we try to reason out our arguments upon any logic other than that of religious faith. After all, faith's assurance is intimately personal and only those who play fair with their "conscience" really "know" and are assured.

The Pragmatic Argument of William James

A discussion of contemporary arguments is hardly complete without attention to the pragmatic approach. Though this is involved in other of the arguments (especially in Ritschlianism) we shall set it down as a special type. For an illustrous example we turn to William James (1842-1910). Though he looked with a sympathetic eye upon the mystics who claimed to have direct visions or intuitions of a God,[19] his honest frankness compelled him to assert that for him there was no such kind of evidence or assurance. This, however, did not prevent his *believing* in a God though it did compel him to seek another way to assert such an existence. The way open to him he found to be that of strong probability if not actual certainty. To understand this

---

[18] He goes on to stress the immanence of God and gives what appears to be a metaphysically idealistic tone to his general argument.

[19] *Cf., ante,* p. 53. Also *cf., First Adventures in Philosophy,* pp. 119; 263 ff.

important argument we shall have to give a résumé of his celebrated essay on "The Will to Believe." [20]

The thesis he here defends is the right (and even necessity) to adopt a believing attitude in religious matters even when logic does not compel. His justification for the attitude of faith follows a most fascinating analysis. There are those, he says, who would deem it a veritable sin to accept things where there is lacking sufficient evidence. If this be a definition of sin (at least one definition) we are sinners to the core; for, fundamentally, it is not by evidence (logical or otherwise) that we live but we continually act on faith; in fact, only a fraction of our living is grounded in evidence. Our lives are spent before the evidences come in. Faith is writ everywhere; we are actively asserting ourselves, launching out, driven by our dynamic nature to seek and to assert; and though we find ourselves often mistaken our courage remains undimmed. We are not mere passive, intellectual creatures waiting for evidence. We are biologically constituted *to seek* the truth (not necessarily the capital "T") and it is by our seeking that we not only find but even create it and live. We construct hypotheses and try them; we revise and reformulate; we run into blind alleys; but we keep on. Very little truth is thrown at us; it comes if at all, by and large, through our willingness to act. In fact, our willingness to act creates for us a fact, a truth. We learn for the most part, by doing, experimenting, trying. Such is life, whether we like it or no.

Now, there are different degrees (or should we say "kinds"?) of faith (or beliefs) which we may set up for ourselves in our attitude toward our environment

---

[20] *The Will to Believe and Other Essays in Popular Philosophy* (1897). Professor J. B. Pratt, an outspoken critic of James's pragmatism, pays this remarkable tribute to the Jamesean doctrine here under consideration: "I think I shall be justified in saying that James's 'Will to Believe' has been one of the greatest influences for genuine religious faith that have appeared in the last half century." *What Is Pragmatism?* (Macmillan, 1909), p. 194.

and toward ourselves. We may, *e.g.*, construct an hypothesis which may be anything proposed to our belief. Of such there are two kinds: live and dead. The latter may be a belief, but it provokes in us no willingness to act; it gives no stir; there is no ring to it, no liveness about it. (If we were to offer an example we might suggest: would one be stirred to action on the hypothesis that Abraham Lincoln's picture is hanging on the other side of the moon?) The former, however, appeals to us as a real possibility and stirs our wills to act upon it; it is lively. (The reader can easily furnish his own illustration. If he is a student in college the prospects of graduation should, normally, constitute a real possibility—a live hypothesis). Suppose, he continues, we are confronted with, say, two hypotheses. Now, such a situation calls for a decision, an option (he calls it), and the outcome of such a decision may be very serious depending upon the nature of the option. There are at least three such options: living or dead; forced or avoidable; and, momentous or trivial. If one is confronted with an option that is living, forced, and momentous one is faced with a *genuine* option, the consequences of which, either positively or negatively, cannot be brushed aside.

Consider these options a little closer. An option is a living option if both of the above supposed hypotheses are live ones; an option is forced where action is required on one or the other, from either of which hypothesis there is no escape (*e.g.*, "accept this truth or go without it"); an option is momentous where it makes a tremendous difference either by acting upon the one hypothesis or refusing to act upon it (*e.g.*, some unique opportunity with momentous consequences, an opportunity which may, perhaps forever, be lost by refusing to embrace it—even as it may have been lost by pursuing it and failing).

When an option is *genuine* and it cannot be decided

on logical grounds, we are faced with a live-dilemma, with being forced to act on one or the other hypothesis, the action or non-action on the one being a decision of consequence and a situation which must be determined by our non-intellectual nature (our will). There are thus situations in which we may not only be justified in acting on faith ("will-to-believe") but we may be compelled to act on faith if we are to share in certain possible consequences. A failure to act in such a situation—*e.g.*, leaving "the question open"—may be as much a "passional decision" against that one promising hypothesis as that of acting upon it; not acting is accompanied by as much risk of losing as that of acting. It may well be that the truth is found only by launching out into the deep. Should we fail to cast out the net we may have unwittingly cast our lot with those who go about empty-handed.

Skepticism may, accordingly, not only be the avoidance of an option but an option in itself; if, faced with a *genuine* option, we take the skeptic's attitude, the consequences are very possibly far-reaching. *"A rule of thinking"* says James speaking of skepticism, *"which would absolutely prevent me from acknowledging certain kinds of truth if those kinds of truth were really there, would be an irrational rule."* In other words, a will-to-disbelieve is fraught with as much danger as the skeptics would say of "the-will-to-believe." It may be the greater wisdom in certain situations to believe and act on such a belief.[21]

The religious question, says James, presents a *genuine* option. According to him, in the same essay, when the religious spirit is stripped of its accidentals we seem to find that what it asserts is that the best things are the more eternal things and that we are better off here and now if we believe this to be true. This religious assertion

---

[21] For an evaluation of skepticism, see *First Adventures,* etc., pp. 77 ff.

involves a living, forced, and momentous option; it offers a living possibility of being true, one must act as if it were true or act as if it were not, and it offers to make a difference for life if we act or refuse to act upon it. But this is not all that the religious spirit asserts; it claims that the eternally best in the universe is a *Thou* rather than an *It,* and that one staking himself on the *Thou* is taking the supreme opportunity of getting on the winning side. This is something that logic cannot prove; yet as a *genuine* option one has not only the right voluntarily to choose this belief but one is forced to make a decision *for* or *against.* Not to side with the *Thou* and to reap possible rewards therewith, one may be taking the greater risk! Life seems to hold something in reserve for the heroic spirit; it seems to withhold some of its secret treasures and prizes from the coward and the skeptic.

There is a "faith ladder" which James commends to intellectually weary and skeptically-sick-pilgrims, which follows this "will to believe" doctrine. It is a kind of self-analysis of the way beliefs enter the mind and a way to climb to the heights of assurance when faith must take the place of evidence. It is worth quoting:

> A conception of the world arises in you somehow, no matter how. Is it true or not? you ask.
>
> It *might* be true somewhere, you say, for it is not self-contradictory.
>
> It *may* be true, you continue, even here and now.
>
> It is *fit* to be true, it would be *well if it were true,* it *ought* to be true, you presently feel.
>
> It *must* be true, something persuasive in you whispers next, and then—as a final result—
>
> It shall be *held for true,* you decide; it *shall be* as if true for *you.*
>
> And your acting thus may in certain special cases be a means of making it securely true in the end.[22]

---

[22] *A Pluralistic Universe* (Longmans, Green, 1909), pp. 328-9.

In other early essays James argues for a "rationality" that is practically satisfying as well as theoretically permissible. If two views are equally logical, he would say, that view which favors action or feeling will seem the more rational. The theistic view is thus more rational than atheism (or any such philosophical *isms* that tend to be atheistic) because it is in line of the least resistance for moral action and the life of feeling. God's existence must be postulated to satisfy our practical as well as our theoretic nature. Belief in God allows full play to our entire being; if the intellect will not come around to such a belief by itself it must submit to what is as much a part of us, *viz.*, our practical needs and the life of action. For, we are not mere intellects; we are behaving and feeling creatures, and that which is conducive to the fullest kind of behavior (conduct) has as much claim upon us, even though all that is involved in that behavior cannot submit to the approval of the intellect. If the (theoretically permissible) belief in God and a moral universe works well (in the widest sense) we are not bound to wait upon reason's final stamp of approval. And the God of which James here speaks is the power "other than me" which makes for righteousness and which is a "mental personality." [23]

The Moral Optimism—Religious-Empiricism Argument of Macintosh

As a final argument we shall set down the position of Professor Macintosh of Yale who builds his constructive view concerning the existence and character of God after a critical analysis of the various conspicuous ap-

---

[23] *See* his essay, "The Sentiment of Rationality" and the ingenious elaboration of a psycho-physiological argument in his "Reflex Action and Theism," both essays in *The Will to Believe and Other Essays in Popular Philosophy*. For a further statement and development of his views on God (especially his famous doctrine of the MORE) see *The Varieties of Religious Experience* (1902).

proaches. Suppose, since we have just been considering the pragmatic view as represented by William James, and since Macintosh draws inspiration from it, we begin with his critique and evaluation of the Jamesean view and especially of the-right-to-believe doctrine.

It will be remembered that James admitted that he could not (though he wished he might) share the mystic's claim (however mild) of an immediate awareness of God.[24] Thus, says Macintosh, the Jamesean argument has cut itself loose from the ground of verification-which-comes-by-way-of-experience and is sailing in mid-air of theoretical probability and of practical possibility. Admitted, such an argument is wholesome and strong where there is lacking any immediate awareness of the Divine Reality; but, would it not be still stronger if it could be grounded in such an experience? That it can thus be coupled with such an immediate experience is the claim of Professor Macintosh; and, thus grounded, it becomes a strong ally to a more adequate argument.

For men like James who, lacking kinship with mystical experience, have disciplined minds and who have a high regard for the rigors of scientific thinking, the will-to-believe doctrine carves out a respectable place for the faith-element in life; but how about the general run of folk who are not careful in their thinking; may not such a doctrine serve them as a guise to a will-to-deceive? Can, in other words, everyone employ such a doctrine in such a wholesome way as did James? How can one determine (without a great deal of self-discipline) where one should draw the line between the duty to doubt and the will-to-believe? Are there not grave risks involved in such a Jamesean doctrine standing alone? And once more, would it not seem to be a more valid argument for the existence and character of a Divine Reality if one could assert that

---

[24]*Ante,* p. 110.

one may come into an immediate contact with it and employ theoretically defensible beliefs about such a Reality where the empirical evidence suggests and permits?

When Professor Macintosh attacks pragmatism-standing-alone he is but carrying out his characteristic criticism of all arguments that are built up without some empirical grounding. For him there is no completely valid argument without an appeal to an immediate experience of Divine Reality, however small an area that experience may cover. As such, he criticizes the moral-argument-standing-alone, Ritschlian schools wherever there is a characteristic distrust of all mystical claims (as well as where there is an anti-metaphysical bias), and any appeal to faith-standing-alone. He contends that the idealistic argument (of the type above considered) is too costly since it involves metaphysical idealism. The appeal to an *a priori* in the pre-Kantian sense,[25] he, of course, holds is indefensible; and an appeal to an *a priori* in some empirical sense though more defensible needs further critical examination.[26] It is the ontological argument that he favors especially; but it is not the older form, of course, nor that of Hocking with its idealistic setting,[27] nor a vague appeal to "mystical experience" but his own form of it which he expounds in a doctrine of knowledge (general and religious) called *critical monism*.[28] Let us turn from his opposition-to-other-of-the-arguments and set forth his own constructive position. We shall see that he draws freely from what he regards as the good elements in opposed views. There are two main approaches in

---

[25] *Ante,* p. 101, foot-note.
[26] *Ante,* pp. 100 ff.
[27] *Ante,* p. 97.
[28] For an exposition of critical monism as a doctrine of knowledge *see* his *The Problem of Knowledge* (1915). I have given an exposition of his epistemological position in my *First Adventures,* etc., pp. 491 ff. We shall confine our remarks here to his use of that doctrine in terms of an awareness of God.

the Macintoshian argument: moral optimism and religious empiricism, the one sustaining the other.

There are a number of attitudes one may take to life, he suggests. One may be a rollicking optimist, or a grumbling pessimist—either of which attitudes is disastrous in its effects so far as a normal, vigorous life is concerned. Should anyone adopt either attitude seriously (I may add: without the saving sense of humor) one would not get far; in fact either undue optimism or undue pessimism is a defeating program of life and suicidal. The exigencies of living require something else. Theoretically, one might adopt a kind of apathetic attitude toward life; but practically this will not do since the environment seems not to tolerate any individual that fails to make a satisfactory adjustment to its requirements. (The principle of Natural Selection has made this clear enough). One may, again, adopt what James called the *melioristic* attitude—a kind of midway position between extreme optimism and extreme pessimism—by which is meant that we may resolutely take a stand and act heroically toward the world of circumstance in the belief that though there is much evil in it, our world can be made better than it is, that though we cannot be assured of a final outcome we have, with the zest of our ideals and in the response of a plastic, pluralistic world, the assured hope that we can make it better.[29]

But, says Macintosh, not even this last attitude is fully adequate. There is a need to go beyond even the moral earnestness contained in the melioristic doctrine of hope. For consider: man may strive with all his might and still not win, if the current of the Universe is against him. There are factors in the world beyond his control and unless these are favorable, both the world and man are doomed to defeat (though, there may be progress for a while). It may be possible, he

---

[29] *See* James's *Pragmatism* (1907), especially pp. 285, 286.

maintains, in other words, for one to adopt a melioristic attitude for a while; but unless this attitude is supplemented by a trust in the trustworthiness of the Universe to maintain a favorable outcome, such a meliorism will in the long run drift back to pessimism.[30] This attitude of trust which goes beyond meliorism and acts as a steadying influence is what he calls *religious meliorism* or *moral optimism.*

If moral optimism is the one attitude to take toward life and the world of circumstance, an attitude, he says, "which combines the normal optimistic impulse of a healthy mind in a healthy body with an appreciation of the absolute importance of duty and the moral will," an attitude which has been the vital and dynamic factor in the religious history of mankind, then there are certain inferences we can make in regard to it. It is of the essence of the attitude of moral optimism to assert that there is something about the world that responds favorably to man's moral earnestness; if such an attitude is valid (and, we repeat, his thesis is that it is *the one* favorable attitude to take as against any other) then "it is undeniable that the metaphysical proposition that God exists"—"a superhuman Cosmic Factor great enough and good enough to justify an attitude of moral optimism"—"is logically implied in the value-judgment that moral optimism is valid." [31] Such a God of such an attitude is favorable to moral values, is at least one being, is intelligent, is moral, is a causal Factor in relation to man and his values, is a Spirit. Among other

---

[30] There are those who vigorously deny this. Among such we should expect extreme positivists, certain naturalists, extreme humanists, extreme pragmatists, and the like. Professor A. Eustace Haydon, an extreme humanist, for example, maintains that one need not drift back to a pessimistic view if one lacks metaphysical hope. So, also, Santayana, the naturalist, and others. Here is a theme worthy of serious reflection and discussion.

[31] The above quotations are taken from his *The Pilgrimage of Faith in the World of Modern Thought* (University of Calcutta, 1931), pp. 199, 200. *See* especially, in this same volume, Chapters VIII and IX.

inferences of the same attitude, he goes on to say, are personal immortality and moral freedom and responsibility on the part of man.

So far, the argument hangs as a practically justified belief. To leave it here is to allow it to suspend in mid-air along with the Jamesean will-to-believe, with value-arguments, with moral appeals, with the launchings of faith; and this, as this author maintains, will not do as a fully valid argument standing by itself. What then? So far, we may be morally, religiously, and theoretically certain, he says; but can we be empirically certain? Is there something furnished in human experience that will ground us in the realm of fact? Unless God is given (revealed) we are forever enclosed in a realm where we can only say that the existence and moral character of God (necessary postulates of a valid religious outlook, he maintains) are but practically necessary and theoretically permissible postulates.

His *ontological* (empirical) argument now takes shape. In his general theory of knowledge which he calls *critical monism* he maintains that in the sensing-perceiving-knowing-relation an independent object (such as a tree) is immediately presented to the knower (hence, *monism* in this knowledge relation) though the knower qualifies what is given *to a certain extent* by certain qualities characteristic of that knowing-relation (hence, *critical*). Thus, knowing does not wholly create its object; the object exists in its own right and has (probably) many qualities unperceived; yet when that object is sense-perceived it takes on certain sense-qualities (*e.g.*, color, taste, sound, etc.) which it does not have unperceived, qualities which are *produced* by the active subject or knower; yet, through and by means of this sensing process certain qualities of the object are *discovered* which are not due to that relation alone.

In other words, one thus perceives the object in a *complex* of qualities, some of which are found to be subjectively produced but objectively located (*e.g.*, color, taste, sound, etc., *i.e.*, the so-called *secondary qualities* are produced by the knower and yet are referred by that knower to objects) and some of which are discovered to inhere in the object (*e.g.*, shape, size, location, number, etc., *i.e.*, the so-called *primary qualities*). Now, such sense-perceptions must, however, not be taken uncritically; for, as is well known, some of our perceptions do not stand the test of critical thought and practical working (*e.g.*, hallucinations); some, however, do stand such tests and are practically trustworthy. In other words, to be completely valid our perceptions must stand the practical test; and so standing, they may be relied upon to give immediate knowledge of objects.

What has been said of sense-perception may be said of perception in general. Using this word in the broad sense (as he does) we may say, he continues, that we perceive ourselves as thinking, feeling, willing, subjects similarly in a complex of elements. We do not point to any particular element and say "this is the self"; but we perceive that self in a complex of elements; the self (undoubtedly) has qualities unperceived; some qualities which are perceived are *produced* by that perception and are not to be considered as aspects of that self while some perceived qualities are *discovered* to inhere in that self. Similarly, we perceive other persons as we do ourselves, objects, activities, in a *complex* of elements none of which standing alone gives us what is given in this "perception in a complex," *viz.*, some elements discovered and some subjectively produced.

Here we come upon the application of this general theory of knowledge as applied to our perception of God. Again employing the term perception (or awareness, intuition, if you will) broadly, we may, he says, be aware in *religious* perception of an Object that exists in its own right and having qualities of its own unperceived; in this perception some qualities are produced which do not belong to that Object (*e.g.*, the sense of "eeriness" or that *numinous* quality of which Otto speaks,[32] as well as other feeling-qualities, sometimes referred to as *tertiary qualities*) and some qualities are discovered in that Object (*e.g.*, worthy ideals and values). Such a religious perception, too, needs the further test of critical thought and practical working; meeting such a test it may be relied upon practically as giving immediate knowledge not only of the existence of the religious Object but knowledge as to its character.

But, notice, it is in *religious* perception that we intuit the presence of the Divine. That is to say, God is not given in a way in which one intuits the presence of a tree (though the mechanism of perception, above described, is similar). There is an appropriate way by which we perceive trees (by senses of sight, touch, etc.) and there is an appropriate way by which we perceive God. This latter way he calls "religious perception" or "the right religious adjustment." What then is meant by such an adjustment or religious perception? Here, the argument turns back and takes up the thread where it was left in the discussion of moral optimism or religious meliorism.

If we adopt moral optimism as an attitude toward the world (and we should, says Macintosh), not only is the existence and character of God logically assured in such an attitude (as was pointed out) but moral optimism itself furnishes the background to the kind of attitude involved in giving such an experience (or empirical assurance) of God. Even as we must have a certain attitude to come into a knowledge-contact with a tree (such as willingness to open our eyes and see, or to stretch forth a hand and touch, etc.) so it is essential, to become aware of God, that we take on the right kind of attitude. Such an attitude implied in moral optimism involves certain phases. First, one must aspire—*i.e.*,

---

[32] *Ante,* pp. 41, 42, 101, 102.

set before one's self ideals that are worthy of realization; secondly, one must concentrate—*i.e.*, direct attention toward a Reality which is regarded as absolutely favorable to one's true well-being and worthy of one's worship and adoration; thirdly, one must surrender— *i.e.*, dedicate one's self in full devotion to such a Reality; fourthly, one must appropriate—*i.e.*, become receptive, have faith, not only in the sense of acquiescence but of deliberate and confident assertion of one's will; fifthly, one must respond—*i.e.*, remove any inhibitions and let one's self go in readiness and in obedience to the awakening impulses that come in the contemplation of such ideal Reality; and, sixthly, one must persist—*i.e.*, one must not "give up" too readily but, if necessary, continue to wrestle until the "blessing" is forthcoming.

Such an analytic acquaintance with procedure as is here given, is, in itself, no guarantee that one will come into an immediate contact with the Divine; after all, one must practice and learn the art itself. If one so does (and granting that one has overcome one's prejudices and the *impedimenta* of erroneous ideas,[33] etc.) one has opened the way for such a "religious perception in a complex" through which comes an empirical awareness of a dependable Factor which is both great enough and good enough to meet the needs and hopes suggested in the right kind of an attitude involved in moral optimism. Such a God as is thus experienced will match, he says, the kind of God that is a practically necessary and theoretically permissible postulate of religious meliorism.

It may well be asked of Professor Macintosh: which is the prior assurance of the existence and character of God, the moral optimism or the religious perception?

---

[33] The trouble with many in this matter of a belief in and the assurance of God is, he suggests, the presence of wrong ideas which they have picked up, notions which actually stand in the way, crowding out appreciations and blinding perceptions. What is here true of ordinary appreciations and experiences is true in religious matters.

His answer is: the religious perception makes for moral optimism and moral optimism makes for religious perception. This, he admits, is paradoxical from the point of view of thought and a dilemma from the point of view of practice.[34]

He holds, further, that there are defensible considerations in the *cosmological* and *teleological* arguments, first, by an appeal to religious experience and, secondly, by an appeal to metaphysics.

In behalf of a defensible *cosmological* approach he asserts: in religious experience at its best there is an awareness of a dependable Factor that is a *causal* agency, creative and sustaining; in metaphysics it is necessary to affirm a First creative Cause (though such a cause is beyond our experience, as Kant said,[35]) since any other alternative involves a contradiction;[36] moreover, though we may not experience a First Cause (*i.e.*, on a large scale), we do, in our experience as free agents, have a

---

[34] *See* his essay "Toward a New Untraditional Orthodoxy" in *Contemporary American Theology* (1932), edited by Vergilius Ferm, Vol. I, p. 277 ff; especially pp. 312-313. For a further elaboration of his arguments, especially related to metaphysical theory, *see* his essay in *Religious Realism,* edited by himself (1931), pp. 307 ff.

[35] *Ante,* pp. 82-83.

[36] Even Kant himself, as we have seen, smuggled in a First Cause (*see ante,* p. 91.) It was Charles Renouvier (1815-1903) whom James characterizes, in tribute and gratitude, as "the strongest philosopher of France during the second half of the nineteenth century" who suggested the contradiction involved in connection with the problem of an infinite series of causes and effects. If there were an infinite series of causes (and hence no First Cause) leading up to a present event, the sum-total of events then would now be an infinite sum. However, if the sum is already infinite, nothing more can be added since the infinite cannot be made greater than itself. Thus no further events would be possible since the infinite is already reached and cannot be added to or increased—a *reductio ad absurdum.* Thus, it is necessary to conclude, insists Renouvier, that the sum of the total events up to the present is a finite sum, which is to say that there is a First Cause (also that the world is finite in time and space, etc.). For a more exact exposition and critical evaluation of Renouvier *see* James's *Some Problems of Philosophy* (1911) and R. B. Perry's *Philosophy of the Recent Past* (1926). The interested, critical reader should compare the notion of infinity here involved with that of the modern mathematician. *See* "The Puzzling Infinite," Chap. XIV, in *First Adventures,* etc. Also, the Kantian antinomies, *ibid.*

first-hand experience of a first cause (within narrow limits) and thus have a fairly definite picture of the real possibility of a First Cause; and finally, he asserts, the God of religious experience may be identified (with certain modifications) with Whitehead's metaphysical theory of "principle of concretion." [37]

In behalf of a defensible *teleological* approach he asserts: in religious experience at its best there is not only an awareness of a causal Factor which creates and sustains but which guides and directs the individual toward a fuller realization of the values that lead to the Divine Ideal; in metaphysics a teleological interpretation of the world-process as value-producing, as being progressively integrated (*cf.*, Whitehead), is highly defensible; that such a process may be crowned with a superhuman conscious purpose is (although not capable of logical demonstration) reasonably permissible; and these two appeals, mutually contributory and supplementary, furnish a strong setting, in modern dress, for an immanent-teleological argument for God's existence.[38]

---

[37] For a brief exposition of Whitehead's "Philosophy of Organism," see *First Adventures*, etc., pp. 182 ff. A. N. Whitehead is professor of philosophy in Harvard University, a vigorous and influential metaphysician. For Macintosh's appreciative discussion and modification of Whitehead's views see *Religious Realism*, pp. 389 ff. It is to be pointed out that Professor Macintosh's fundamental view is that while a respectable metaphysics (*i.e.*, one that takes into consideration the best findings of scientific research, etc.,) should contribute to theological theory, theological theory (which in turn rests upon certain empirical foundations—the deliverances of religious experience at its best—) is qualified to contribute to metaphysical theory. This is the burden of his well known volume *Theology as an Empirical Science* (1919).

[38] Professor H. N. Wieman (of The University of Chicago), also influenced by the metaphysical thought of Whitehead—though, with considerable modifications—makes much of the teleological argument for the existence and character of God. He identifies God "with that process [and structure] of existence which carries the possibilities of greatest value," and he calls such a process "progressive integration." Such a God, he claims, is scientifically knowable because such a God is found by the method of observation and critical reason. Moreover, such a God, he maintains, is more-than-personal since (among other reasons) progressive integration is not limited in its

Thus, we note, in the thought of Professor Macintosh there are numerous strands coming together. One notes, for example, such strands as pragmatism, intuitionism, mysticism, Ritschlianism, Kantianism, moralism, empiricism, religious faith, a high regard for metaphysics—all, however, considerably modified; one notes also the traditional arguments (ontological, cosmological, teleological, moral) recast; and one is quite aware that though the result is largely synthetic, it is not purely so, for there is considerable novelty in his view both by way of criticism and constructiveness. For Christian theism Macintosh has furnished a vigorous, contemporary apologetic.

---

expression to that kind of social interaction which generates and sustains personality. For an acquaintance with this vigorous thinker *see* his books and essays: *Religious Experience and Scientific Method* (1926); *The Wrestle of Religion with Truth* (1927); *The Issues of Life* (1931); "God and Value" in *Religious Realism* (1931), edited by D. C. Macintosh, pp. 153 ff.; "Theocentric Religion" in *Contemporary American Theology* (1932), edited by Vergilius Ferm, Vol. I., pp. 337 ff.; and *Normative Psychology of Religion* (1935), in collaboration with Mrs. Wieman.

Cf. James Ward's teleological argument—the tendency toward a higher Unity in a pluralistic world, a résumé of which is given in *First Adventures*, etc., pp. 176 ff.

CHAPTER VI

CURRENT THEORIES OF VALUE

It is characteristic of the mind of man to take on certain attitudes and to make certain qualitative judgments about himself and the world of circumstance. His experience and his world are not colorless existences. Man is a feeling and quality-judging creature. The world of his experience is not something to be observed, remarked about, and descriptive notes set down; rather it is something which gets colored and "touched up" by his loving, his hating, his favoring, his disfavoring, his approving, his condemning it. Such attitudes and quality-judgments constitute the process which goes under the name of valuing and it is one that gets expressed in innumerable ways. In the religious response, values play a dominant rôle.

So characteristic is this evaluating tendency in human behavior that Ritschl made the claim, as we have seen,[1] that there is no such thing as a mere descriptive and disinterested attitude or judgment which the modern sciences have set up as their ideal technique. We are by nature given to take on attitudes of *for* or *against* objects, events, circumstances; we are "passional" beings (to employ the Jamesean expression) given to a natural bias of likes and dislikes through which our experiences become dyed with colorful meaning.

A study of this important phase of mental life raises the whole question of the nature and status of value, one that is immensely complex psychologically and of far-reaching consequences metaphysically. The whole question of the nature of good and evil, for instance,

---

[1] *Ante,* p. 106, footnote.

revolves about a theory of value. When we say that a thing is good, is that thing really good or is it merely an expression of our attitude or qualitative judgment? The same question applies, of course, to the notion of evil. Both are expressions of value. Are there such things as values *per se*, independent and objective, unchanging and absolute; or are values merely expressions of human attitudes and wholly relative? In what does value consist? Perhaps a thing is without value—neither good nor bad in itself "but thinking makes it so." What makes for such valuing as when we say the good, the better, the best, or, the bad, the worse, the worst? How explain the evident fact that values change? For one person a thing may be bad and for another good, and for the same person a thing may be bad at one time and good at another. If there were no such beings as humans or any being approaching their kind, would the world or anything have value, be good or bad, beautiful or ugly?

A serious study of such questions in terms of a general theory of value is a rather recent effort of philosophic thought and to it some of our ablest thinkers are giving their whole attention. Recognition of such problems has, of course, occupied men throughout the history of classical thought, but such problems were considered especially in connection with ethical theories. It is now becoming recognized that here is a prior question that deserves treatment by itself inasmuch as it is so complex and fundamental to any general philosophical theory. We shall, in this chapter, outline and classify some outstanding contemporary theories of the general nature of value, suggesting as we go some implications in terms of one's general philosophy. The reader will understand how basic such a study is to a religious philosophy.

Some Contemporary Theories of Value

First, let us outline what may be called *relative* and *relational* theories of value.

When we come to speak of value we may strike toward the very bottom by saying that there are (at least) as many kinds of value (social, economic, religious, educational, esthetic, moral, cultural, and so on indefinitely) as there are human attitudes of conscious interest. What one is consciously interested in has value; and such conscious interests depend largely upon one's likings, desirings, wishings, and feelings in general. This view is called by Professor John Laird the *appreciative view* of value.[2] Anything, accordingly, has value if it is *related to* any such conscious interests and, conversely, anything lacking such an interest is lacking in value.

The obvious criticism of this view lies in the possibility of things having value without humans taking conscious interest in them. May not the foundation-stones of the building in which I now find myself have a value independent of my conscious interest or appreciation of them? Of course, in answer to this, it might be said that it is not meant that the appreciation in question has to be that of a present conscious appreciation; it may have been a matter of past conscious interest and hence by that relation, foundation-stones continue to have value in that they have been gathered together for an expressed purpose which in turn rests upon conscious interests. But, it may be further asked, how about such things which we discover to have been of tremendous value, which we have enjoyed, even though we were never aware of them? Have not the so-called "vitamins" been of value to the human body long before they were ever appreciated?

---

[2] References here to Laird are to his *The Idea of Value* (Cambridge University, 1929).

Professor Laird believes that the above theory while obviously too narrow is, however, to be included in a more favorable theory which he calls the *elective theory* of value. This theory rests upon the thesis "that whatever *matters* to a thing, or concerns it, is a value or disvalue to that thing; and that whatever does not matter to it, is, for it, no value but wholly indifferent." [3] Obviously, this is a very broad conception of value and extends far down the scale beyond the organic to the inorganic. Values are *relative* to any elective agent. The behavior of planets, of crystals, a magnet attracting iron filings—in fact anything that reveals natural election or prizing, such as attraction, repulsion, selection, response, affinity, non-indifference, anything from natural infra-conscious entities or processes up through organisms and including consciousness, exhibits value (or disvalue).

Plainly, this is about the limit of extension of the category of value and one that is open to the criticism of being too broad. The merit of such a theory, insists its proponent, is its taking into consideration the wide variety of values that appear in this complex world together with all their intricate relativities. Has not the sun value for certain plants under certain conditions and to a certain degree as much as certain kinds of food have value for hungry boys under certain circumstances; similarly, do not certain flowers have value for bees and bees for flowers under certain circumstances? Shall we confine the category of value only to beings with conscious interests? May not the world have had countless values before the appearance of man or sentient beings?

Between the above views stands the view of Professor R. B. Perry of Harvard who limits and *relates* values

---

[3] *Op. cit.,* p. 302. He goes on to say: "Since everything matters to itself, self-maintenance is a value to every existent."

to interests, human and organic.[4]   As against the appreciative view (as above defined) he defines interest in a much broader sense, recognizing its contextual setting in the biological level and beyond the category of mere cognition at the human level (*vs. conscious* appreciation); as against the elective view he limits the category to the organic (including human).   It is possible, he would probably say, to define value as anything whatever that matters to a thing; but such a definition is to make the category colorless and to rob it not only of its general meaning but of any characteristic meaning. For, may not anything and everything conceivably matter to anything and everything and thus any- and everything have value?   And if so, nothing is gained by the definition.   If, however, by "mattering" we mean something more definite, then it becomes necessary to say what is meant.   In other words, we need more definite definitions.   Conceivably anything *may* become valuable; but this is not to say that because any- and every-thing matters to any- and every-thing, any- and every-thing has value or that the category of value is appropriate for such relations.   Whatever value may be said to mean, it should not be robbed of the meaning of that "something peculiarly characteristic of the human and social sciences." [5]   We shall consider Perry's view more in detail later.

It has been suggested by Professor A. P. Brogan that value itself is indefinable.   Nevertheless, may we not say something of it in terms of comparison?   For instance, suppose we start with the relatively indefinable

---

[4] Perry's theory is a "bio-centric" as well as a "psycho-centric" theory of value. *General Theory of Value* (Longmans, Green, 1926), p. 139.   Though, strictly speaking, he would limit interest to "living mind," broadly speaking, he gives to interest a wider meaning by a consideration of the living organism which provides the context of interest. *Op. cit.,* p. 180. Also *cf.* below p. 138.

[5] *Op. cit.,* p. 153.

term "betterness," can we not then define "worseness" as its logical counterpart? The fundamental characteristic of value, then, is the relation of comparison, between betterness and worseness, without there being an absolute best or an absolute worst. Value consists merely in the comparison of a thing with another in terms of betterness ("the fundamental value-universal"). The critic may feel like asking what is meant by "betterness" to which there is no answer by way of further analysis.[6] What we *can* say, this author holds, is relative.

Second, consider next the theory that value is absolutely *indefinable*. To define any term exactly, is it not necessary to find another term or set of terms which could be taken as equivalent? Now, one may define a term approximately by putting it into a class with other similar terms; but to define it completely, is it not necessary by a close analysis to find its equivalence in other terms? But suppose the term represents a simple feeling quality, something ultimate, *sui generis*, what then? Moreover, granted that we may define, say, "yellow" approximately by finding its "class," how could we define it exactly if it is a simple rather than a complex quality, or if it is a simple feeling quality? Is there something that has the exact equivalence to "yellow"? It may well be that, by the rules of strict and exact definition, many concepts and categories are thus indefinable. That "value" is one such category is the claim of some notable thinkers. Professor G. E. Moore, for example, defines *good* as a simple notion (just as yellow) which can be understood by anyone who has perceived it, but inexplicable to one without such an experience. It permits of no exact equivalence; nor does it need any further definition. The good, like

---

[6] *See* his article "The Fundamental Value Universal," in *The Journal of Philosophy,* Vol. XVI; also, "Objective Pluralism in the Theory of Value" in *The International Journal of Ethics,* Vol. XLI.

yellow, is a distinct *quale*. Santayana, similarly, holds that goodness is indefinable, an unanalyzable datum.[7] The implication here is that such a concept as value, similarly, is an ultimate that is indefinable.

Against this general theory Professor Perry remarks: To say that value like yellow is a simple quality "out there" which is perceived and indefinable is to hold that *tertiary qualities* are objective and to commit oneself to a too extreme pan-objectivism. But, asks Perry, is there not a real difference in ordinary experience between secondary and tertiary qualities which prevents our linking them together in an objective world? Do not tertiary qualities point emphatically to the moods and attitudes of observers (not so characteristic of secondary qualities)?[8] Again, some who hold the indefinability view seem to suggest that value depends upon a unique feeling-experience by which value is apprehended, an experience which is unanalyzable. But, says Perry, this is not so. Feelings are not simple but complex and hence analyzable. Such an analysis will reveal the very nature of value in all its complexity. Moreover, to say that value is indefinable is to admit failure to set up a defensible theory of value in general. To say that value has not been adequately defined is not to say that it cannot be so defined.[9]

Third, consider what Laird calls the *timological view*. In opposition to the theory of election which makes value relative to the elective agent, the timological view emphasizes the point that value has a certain intrinsic

---

[7] The concept of *ought,* similarly, is held by H. Sidgwick in his *The Methods of Ethics* (1874) to be fundamentally indefinable. Laird, too, admits that the principle of "natural election" is ultimately indefinable. *Cf.* Urban's view, a discussion of which follows later. The reference to Moore is to his *Principia Ethica* (1902). For Santayana's views, *see* his *The Sense of Beauty* (1896) and his *Winds of Doctrine* (1913).

[8] On the distinction between *primary* and *secondary qualities see ante,* p. 121.

[9] For Perry's elaborate criticisms see *General Theory of Value,* pp. 28 ff.

worth apart from considerations of any particular point of view. The term timology (from the Greek τιμή-esteem, dignity, and λόγος-study of) then emphasizes value as inherent worth or excellence, the valuable in itself. But, what is this intrinsic excellence? Laird summarizes the answer by saying that "the character of excellence . . . or again the character of badness, interpreted as timologists interpret it, is a mysterious, unintelligible, unverifiable, noumenal predicate, out of all relation to life or actuality." A thing may have value as an intrinsic part (uniquely so?) of its nature as much as four plus four equals eight no matter who views the matter or under what conditions. This may be known either by rational insight or intuition.

As an example of the timological view we shall cite but one case (one among many). G. E. Moore argues that organic wholes, organic unities, furnish examples of that unique and inner excellence which is not conditioned by anything apart from itself; such wholes *per se* possess value independent of the values of its separate parts and independent of time or circumstance. He defines his view in terms of intrinsic value, a unique predicate of wholes which is constituted by the peculiar organization of organic unity. *"To say that a kind of value is 'intrinsic,'"* he says *"means merely that the question whether a thing possesses it, and in what degree it possesses it, depends solely on the intrinsic nature of the thing in question."* He sets up two propositions to explain what he means by *"depends solely on the intrinsic nature of the thing in question"*: First, it is impossible for what is strictly *"one and the same thing"* to possess its value at one time (in a given degree or in a given circumstance) and to possess another value at another time (in another degree or in another circumstance). If its value changed, the thing is no longer *one and the same*. Secondly, any other given thing that is *exactly* like that *"one and the same thing"* must possess the same value in the same degree.[10] Moreover, intrinsic value must not be considered as a quality or property of the whole. If it were, this would mean that such a value would be a part of the whole which must then be included in a complete description of the whole. A complete description, however, of the whole could be given if all qualities or properties of the whole were enumerated, without mentioning any predicates of value it possessed. Hence, intrinsic value cannot be a quality or property but a *unique* (and further indefinable) predicate of the whole.

Laird's Evaluation of the Elective and Timological Theories

The two types of contrasting theories, the one relative and the other absolute, will, no doubt, seem reasonable to the reader. Both have important consequences, for example, for such problems as those of good and evil. Let us consider Laird's evaluation of both since it affords a sympathetic appreciation of the "values" of both.

Laird suggests the following illustration. Consider the spider and the fly, each of which has its own viewpoint. From the point of view of the spider the escape of the fly from the web is an evil (a disvalue); but from the point of view of the fly, a good (a value). A given event, such as this escape, is both a good and an evil at the same time. So far as the particular escape is concerned and so far as the view-point is considered, the good and the evil which co-exist are absolute good and absolute evil as events and yet the good and the evil are relative to a particular point of view. (If this sounds too much like an apparent contradiction consider

---

[10] *See* his essay "The Conception of Intrinsic Value" in *Philosophical Studies* (Harcourt, Brace, 1922). Other names which may be cited favoring (at least in certain aspects) the timological view are Plato, Aristotle, J. M. E. McTaggart, W. M. Urban, E. G. Spaulding, and G. H. Palmer. *See* Perry *op. cit.*, pp. 43 ff.

a curved line which at the same time is both concave and convex and yet relative to a given perspective).

On the timological view the good is simply good; on the elective view the good is relative to a certain view-point. But, are these two views, after all, really irreconcilable? Answer: with proper interpretation, no.

For, consider another of Laird's analogies, the absolute view-point of God as it possibly relates to relative views. A tiger catches a man. From the tigerish view-point this is a good; from the man's, an evil. The man, let us say, escapes the tiger; from the tigerish view-point this is an evil, and from the man's view-point a good. Either way considered, both good and evil exist simultaneously. But, how is this to be viewed from the point of view of the Absolute? Answer: God must recognize the tigerish good from the point of view of the tiger and the man's evil from that point of view (and vice versa). But, if the one good is better than the other, it is necessary to go beyond this relative comparison to something beyond mere relativity. In other words, the-man's-escape-as-a-good may be better (or more excellent) in itself than the tiger's-satisfaction-of-hunger-as-a-good, from a higher view-point; a higher excellence is required which only the timological view can furnish, an excellence not guaranteed by the elective view itself.

The timological view supplies the lack involved in the elective view. On the other hand, the timological view-point can hardly deny that there are goods and evils which depend upon relativities and relevancies. And further, it may well be that certain elections (values) are quite worthless from the timological view-point. There may be higher or superlative excellences (timology) which deeper insight may grant vision of, but which lie beyond the purview of the elective view; at the same time there may be lower and positive values (election) which a higher insight may fail to consider or even to deny. Both views are thus supplementary to each other if lines of exclusion are not drawn, and proper interpretations made.[11]

Let us move on now and consider at closer range two opposing theories of value as they are set forth by two vigorous contemporary thinkers who have given special study to this general inquiry. We shall but touch upon some of the implications of these views; the reader can "follow through" at his own leisure.

Perry's Relational Theory of Value

In his great work, *General Theory of Value*, Professor Perry, behaviorist and new realist, offers a detailed analysis of the complexities of *interest* as the key to the understanding of the nature of value. We first ask of Perry: what is an interest? When one has an interest (or, shall we say, when one is interested?), Perry answers, one is, first of all, motivated and governed by a dynamic and determining tendency, a set, or a "propensity" (whatever in the organism that initiates and incites effort) which seeks the fulfilment of its unfulfilled phases. As such, this propensity issues in anticipatory responses (which are subordinate to it) by which this propensity is to be executed. Now, these anticipatory responses ("active" and "teleological" as is the whole process) are tentative, selective, experimental, expectant, and fallible, and make for actions that are thus interested; they determine behavior in that they act as the link between the propensity unfulfilled and the propensity to-be-fulfilled. It makes no difference if success or failure comes to the interest; the interest lies not in the result but in the process of expectation (which makes for action) and its concomitant relation to its governing propensity. In the act of interest there

---

[11] Laird, *op. cit.,* p. 320.

is thus an end in view to which means are subservient (though a means itself may become an end).

Now, for Perry, the genetic setting for interested behavior extends down the scale wherever in life there is that capacity to act in the light of expectation. If an amoeba, for example, responding to food, reveals such a capacity, it may be said to have a "prospicience" (incipient interest) for food; if a plant, similarly, responding to sunlight with simple tropistic adjustments reveals such a capacity, it may be said to have "prospicience" (incipient interest) for sunlight; and so on up through higher organic forms until at the level of intelligence among some animals and with man interested behavior becomes highly complex in that action is motivated by thought and by a great variety of special desires.

What, then, we may next ask of Perry, is value? Anything, he replies, has value *conferred upon* it when it is an object of such interested response even "as anything whatsoever becomes a target when anyone whosoever aims at it." One does not have to *judge* a-thing-to-have-value to make it valuable; value is independent of any *judgment* (though judgment may affect interest) even as an interest in anything may obtain without our judging ourselves to be interested. Are then, we ask, values merely subjective, that is, "wholly within" and not "out there"? His answer: values are objective in the sense of being independent of any judgments about them and subjective in the sense of being functions of interest. A value *takes on existence* when an interest is generated (regardless of anyone's knowledge concerning it); it ceases to exist when its sustaining interest is withdrawn or changed. Moreover, even as interests when generated (and therefore come into existence) can be known like any other facts, so values can be known and thus acquire an existential status though related to interests. In other words, values as existences have objectivity while they last; and they last so long as interest sustains them; or, again, an object (real or ideal) takes on the character of value when an interest is taken in it; it loses value when the interest is withdrawn.[12]

Among the many distinctions which Perry draws among interests, there are two that are of special interest. It is the distinction he draws between *positive* and *negative* interests, the former, in terms of value, are defined as *good* and the latter as *evil*. What then, is the distinction between these two types of interest? The reply is that the conception of interest (given above) forbids our saying that a negative interest is a lack of interest and hence evil is not to be considered as a lack of value. The distinction can best be put this way: in a positive interest one is controlled by a governing propensity which incites an anticipatory response that is *attracting* one *toward* an object (real or ideal), such an object taking on then a positive value of *attractiveness* (such as "desired," "loved," "joyous," "charming," "alluring," "auspicious," etc.,) or the character of good; in a negative interest one is similarly controlled by a governing propensity which incites an anticipatory response that is *repelling* one *away from* an object (real or ideal) such an object taking on then a negative value of *repulsiveness* (such as "odious," "alarming," "portentous," "distasteful," etc.,) or the character of bad. The difference, in other words, lies in the kind of anticipation or expectation. An object may thus have the value at the same time, of being good and bad,

---

[12] There is much similarity here with Professor Macintosh's theory that secondary qualities (such as color, taste, sound, etc.) are subjectively produced but objectively located. *See ante,* pp. 120-121. There is, however, a marked difference between the two in that Professor Perry is a new realist and Professor Macintosh is not. The striking dissimilarity between them, of course, lies in their doctrines of mind or self. For Perry, as a new realist, primary qualities (such as shape, size, location, number, etc.) and secondary qualities are externally real (independent of their being known) while values are also a part of the world (while they last) relative to interest. On New Realism see *First Adventures,* etc., pp. 221 ff. On Perry's New Realism see *ibid.,* pp. 273 ff.

depending upon the fact that it is the object of both positive and negative interests of people. Such a doctrine conceivably involves no more strain on the imagination (the possession of opposite characters at one and the same time) than the apparently simple fact of an object which is, at the same time, "to the right of," "to the left of," "above," and "below" other objects.

Plainly, the merit of this theory lies in the fact that it accounts for the evident varieties, fluctuations, and the relational character of value which experience seems to teach. It has long been recognized that what has value for one does not necessarily have value for another; what may be good for one is not necessarily good for another (a point that St. Paul clearly made in one of his well-known epistles). A whale may be bad for a Jonah, but may be good for those engaged in the oil business. But, granting this relational character, shall we then say there is nothing at all stable and solid about value in the world?

Perry faces this latter question by offering some metaphysical suggestions. Let us take one such. Suppose we say that this is a pantheistic Universe; and, if so, consider that the great Subject has itself for object; may not, then, if the Subject takes an interest in itself, the Universe have value, and if the Subject takes on a positive interest, the Universe take on the value of good, or if the Subject takes on a negative interest the Universe take on the value of bad? At least, may not the Universe have value by virtue of an all-embracing interest? Let us add our own metaphysical suggestion. Suppose we think of this world in terms of theism; then, if God takes an interest in the world, is not, by definition, the world valuable, independent of any human interest? In other words, it seems possible to apply Perry's relational theory of value and still maintain an objectivity independent of such interests which emerge only in certain phases of the world-order itself.

What, then, may be bad from the human point of view may be good from the side of Deity, and vice versa; or, what is without value from the point of view of the natural order may be valuable from the side of Deity, and vice versa. (The implications are too evident to need further elaboration). On such a metaphysical view and with such a theory of value, the question as to a favorable destiny for human beings would depend upon whether or not it can be maintained that there is the kind of a God (assuming adequate power) having sufficient positive interests in them to outweigh negative interests; to maintain this latter hypothesis, one is compelled to fall back upon the arguments (already considered) for a God having a validly moral character and upon the possible evidences of positive teleological factors (*e.g.*, progressive integration) at work in the world.

Leaving the reader to work out his own thought on the religious implications of this theory of value we may say, in conclusion, that Perry's view (so far as his theory of value is concerned) turns out to be far from radical as many of his critics have assumed it to be.[13] A suggestion, however, may be made concerning comparative values by the mention of Perry's view in this matter. Four principles are suggested by which we are systematically to set up a gradation of generic values, *viz.*, correctness, intensity, preference, and inclusiveness —all relating to interest. The first criterion suggests whether or not the value is judged to be founded on truth or error, but does not furnish a criterion of comparison of values (since it does not yield a judgment of

---

[13] For a discussion of Perry's general theory (including his reply to some of his critics) the interested reader is referred to the following journals: "Symposium on R. B. Perry's *General Theory of Value*" by DeWitt Parker, H. H. Dubs, Charner M. Perry in *The International Journal of Ethics,* Vol. XL, No. 4, pp. 465-495; *ibid.,* Vol. XLI, No. 4, pp. 429-442; *The Journal of Philosophy,* Vol. XXVIII, No. 17 and succeeding issues.

better and worse, more and less). The other three criteria suggest principles of comparison, each one of which is not reducible to the other.

An object, such as wine, says Perry, is better than an object such as water if, first, the interest in the wine is more intense than the interest in water, secondly, if the wine is preferred (*e.g.,* taste) to the water, thirdly, if the interest in the wine is more inclusive than the interest in the water.[14] Intensity means the degree of the interest's arousal such as waxing and waning—a more or less than; preference means simply that some interests are preferred to others—a rather than; inclusiveness means that objects take on augmented value from the summation of interests taken in them: such as the case where the same object becomes the object of the interest of two or more people (rather than of one person) and thus derives *additional* value; or, the case where the self is exalted above its fleeting interests or group-interest is exalted above the interests of its members.

Of the various *kinds* of value (functions of interest) Perry speaks of positive and negative, progressive and recurrent, potential and actual, independent and dependent, playful and real, submissive and aggressive, subjective and objective, immediate and mediate, personal and social. These constitute what he calls the psychological classification and is admittedly complex and detailed. The historical classification which follows the social sciences are: cognitive, moral, economic, political, esthetic, and religious values.

Urban's Absolutistic Theory of Value

An American pioneer in the subject of a general theory of value, Professor Urban of Yale, has published some notable books on the problem, revealing the development of his thought toward a view which is to be

---

[14] *Op. cit.,* pp. 615 ff.

distinguished sharply from the one just discussed.[15] The term "axiology"— (ἀξία —worth and λόγος— science of or study of) or the science of value (norms) —which has come into philosophical vogue, was coined by him. He refers to his own axiological theory as that which pleads the cause for absolute values. For him, value is essentially indefinable in terms of anything else and is, accordingly, an ultimate category. Instead of trying to understand value in terms of some existent-other-than-itself, it is necessary, he insists, to employ the category of value to understand existence itself. Value and fact are inseparable. The very reality we know is not valueless stuff; it is stuff charged with value (or, should we say, value charged with stuff?). The very act of intelligibility is that of a valuing process; without our being able to appreciate values (meanings) we should not understand. "I hold," says Urban, "that there can be no existence without value and no value without existence." [16]

We do not paint values on to existence; they are already there. Axiology accordingly takes one into the very heart of metaphysics. It may be admitted that the relation of value and existence is a mystery; but to separate them is not only to distort reality but to make for no meaning (unintelligibility). Value, then, is not relative to something else, such as interests, human satisfactions, a Divine will, but is part and parcel "in the nature of things"; it is not a quality of an "is" (being); rather, it "is" beyond any "isness" having a validity of

---

[15] Professor W. M. Urban was for a time a student under the celebrated German philosophers, A. Meinong and C. von Ehrenfels, pioneers in the field. A reliable exposition of the views of these men may be had in H. O. Eaton's *The Austrian Philosophy of Value* (1930). Urban's early publication is entitled *Valuation, Its Nature and Laws* (1909); for his later views (to which our exposition is confined) see *The Intelligible World: Metaphysics and Value* (1929); "Metaphysics and Value" in *Contemporary American Philosophy* (Macmillan, 1930), edited by G. P. Adams and W. P. Montague, Vol. II, pp. 357 ff; also *Fundamentals of Ethics* (1931).
[16] "Metaphysics and Value," *op. cit.,* p. 375.

its own. Hence, if one should ask "Where is value?" or, "What is value?", one is confronted with an unanswerable enigma so far as trying to relate value to such categories (other than itself) as *whereness* or *whatness* in terms of *isness*. Values simply "are" and are acknowledged by value-judging subjects.

This doctrine may seem both difficult and strange. It is admittedly difficult to conceive of objective value apart from the category of "being" [17] and strange to behold the alleged union of such unlike sets of categories as value and being. Nevertheless, one is reminded that what may seem philosophically difficult and strange is not impossible. Professor Perry reacts strongly against this view since he thinks it lands one in a kind of worshipful mysticism and makes impossible a defensible *theory* of value. To which Urban might well retort: One should try, indeed, to press a logical theory as far as it goes; but there is a limit to such logic. Is not the pressing of logical analysis to the hopeful point of limitless possibilities as much a worshipful attitude (toward such logic)? To try to make value conform completely to logic when, indeed, it may have a logic of its own, is to commit an unpardonable philosophical sin. And so the issue is squarely joined.

---

[17] *Cf.*, the metaphysical view of H. Münsterberg in this matter. *First Adventures,* etc., pp. 163 ff.

CHAPTER VII

EVIL, THEODICY, AND PESSIMISM

EVIL AND THEODICY

A consideration of a general theory of value lands one immediately, as we have seen, in that morass of vexatious questions which revolve about the problem of evil. Indeed, there would hardly be such a problem if one did away with the notion that, at the heart of the world, there is the good (a good God). We have found in our discussion of God that the question of God's existence is not the only question bound up in an inquiry into the theistic view but there is the further important inquiry into the character of such a God. So far as a valid religion is concerned, the latter question is of equal importance with the former. The traditionally religious spirit has tended to assume (perhaps tacitly) a certain *kind* of God wherever theism has been affirmed, a God possessing the quality of goodness (although not always have such views been valid); especially so is this the case of Christian theism. At once, this raises the perplexing problem of the relation of God to evil (assuming evil to be real), one of the "knottiest" problems in the philosophy of religion. *Si Deus bonus est, unde malum?* If God is good, why evil? The technical term for the problem of justifying the character of a good God in the face of such doubts as arise in the fact of evil (and other problems) is *theodicy* (Θέος-God and δίκη-right, justice).

Concerning a Classification of Evils

When we come to speak of evil we may begin at the very bottom by saying that there are (at least) as many kinds of evil (assuming these to be real) as there are negative responses. In terms of the human level we should then speak of negative interests (with Perry). Any object, situation, event, may thus become a candidate for the category of evil since it is conceivable that a negative interest could apply any- and everywhere. The relational character of this doctrine has already been sufficiently pointed out; the merits of this view undoubtedly lie in the ready explanation of the obvious fact that what is evil to one may be a good to another, and so on.

It is now common to speak of certain broad classifications of evil, each one of which has reference to a certain set of relations. There is what is known as *metaphysical* evil, *i.e.*, evil considered from the point of view of ultimate Reality—evil in terms, *e.g.*, of imperfection; there is what is called *physical* and *natural* evil, *i.e.*, evil in relation to the physical and natural order—those natural elements and events which are hostile to life— evil in terms, *e.g.*, of frustration of life, pain; and there is what is called *moral* evil, *i.e.*, evil in relation to human conduct and relationships. Further classifications reflect the multitudinous character of specific human interests, such as, intellectual evils, mental evils, economic evils, political evils, religious evils, educational evils, etc.

Metaphysical evil is concerned with a discussion of the cosmological and ontological questions.[1] Such solutions have ranged from an outright denial of evil by certain idealistic monists [2] (which is one kind of solution) to its re-interpretation in the light of a higher

---

[1] On this point, see *First Adventures,* etc., pp. 124 ff.; 128; 131; 136 ff.; 139 ff.; 145-146; 153 ff.; 161 ff.; 167 ff.; 219-220; 373 ff.

[2] Spinoza, *e.g.*, held that evil is due to inadequate knowledge. If we possessed the *sub specie æternitatis* outlook we should have no such conceptions as good or evil. Evil, accordingly, is an illusion. The doctrine of Christian Science may also be referred to.

good by other idealistic monists.[3]   Then, there has been
the metaphysical dualist's solution which though it, in
certain respects resolves the problem, gives birth to
others.[4]   By many, the problem of evil is declared insoluble.   Or again, it is held that evil is relative only
to organic forms (their maladjustments) and that there
is nothing ultimate or metaphysical about it.[5]   Pluralistic philosophers, such as James, who hold to a theistic
interpretation have insisted upon the reality of evil and
at the same time have held that, though God may be
good enough, God is not powerful enough (hence finite
in this sense) to have prevented it.   Evil is bound up
with the crossings and conflicts, the zest and uncertain-
ties, in a world that is in the making.[6]

Theistic solutions to this question have varied greatly.
We shall consider some important views and names.

---

[3] Absolute idealists in general, for example, have found this problem
one of serious embarrassment.   Perhaps no one has wrestled with it,
from this point of view, in a more frank and fearless manner than
Josiah Royce.   For specific literature and an interpretation of Royce's
solution, the reader is referred to an article entitled "Royce on the
Problem of Evil," by Howard B. Jefferson in *The Journal of Religion,*
Vol. XI, No. 3, pp. 359-377.   Also, *cf., Hocking's views: The Meaning
of God in Human Experience,* Chap. XXXII; article in *The Journal
of Religion,* Vol. III., No. 6, pp. 582-589.

[4] The personification of an evil principle, referred to as Satan and
the Devil (as well as by other names) has been a mode of explanation
in Jewish-Christian tradition (Persian influence).   In II Enoch (18:3;
29:4 ff.) Satan is referred to as a rebel-angel cast down from the
heavens.   This conception has been made especially popular through
Milton's *Paradise Lost.*   The cosmological dualism here is of a modified type; the question of how the "great fall" occurred is an enigma.
The New Testament, as is well known, refers to this prince of darkness as the chief cause of all ills but one that shall ultimately suffer
defeat.

[5] This is the positivistic, naturalistic, extreme (religious) humanistic
solution.   *See e.g., Reconstruction in Philosophy* (1920), John Dewey,
p. 177; *The Quest of the Ages* (1929), A. Eustace Haydon, Chap. VI.

[6] James's notion is that the problem of evil is explicable only on the
assumption that a good God is finite and is struggling with an imperfect world.   In the pluralistic scheme the element of chance is held
to be real; physical evil is always an open possibility in a world
where there is so much loose play.

Jewish-Christian Attitudes Toward Human Suffering

Undoubtedly, the experience of human suffering, mental and physical, has been man's chief concern in this whole question.[7] In cruel pain the seamy side of life is revealed. It has brought man not only to wonder at its meaning and significance but to question the primacy of the good. To physical pain has been added the horrors of mental anguish: chagrin, failure, disappointment, frustration of hopes, injustices, and a thousand other forms of invisible suffering. For most of the children of men, the sun of goodness, at some time or other, has been completely hid behind clouds of frustration and despair, and doubts have been raised whether or not there really was such a thing as the sun. For some, such experiences have meant an untempered pessimism; for most they have brought a *tempered* optimism.

In Western thought, Jewish and Christian traditional interpretations of the meaning of human suffering have played an influential rôle; a glance at these ideas will serve to show how millions have understood (and even now interpret) their afflictions. To get this picture before us, we shall follow the lead of contemporary scholars who are attempting to trace the actual historical development which tradition, for the most part, has enveloped in a cloud.

It is now common knowledge that there has been a marked development throughout early Hebrew, Jewish, and Christian thought, bearing on religious, on theological, and ethical questions. It is now expected of one who inquires into their several sacred writings, that he will compare utterances with time, place,

---

[7] This is undoubtedly because (as Professor Wieman observes in his *The Wrestle of Religion with Truth*, pp. 164 ff.) pain so often involves a frustration of some interest. If suffering were "enjoyed" or if there were no interest frustrated, it would doubtless have no evil connotation.

authorship, and circumstance.[8] It is also common knowledge that, unlike the Greeks who developed their strong metaphysical bent into interpretations which had strong metaphysical coloring, Hebrew and Jewish thought (before it became mixed with the Greek) was less metaphysical and more theological, moral, and religious in emphasis. There is a conspicuous absence of inquiry into the nature of Nature in the latter tradition; but this does not make it of any less consequence

---

[8] There are two sets of questions which deal with the matter of an adequate understanding of this literature. The reader should have at least a passing acquaintance with these disciplines.

Lower criticism, so-called, undertakes to find out the most nearly perfect text or book and to examine critically and compare ancient versions. Lower here means primary, fundamental. It is now well known that no portion of the Old Testament has survived in the form of original documents. The so-called Massoretic text (the Massoretes were Jewish scholars who labored upon and fixed a standard text) dates back to about the third century A. D. and forms the basis of the present Revised Version and the King James version. The most ancient copy of the New Testament extant goes back no farther than the fourth century. Two sorts of manuscripts are known to scholars: the so-called known *uncials* (written in Greek capital letters), dated from the fourth to the tenth centuries, survive to the number of about 160; and the so-called *cursive* (written in running script) which date later, survive to the number of some three thousand and more.

Higher criticism, so-called, undertakes to find out about the authorship, integrity, historicity, and chronology of the books. Its task is to compare references to dates and names with other sources, to verify quotations, to validate if possible claims to authorship, to understand meanings (historical and literary) in the light of the thought-mold, language, and customs of the times.

Biblical criticism as we now know it is a comparatively recent discipline. The books came into existence without any such criticism. Among the findings of modern critical scholarship we may mention: the order of the books is not chronological; the name of the book is not a necessary indication of authorship; a given book frequently is a patchwork of more than one writer; many emendations and corrections appear; the form of the literature employed varies greatly, such as stories, traditional fables, romances, fiction, poetry, hymns, etc.

The list of the Hebrew writings was not fixed at the time of Jesus; that list was completed about 113 A. D. (Council of Jamnia). The New Testament books also appear gradually; by the time of Irenaeus of Lyons (177-202) most of these books became recognized. It is plain that modern scholarship has merely begun its important work in coming to grips with this body of significant literature. For an introductory survey the following book is recommended: *The Bible Through the Centuries* (1929), by H. L. Willett.

in its effect upon subsequent development of thought.

The earliest interpretation of human suffering revealed by this tradition was to the effect that all suffering is punishment either of one's own sins or the sins of parents. Underlying this interpretation was the notion that all retribution took place in "the here and now" (there being no idea of retribution in the future). Doubts concerning this theory arose with the changing social order of the Hebrews. In the relatively simple pastoral life the good were observed, on the whole, to prosper, while the wicked suffer; but in the more complicated life which came with developing social contacts with other groups, with the growth of monarchy, and especially by the cruel experiences of exile, it became more and more obvious that the worthy not only suffer hardships with the unworthy but prosperity seemed to be held out particularly to the wicked! Skepticism concerning the old notion which is evident before the exile came to the fore during and after the exile with the result that the interpretation of human suffering underwent a number of modifications.

In the prophetic writings (so-called), the theme of human suffering takes a prominent place. The prophets were themselves sufferers and knew intimately the bitterness of life. There was the morally sensitive Amos (ministry, *circa* 750 B.C.), the prophet of doom; the gentle Hosea (ministry, *circa* 745-735) who bore the misery and shame of an unfaithful wife whom he ardently loved; the majestic Isaiah of Jerusalem (ministry, *circa* 738-700) grieving over the impending ruin of Judah; Micah (ministry, *circa* 730-722) public defender of the poor, denouncing social injustices, and suffering persecution; Jeremiah (b. *circa* 650), the typical sufferer, rejected and despised, lamenting the day he was born, and yet a great preacher of righteousness; Ezekiel (ministry, *circa* 597) an invalid, captive, man of faith, and shepherd of a bewildered flock, optimist among the disheatened—to name only a few among the great prophetic spirits. From the point of view of tradition these men were great sinners and their suffering bore the mark of the sins of the past. Such a solution, however, did not square with their own experience. Habakkuk (ministry, *circa* 605-590), bewildered by the non-interference of Yahweh in the cruelties of life and wholly dissatisfied with ancient explanations, comes out challenging God and demanding a real explanation.

The solution which gradually dawned in their sense of mission in spite of so many obstacles was that they were not being punished either because of their own or because of their fathers' sins but they were servants of God sharing with their King in a sacrificial ministry of redemption. The new note which was struck and which came later to be the chief burden of the ministry of Jesus was the strange doctrine that God suffers and those who follow the path laid out by the Divine markings must also suffer. The great unknown prophet (Isaiah 40-55), known to scholars as Deutero- (Second) Isaiah, or the Isaiah of the Exile (ministry, *circa* 546), proclaimed this doctrine in the famous theme of the "Suffering Servant of Yahweh" and thus linked post-exilic thought with pre-exilic in a revised conception of the meaning of pain.[9]

In the so-called Wisdom Literature, we find two classic examples of this wrestling with the mystery of pain and suffering. The Book of Job (*circa* 400 B.C.) and the book called by the Jews "Koheleth," called by the Greek translators "Ecclesiastes" (*circa* 200 B.C.)

---

[9] Considerable dispute has centered about the interpretation of the meaning of the phrase "Servant of Yahweh." Though Christian tradition has seen in this a reference to an individual and associated it prophetically with the regal Messiah and with the historic Jesus, modern scholars find this untenable. It is now generally interpreted to refer to the remnant of Israel which realizes the ideal of redemptive suffering in fellowship with God (an ideal however, which may be said to have been singularly fulfilled in Jesus).

reveal such pessimistic conclusions that more than one scholar wonders how these came to be included in the canon of sacred Writ. The suffering of the righteous and the prosperity of the wicked form the burden of both discourses.

The unknown author of Job (an Arabian?) depicts his own misery and the enigma of pain by taking as his hero a blameless man who suffers the taking away, in turn, of his wealth and health, and the scoffing of his orthodox friends. He is reminded of the traditional teachings, especially the old doctrine that all suffering is punishment and that he is a vile sinner; though he agrees that God is the ruler supreme, that there is a Sheol where memories are lost and other of the traditional doctrines, he rebels against the traditional meaning of pain and insists that his sufferings are out of all proportion to his deserts and that Nature and history hold out no evidence of a power that makes for righteousness. Where then is justice? Answer: there is none. God is arbitrary and cruel and an avenger of innocent blood. God only knows the reason for human suffering; for man it is an enigma. And yet—God is righteous and, in the end, man's miserable life will be vindicated by the great Vindicator who lives and moves in mysterious ways. The dilemma he finds lies in this: either God is unjust or the relatively blameless man is a vile sinner. For Job there is no positive solution to the meaning of suffering. Not all suffering, he feels assured, however, is due to sin; a man may still suffer and stand in favor with God; why he should suffer remains an enigma. The answer is hid with God. Modern scholars see, in the present form of the book of Job, the revisions of later orthodox hands (*e.g.*, the long speeches of Elihu, and the epilogue containing an account of Job's later prosperity) where orthodoxy takes its last stand to vindicate the old theory.

In Koheleth (meaning the master of a school), the

philosophy of determinism is affirmed. Everything has
its appointed time; Nature behaves in monotonous uniformity with no progress or aim. The righteous suffer
and even perish by their own righteousness. Wisdom
brings no happiness. The great reward of wealth
promised in antiquity (long life, much cattle, and many
children) brings delusion and despair; all is vanity.
We bring nothing into the world and we take nothing
away. Long life is a curse. Death ends the sorry tale.
The wise are forgotten; the wicked rule and go unpunished. There is no advantage in being good. Better
would it be not to have been born. And yet, God rules;
not however, by righteousness but by ways mysterious.
Morality is not characteristic of the heart of things;
man can do no better than to accept the inevitable cruelty
of it all, play his part, and enjoy life while it lasts in
work and moderation. (*Cf.* Epicureanism and the
philosophy of Omar Khayyam). There is no explanation
of suffering; of only one thing are we sure: the traditional theory is untenable and there is nothing to take
its place. (It may be remarked that modern scholars
have noted the touch of other hands in this pessimistic
book, such additions and interpolations as tend to soften
its tone).

As is well known, Jesus came into cruel conflict with
much in Jewish tradition. His special kinship with the
prophetic tradition is easily seen, and, so far as the doctrine under consideration is concerned, his teachings are
especially noteworthy. Three interpretations of human
suffering are discerned in the record of his teachings.
First, there is no doubt in his mind that sin is punished
by suffering, that God rewards the righteous and pun-
ishes the wicked (*e.g.*, Mt. 25:14-30; Lk. 19:12-26;
Mt. 5:3-12); that retribution comes partly in this life
(Mt. 6:33; Mk. 10:28-30) and that retribution continues in the future life (Mk. 12:18-27; in terms of
rewards: Mt. 5:12; 6:19-21; 7:13 ff.; 18:8 ff.; 19:16

ff., 29; 25:46; in terms of punishments: Mt. 5:22, 29
ff.; 10:28; 13:41 ff.; 18:8; 23:33; 25:41, 46; that
retribution is individual and not collective (Jn. 9:1-3;
Mt. 16:27); that punishment is not vengeance (Mt. 5:
43-48; Lk., 6:35 ff.; Mt. 6:14 ff.; 18:21-35); that retribution is not arbitrary (Mt. 5:3-11, 44; 10:39; Mk.
10:30 b; Mt. 10:22; Lk. 23:43; Jn. 14:1-3; Mt. 13:
43; Mt. 5:22, 25; 7:1 ff.; Lk. 15:16; 16:1 ff.; Mt. 25:
28 ff.; Lk. 14:24; Mt. 8:12; 25:10). Second, he takes
issue with the ancient doctrine by teaching that suffering
is not always punishment (*cf.* Lk. 13:1-4; Jn. 9:3; Mk.
13:9-13; Mt. 10:24 ff.) Moreover, his own conviction
of sinlessness (*cf.* Mt. 3:15; 4:1-11; 11:29; Jn. 14:31;
8:46), his silence with reference to admission of sin,
his consciousness of sonship with God, together with
the testimony of his disciples and enemies, could hardly
be squared with the ancient doctrine. Third, he definitely links himself with the prophetic doctrine that it
is characteristic of love to suffer and that because God
loves there is suffering in the very heart of the Universe.
(*Cf. e.g.*, Lk. 15:4-10, 32; Mt. 18:14). He identifies
himself with the suffering prophets and especially with
the Suffering Servant of the Lord (Lk. 4:16-22 *vs.* Is.
61:1-3; Mk. 10:45 *vs.* Is. 53:11 ff., etc.), rejecting
sacrifices (Mt. 9:13; 12:7; Mk. 12:32-34; etc.) and
regarding self-sacrifice as the way to the higher life
(Mt. 10:38 ff.; 16:24 ff.; Mk. 8:34 ff.; Lk. 9:23 ff.;
Jn. 12:24 ff.; 12:32; 15:13).

It is curious to note that the Church minimized (when
it did not frankly ignore) this interpretation of the
meaning of pain in terms of a suffering God, in its
great credal expressions. The reason, of course, is to
be had in the influence of subsequent Greek thought.
Such a conception as a suffering Deity is foreign to the
Greek conception of perfection; it was enough to portray
Jesus as a substitutionary sacrifice after the analogy of
animal sacrifice, as suffering in behalf of man and his

guilt; but to transfer this suffering to the heart of the Universe, a God participating in that suffering, was going beyond the bounds of propriety and dignity, and hence this solution was almost hidden away by the orthodox interpreters of the oral and written tradition.[10]

Human suffering, then, has its setting not in the arbitrary will of Deity but in the very nature of Deity. This is as far as the constructive solution of Jesus goes. It is a religious and moral rather than a scientific-metaphysical solution. There is no attempt to explain the *dysteleologies* (bad purposes) of nature, the ugly scars and catastrophes in the physical world, nor the evils which, perchance, lie at levels below the human. Though it is undoubtedly an exalted interpretation of some of the great ills of mankind and a morally elevating conception of God, it stops short at certain points crucial for philosophy, points characteristically neglected by the Hebrew-Jewish mind. Features of the problem of evil still remain untouched in this religious outlook, features which continue to vex the inquiring mind of man. The prophetic tradition marks a step toward a possible solution, but there remain many more steps before a completely satisfactory theory has been reached.

Catholic Traditional Views of Sin and Evil

We shall consider two notable interpretations of the problem of evil in connection with the development of historic Christianity. There is, first, the influential view of St. Augustine (354-430) of whom it has been said that "men of every variety of school look back to him for their inspiration . . . Romanist, and Anglican, Mystic or Covenanter, Lutheran and Methodist, to say nothing

---

[10] The doctrine of the *Patripassians* is a notable exception. However, this doctrine was acclaimed heretical in the developing Christian orthodoxy.

of other schools, all . . . [of which] revere his memory, and are eager to quote his authority." He reverts back to Adam as a background for his theory. The "first man" possessed in his unfallen state a perfect free-will and a holy inclination to do right. And yet implicitly embedded in that free-will was the possession of the power to do wrong (*possibilitas peccandi*) which, however, did not become explicit until Adam was put to the test.[11] Under the test Adam "fell" thus originating sin *ex nihilo*, possibility became a permanent actuality, and the perfect will became a perverted will. This perversion was transmitted to the race and human nature became corrupted, an inherent bias, the root of evil. Thus "original sin" (his own term) gained entrance into the world and played havoc, corrupting not only human nature but nature itself. Helpless and prostrate, man's salvation is wholly the work of Deity, the gift of grace (irresistible and predestined) without any merit on the part of sinful man.

Two strains of thought (other than the record of sacred writings) creep out in the Augustinian view. He began as a student and disciple of Manichæism—so-called from the founder of the sect, Mani (b. *circa* 215 A.D.)—with its teaching of an eternal dualism between good and evil, the latter getting expressed in nature, in the body of man as well as in half of his soul. The Augustinian emphasis upon identifying original sin with sexual lust carries this Manichæan trait (as well as the imprint of his own previous licentious living). The other influence is that of Neo-Platonism with its idea that evil is a negative state, a lack, and not something

---

[11] It has been suggested that the difference between Eastern and Western thought on the matter of free-will and moral responsibility is that among the Greeks moral freedom is possible only in the face of alternatives, while the Latin (Augustinian view) holds that a will is free if it is self-determined (*i.e.*, without external compulsion) in spite of the fact that there is but one alternative. *See* R. S. Moxon *The Doctrine of Sin* (1922), p. 82.

in itself to be accounted for by the just judgment of God against fallen man.

The inadequacies of these views have been pointed out again and again. Augustine is not consistent; his logic is at fault; he throws back the problem of the origin of evil upon a mythical figure (mythical particularly from the evolutionary view-point) and leaves it there inexplicable; his notion that sin is punishable hardly squares with man's alleged impotence; he confuses original sin with guilt and renders his theory immoral; his Scriptural exegesis is faulty; his inheritance-theory is artificial and unsound (his notion that the results of the Fall are passed on to children implies the *traducianist* view *viz.,* that the soul of a child is generated from the souls of its parents); and no satisfactory account (other than a curse on the part of Deity) is given to explain the evils in nature; failing to recognize the spark of good in man he sinks too easily into a dismal pessimism; and so on. And yet, it is maintained, there is profundity in it all; Augustine recognizes the brutal reality of evil and the unpleasant fact that man is far from a saint.

St. Thomas Aquinas, the great system- and norm-maker for Catholic orthodoxy [12] took over the main principles of Augustinianism (including the doctrine of "original sin") and yet introduces important modifications under the spell of the revived studies of Aristotle. He presents three possible explanations of the origin of evil. First, evil is permitted to furnish a contrast to the good, by which the good is shown to greater advantage. Second, the differentiation of nature into a variety of forms (which is evident throughout nature) would seem to require that some aspects of nature should be nobler than others, some finer and some stronger, some better, than others. The presence of evil thus

---

[12] *Ante,* pp. 76 ff.

lends itself to the law of variety. Third, evil is not an entity; it is a lack. (*Cf.* Neo-Platonic-Augustinian views above). Since it is a departure from real existence, from God, it is outside the category of substance and hence "is" no-being, it "is in reality" nothing. And, having no existence *per se*, evil has no cause and having no cause cannot be attributed to the Universal Cause (God). Moreover, it is nothing in the sense that it is a defect (like saltless salt).

The Doctrines of Sin and Original Sin Re-interpreted

The term "sin" in modern thought generally is reserved to mean a conscious deliberate failure on the part of a person to be or to do what in the light of his ability and opportunity he ought to be or to do. This is to be distinguished from failure due to ignorance, mistake, or impotence, to uncontrollable circumstances such as heredity, physical, psychical, or social handicaps. Now, it is a recognizable fact that to sin is easy and some reasonable account ought to be given to explain this universal tendency on the part of man to choose deliberately the worse instead of the better. The insistence, in ancient theory, upon a recognition of this tendency has had the merit of frankness in facing an ugly fact and has acted as a check upon any undue or shallow optimism. Yet, the form in which the account was cast is now widely given up. The answers given were either too easy or too artificial in the light of present-day psychological and biological view-points.

One theory which reveals how the doctrine of original sin might be recast in a more acceptable form is that offered by F. R. Tennant.[13] Briefly, it is suggested that the origin of sin has a long history which goes back racially to those unmoral natural impulses and habits

---

[13] *Hulsean Lectures* 1901-1902.

which precede later stages in the development of the mores and of ethical norms.

Habits and tendencies which were a-moral at an earlier stage become moral and sinful at a later; and this holds for both the race and the individual. A child is non-moral; not until the child is faced with the possibility of deliberate choice of aligning himself either for or against what, in his environment, is recognized as of higher worth as over against his own immediate claims (his impulses, etc.) is he a moral creature. Sin thus implies moral choice. But, to moralize his natural impulses and desires is not an easy task; these impulses "hang over" and render the new alignment difficult. Sin consists in the failure to check these habits and tendencies in the face of ethical sanctions. It has its setting, accordingly, in the past. Man is sinful because of his failure to moralize the raw material of morality; that raw material is out-of-step with later developments; thus, the expression and the misuse of ancestral habits and tendencies, as viewed from a later context, constitutes sin. This theory has been criticized for its emphasis upon the negative character of sin (failure) and lack of emphasis upon its positive side; if sin is essentially an anachronism, such a theory (so the critics say) fails to take into adequate account the responsibility on the part of a sinner (who is pretty much chained to his past) and his sense of guilt.

Consider another expression of this attempt to reinterpret the doctrine of original sin in terms of the evolutionary and social processes by and through which men are linked with the past and with each other in a corporate manner. Consider, collectively, the views of that notable group of clergymen, psychologists, psychotherapists, neurologists, and physicians in England and Scotland who, a decade or more ago, almost succeeded in forming a special school of religious and moral psychology, based upon reflections on the grim realities of World War experiences. Such writers (*e.g.*, T. W. Pym, C. E. Hudson, E. J. Bicknell, R. S. Moxon, R. H. Thouless, W. M. Mackay, E. R. Micklem, F. R. Barry, William Brown, and J. A. Hadfield [14]) have made much of the fundamental drives (instincts or instinctive emotions) which form the raw material of human behavior.

These instincts, of course, are the biological heritages of the past (residing, as some maintain, in the subconscious); they have served useful functions (*e.g.*, protective). They continue to operate, but are excessively strong so far as man's present social environment is concerned. As such, man comes into conflict both with himself and with his social order. The result is maladjustment. These elemental drives though they are in themselves non-moral have "moral tendencies." It is what human beings through deliberate effort do with their biological equipment which makes for the possibility of sin. Free expression brings trouble; repression also. Intelligent sublimation (re-direction) is the only solution. Original sin consists in this universal tendency inherited from man's animal ancestry to gratify natural instincts and to employ them for selfish ends. Actual sin is not to be confused with this setting, though the setting explains it; actual sin is a refusal to moralize these inherited drives.[15]

---

[14] Hadfield's *Psychology and Morals* (1923) which deals with case-studies (*e.g.*, shell-shock) contains some important observations of the relation of psychology to moral questions. It is highly recommended in connection with this topic. *See* his famous essay "The Psychology of Power" in *The Spirit* (1922), edited by B. H. Streeter, pp. 68 ff. W. M. Horton's *A Psychological Approach to Theology* (1931) should also be consulted.

[15] There is considerable dispute today among psychologists over whether or not there are "instincts." This is a discussion into which we cannot here enter. A classical definition of instinct formulated by Professor Wm. McDougall is worth setting down: "an inherited or innate psycho-physical disposition which determines its possessor to perceive, and to pay attention to, objects of a certain class, to experience an emotional excitement of a particular quality upon perceiving such an object, and to act in regard to it in a particular manner,

Actual sin is not mere failure (negative); it is sheer selfishness (positive). It is easier to sin than to do good because the latter requires intelligent effort and self-control while the former consists merely in slumping back on the wave of inherited drives. Social sin operates (propagates) because of man's corporate relations to his fellows through the psychological laws of suggestion, imitation, sympathy, authority — all of which complicates matters. Moral disease (organic diseases, functional nervous disorders) is to be distinguished from sin in that the former is compulsive and beyond the individual's control (and hence beyond responsibility). Thus, in accounting for sin and guilt (horribly confused terms) one is forced to recognize a host of factors, among which man's biological equipment and social inter-relations are significant. That it is better that men are so interwovenly related to the past and present than if they were biologically and socially isolated, is a thesis which can be easily maintained, involving the corollary considerations of natural laws (hereditary and social) and orderly processes—points which will receive consideration later.

The Theodicy of Leibniz

A word, in passing, about the celebrated metaphysical explanation of evil offered by Leibniz (1646-1716).

---

or, at least, to experience an impulse to such action." *Social Psychology* (Luce, 1921), 14th ed., p. 30.

On the modifiability of instincts through the growth of habits and the development of ideas there has, of course, been considerable debate. A most suggestive treatment has been given this subject by L. T. Hobhouse in his *Mind in Evolution* (1901, 2nd ed. 1915). According to him, intelligence is not something that has grown up apart from instincts but intelligence is the name for the variable side of instincts. Accordingly, instincts change their character (*e.g.*, become less specific in the course of evolution) by means of intelligence which has been evolved *within;* modifiability, accordingly, is a part of the process itself.

W. E. Hocking's *Human Nature and Its Remaking* (1918) will be found rewarding reading upon this general topic.

Created beings are finite and this finite-nature is imperfect and this imperfection is the source of evil, an evil which is not the result of the direct will of God but a necessary concomitant of the nature of the finite. The limitations of this finite are, however, in comparison with the good, relatively small; they are like the discords which enter into and give fullness to the symphony. Now, says Leibniz, this is the best of all possible worlds since, first, God's creative laws are without blemish since God is infinite perfection and his purposes are those of perfect satisfaction; and second, a created world necessarily involves other-than-God and finiteness, and thus, imperfections play a necessary and enhancing rôle in that glorious symphony of the whole with its perfect laws.

The best possible world might, indeed, include evil if it could be maintained that only by such evils could certain goods be achieved (involving "higher interests"). This is the favorable side of Leibniz's picture. But, granting such a *theory of transmutation*, it is well to ask whether this interpretation satisfactorily accounts for *all* evils. In other words, suppose it is possible to say that many evils may be transmuted into a higher good and thus turn out to be good-in-disguise, can *all* evils be thus transmuted? Indeed, here is the rub!

Contemporary Considerations in Relation to Theodicy

In the solution of the vexatious question of theodicy, two (among a number of) ideas have come to the front in recent thought: the notion of evolution has considerably altered the older "solutions," and, with that notion, there is a prevailing tendency to revise the conception of God. Let us look at these notions, first in a general way, and then consider two concrete examples.

The evolutionary picture as drawn by the modern natural sciences has shown that, in the struggle for existence and the survival of the fittest, the principle of evil has played a necessary rôle in progress. And this picture has been widened to include the whole sphere of existence. In man it is only through conflict that achievement comes. It is progress through risk; and yet, progress. The question at once presses upon us: could progress have come in any other way, by way of less cost? Perhaps its price has been too high. Granting that any genuine, spontaneous progress involves costs and risks, has not Nature been unduly exacting? If the answer is that there is no ultimate meaning to the struggle and attending evils and that there is no worthy teleological factor at work to furnish the means by which an end may be ultimately achieved or that the end is wholly unworthy or out of proportion to the price, pessimism is the likely result. Theodicy thus becomes no problem. Either there is no God; or, if there is a God this God is not good enough. The first alternative solves the problem by dismissing it. The second alternative, of course, solves the problem by making it irrelevant and meaningless, since such a God would then be a *quasi*-Devil.

If we suppose that God is and that God is good enough but that God is limited in power, then a number of interpretations may legitimately be offered. That limitation may be a self-limitation in the interest of "higher interests." In other words, God may have deliberately willed the drama of evolutionary struggle to produce a certain type of being (related in an orderly way to a natural order) which achieves a certain "stature" through a long and rigorous discipline, a stature which can only be accomplished by the pervasion throughout of struggle and risk. To achieve this, however, would imply a continuation of the struggle, at the human level, beyond the (too) narrow time set by the "here and now"—a continuing process in which beings worthy in such a plan could find the necessary time and opportunity for the realization of the fundamental creative purpose. Or, that power may be limited by another paired-power in which case we should have dualism and undoubtedly ultimate pessimism. Or, that power may be limited in that it is, itself, developing and maturing, in which case we should have Deity included in the evolutionary process itself. In this case it is difficult to see how, if God's power is developing, God's goodness is not also in the process of development; if God's goodness is stable, how reconcile this with God's evolving nature; if God's goodness is growing, then there must have been a time when God was less-good (a view which would tend to render the whole question of theodicy less acute if not irrelevant—since, then, it would not be necessary to relate evil with a completely good God).[16] Or, again, that power may be limited by a peculiar character of God's self in which case though God is completely good there is an element in the nature of Deity which makes for limitations and frustrations. The two special views which we shall consider are those which follow, in the main, the first and last of these alternatives, those of Professors D. C. Macintosh and E. S. Brightman.

The Theodicy of Macintosh

According to Professor Macintosh,[17] this world with its evils does not render a theodicy impossible. We may still believe that it is the work of a good God. It is not the best possible world as it now is (since the better has not always been followed), but it is the best possible world under the conditions of creative freedom and in view of the kind of a world implied by such a drama supposedly purposed by Deity. At least, he says, it is as good as any other when one takes into consideration

---

[16] This view of God's evolving nature is maintained, *e.g.*, by John Haynes Holmes in an essay "A Struggling God" in *My Idea of God* (1927), edited by Joseph Fort Newton, pp. 109 ff.

[17] *Ante,* pp. 115 ff.

the kind of a world (in the purposes of Deity) involving creative freedom and the risks involved in such a procedure.

What kind of a world do we find? Answer: it is a world that is quite dependable, *i.e.*, there are physical, mental, and social laws which govern even in change. To have a world which lacks order would imply chaos; and chaos, of course, is confusion confounded, a world in which purposes would be wholly irrational, arbitrary, or impossible. But, if law and order are a part of this best kind of a world, what does this imply? Answer: either it implies rigorous determinism and a denial of spontaneous freedom or, if spontaneous freedom is asserted, it implies a qualified kind of order. In the first case, we should have a world that churns away producing puppets, a world which could not produce creatively free beings, a world which conceivably would be "worse" from the view-point of a Divine plan than one where creative freedom is allowed (even with its attendant risks). In the second case, we should find that enough spontaneity is made possible to produce, in the course of time, such beings (which nature has produced up through the animal kingdom) as man with the power to make choices. In other words, the spontaneity in nature forms the evolutionary background for that spontaneity in man which is asserted of his freedom. The risk of such spontaneity both in nature and man is, of course, evident.

Physical catastrophes (such from the view-point of organic forms) may be looked upon as the result of physical and chemical laws operating in an orderly way, but interrupting the development of such organic forms as fail to make necessary adjustments; they may be looked upon, in certain instances, as the result (if the element of spontaneity is asserted in the inorganic realm) of blind-alleys which such spontaneity in nature has brought about; in living forms, the production of injurious forms of life, such as poisonous reptiles and plants, beasts of prey, death-dealing bacteria, physical and mental disabilities, may be traceable to this same orderly process, which, from the higher view-point, may be considered as the result of a non-mechanistic factor (vitalism) asserting itself spontaneously and hence not always favorable to higher forms in the world-order. Without this spontaneity it is difficult to see how nature could have produced human free-agents (unless their production was the arbitrary intrusion of the Divine factor in the world order).

Now, if law and order plus some degree of spontaneity are involved in the best kind of a world for the production of human free-agents, our next step is to show how all this affects human beings (since, of course, theodicy is a problem only for those, produced in the natural processes, who are capable of reflection). A human being, as is well known, is constantly running up against what to him is disaster: disease germs, lightning, floods, drought, heat, cold, and a hundred other "ills" of nature, together with the mistakes he and others make because of perverted or ignorant notions. Many such "ills" are patently beyond his control.

Now, it may be (and often is) asked: why does not God interfere and prevent such ills for the sake of man? Answer: By so doing, God would be interfering with the natural order; if he should work a "miracle" (in the sense of law-upsetting) for one person, he should (to play fair) work it for another, and the result is chaos. It is better (in the long run) that the order be maintained than that it be dissolved; and this means that human beings will have to suffer such ills. The problem remains insoluble if the present existence is all there is to the story. If, however, we could maintain a continuance of personal life beyond death (as can be maintained, says Macintosh), then the present handicaps may be overcome with further time and opportunity without upsetting the order. It is better to have such ills with order than to have sheer puppet-like "blessedness," or, chaos. If the purpose of the Universe is to produce beings that are to be self-determining and hence moral (the only way in which moral responsibility is possible), then both order and creative freedom must be maintained at whatever the cost.

Let us put the matter in a concrete way. A man is walking close to a precipice. The sod gives way; he falls to his death. Could this not have been prevented by a good God? So far as the physical law is concerned: yes, if God had interfered with and upset the law of gravitation; no, if the laws of physical nature are to be respected. But, could not God have put it into the mind of that man not to walk there? Yes, if the man is a mere puppet; no, if the man is creatively free. Either the man was ignorant or knew better. If he knew better the situation involves his own responsibility; if he was ignorant and because of it God interfered to save him, then ignorance is made a condition in which to interfere with natural law; everyone then, under similar circumstances, would thus justly expect such interference. But interference is the cancellation of law, and general interference implies natural chaos. Is there then no solution? If we could hold that further opportunity is afforded the man in a continued existence, the present ill could be eventually overcome without upsetting either the law of nature or man's self-determination. And so on with countless other experiences.

There are, says Macintosh, ways in which God, presumably, has allowed for the mitigation of such ills without interrupting the natural processes. Nature has all along been producing means by which many such ills are gradually overcome. Notice well: in spite of the odds, Nature has produced means of survival! Sensation, in the case of biological forms, is a case in point. Sensations have emerged in biological evolution as a means of counteracting possible evils. The fact that an animal can see or smell danger is a way by means of escape and survival. Sensations, however, do not upset law; they merely overcome one set of laws by another set of laws.

Consider pain. Pain is nature's warning signal that all is not well. The biological value of pain (having laws of its own) is evident; were it not for its warning many a situation or circumstance would end in disaster. (The most treacherous diseases, for example, are those that come on and develop without the warning of pain.) Consider thought (where an organism has evolved to the extent of having a brain capable of it). By means of thinking the organism can overcome many physical ills and needless pains without interrupting laws; again, it is a new set of laws overcoming another set. In thought, the organism anticipates danger and prevents many ills. But thought has the possibility of error. To overcome this, Nature has developed the power of attention, the capacity on the part of the individual to *direct* his thoughts to overcome such errors. This implies the freedom of his will which acts as a deterrent to ills. But this is not all. The freedom of the will carries the possibility of moral evil. A man may know what to do and yet, not do it.

Hence, a further element must be introduced: *viz.*, a morally good will. For without such a will a new set of ills (moral and social) come about as a result of misuse of freedom. Such a will to be morally good needs the supplementation of a wholesome religious perspective (moral optimism) [18] to guard effectively against moral evil. Thus, there is an orderly way which Nature has found (up through man) to meet ills without interrupting the order. It is order within order. Each new order while having the possibility of offsetting the

------

[18] *Cf. ante,* pp. 118 ff.

evils attending each previous order brings about the possibility of a new set of evils; and yet, the whole (with its climax in man) represents the way in which nature has been providing means to overcome evils in an orderly way in a setting of creative freedom. Physical death itself may have value, among other reasons, in that it affords release from the burdens of old age and a place for others.[19] But this, too, is not an ill if personal immortality can be asserted.

Thus, on the long look, Nature has produced ways by which ills may be gradually overcome (from the view-point of man) without interrupting the order, by introducing factors which operate in an orderly way and, at the same time, permitting the play and interplay of creative freedom culminating, in its higher reaches, in the expression of moral responsibility. And so, says Macintosh, this is the best possible world of its kind for the orderly production of moral free-agents as a first stage in their development. Assuming a morally worthy God (implied in the doctrine of moral optimism [20]), it is reasonable to expect that further opportunity in time will be given to a further development of moral free-agents—a doctrine that is patently necessary to bring about justice for those who have been caught up in the mesh of physical and moral evils beyond their control.[21]

---

[19] *Cf.* the essay by George A. Coe, "A Realistic View of Death" in *Religious Realism* (1931), edited by D. C. Macintosh, pp. 179 ff.

[20] *Ante,* p. 119.

[21] For an account of Macintosh's theodicy *see* his *The Reasonableness of Christianity* (the Bross Prize Book—1925), pp. 84 ff.

The notion of deliberate self-limitation on the part of Deity has been widely held. Consider the view of Professor G. H. Palmer: Events, he holds, *become* good or bad according as they are used. Any event may become good or ill. God, so far as man is concerned, is a wise educator. He offers opportunity for his children. He expects results not by coercion but through self-discipline. He uses the elective system. Even as a student forced is no student at all so a child-puppet is no child at all. The whole process is that of a high purpose willed by means of self-limitation and at the risk of failure. *See* his essay in *Contemporary American Philosophy* (1930), edited by G. P. Adams and W. P. Montague, Vol. I., pp. 51 ff.

The Theodicy of Brightman

Another way of dealing with theodicy is that offered by Professor Brightman of Boston University, contained in his book *The Problem of God* (1930). We shall give a brief summary of his general thesis.

This book purports to be a revised apologetic for Christian theism. Brightman acknowledges the widespread doubt of the present day in reference to the existence and character of God. Frank atheism, he finds, abounds; non-theistic views are multiplying; and the older theistic conceptions are increasingly being abandoned. Is there, then, no case for theism?—he asks. Answer: Most assuredly; not, however, without certain revised conceptions.

It is one of the peculiar features in religious thought, he continues, that wherever abandonment of the God-concept has occurred, substitutions have appeared. Contemporary doubt has erected its pantheon of substitute-gods before which it worships with characteristic religious fervor. This is truly an idolatrous age. Behold only such names as: J. B. Watson, Everett Dean Martin, George Santayana, Morris Cohen, Clarence Darrow, Harry Elmer Barnes, R. W. Sellars, Harald Höffding, Julian Huxley, John Dewey, Bertrand Russell, S. Alexander, S. Freud, and others—some atheistic, some agnostic, most of whom are idolaters (*i.e.*, have created their own ideal images), all non-theistic, tender-hearted, but tough-minded and fearfully influential.

Whatever semblance of the God-idea has remained among many of the intellectually influential, it has dissipated itself in two directions: either it has been expanded and made so broad (paralleling the expanding horizon suggested by the sciences) that it has come to mean everything and nothing; or else it has been so contracted and made so narrow that it has come to mean little or nothing. Sinners of the first class are the pantheists and absolutists—revelers in a foggy emptiness. Sinners of the second class are the radical finitists —worshipers of lean gods.

Well, what can the traditional theist say to his contemporaries? If he is wise he will not be dogmatic; he will survey the landscape, search out the hidden currents of thought as these are being charged with changing notions (many of which are here to stay) and reexamine his own position. To conserve theism, he will find, thinks Brightman, that it will be necessary to convert theists. Their idea of God will have to undergo change —in the direction of both expansion and contraction. Expansion is necessary in the overcoming of intolerable anthropomorphisms (*i.e.*, making interpretations to conform to man's image); contraction is necessary in making God real and vital for human flesh and blood. For instance, our inherited notion of God as omnipotent, omniscient, immutable, impassible (and such like) which gave to him an Aristotelian sense of dignity [22] may satisfy an esthetic, contemplative consciousness, but it is too far removed from the world of circumstance to be of any vital significance or use to poor, suffering, struggling humanity. To be valuable God must be usable; but to be usable he must be capable of entering into human experience with all its attending limitations. We may paint God in terms of pure form (with Aristotle); but to do so is not helping us in the tough tasks of every day; we may think of God in terms of pure experience, but to do so is to take him out of our own. The traditional view may be more beautiful, but it is less useful. If God is to be made vital for our contemporaries we may have to picture him less as an object of perfect art and more as a rugged though lovable Companion.

Some kind of a limited conception, accordingly, is

---

[22] *Ante*, p. 79, foot-note.

necessary. Here Professor Brightman works into his thesis: God is finite. Consider certain alleged attributes of God in the traditional conception. How about omnipotence? Can God do whatever he wills? Answer: No. In the first place, granted that he has willed free beings he is limited by them; in the second place, he has his own inner difficulties, contrasts, tensions, conflicts (summed up by the author's word "Given"), which are characteristic of anything that savors of personality. This Given is a kind of *an inner other than* upon which the Divine Will works, presenting tasks to be done, meanings to be fulfilled, always stirring the Divine Nature on from more to more and never completely satisfied or overcome. His is a dynamic personality, continually willing, but limited by what he wills and by the factors of stress and strain within his own nature.

His is not a self-determining will alone; it is caught in the mesh of the Given and, accordingly, not all powerful. How about omniscience? Can God know everything? Answer: No. To know ahead of time (foreknowledge) implies a disguised determinism; the classical distinction (set up by Christian theologians) between foreordination and foreknowledge as a solution to a time-honored dilemma no longer holds water; for, how could things be known ahead of time unless there be some kind of causal nexus sufficiently binding to make prediction possible? Of course, we might say that he determines everything; but the consequences are too severe. Why not frankly say that God is limited even here; that whereas he may know all possible moves he does not know which particular move may obtain? (This is William James's view and his analogy of the chessboard).[23] How about immutability? Is God unchangeable? Answer: No. His very character implies potentiality and an inner dualism of process by reason of the

---

[23] *See* "The Dilemma of Determinism," pp. 181 ff., in *The Will to Believe*.

Given; time and change, accordingly, are real with him. How about impassibility? Is God incapable of suffering? Answer: No. His very character implies frustration, tension, conflict, inherent in the nature of the Given.

And here we touch directly upon the problem of evil. Does God have a perfectly good will? Answer: Yes. To say otherwise is to suggest a Devil. But the Yes must be understood to refer only to the Will; the Will, itself, it is to be remembered, is chained to the Given. It is this latter element in the Divine Nature, acting as a "drag" and presenting difficulties, that accounts for the dysteleologies of nature, the evolutionary struggles and delays, as God expresses himself creatively in the cosmic processes. Even as the good will resolves its own difficulties, so will the cosmic difficulties be resolved; but, not fully, for there will always be tasks, trials, tensions.

Our solace may be had in the thought that the good will is sufficiently powerful to bring an eventual outcome of present conflicts. Some may feel a sense of disappointment in not being assured that there will be no further struggles; but, then, would not a "sublimely perfect" situation without struggle, without tasks, be boring and intolerable, with nothing to do but to sit quiet forever and ever? Is not a life of zest better than a colorless one? This is Brightman; and this (the latter point) is William James.

If the reader wonders what Brightman means by his doctrine of the Given, he is referred to his own inner self. Will he not there find that the very fibre of personality consists of an inner duality: an active working upon a passive, a subject acting upon an object, a form shaping a content, a very dualism of process? [24] Such, similarly, is the Divine Personality. It is in this

---

[24] There is, on this point, a similarity with Fichte's analysis of self. See *First Adventures*, etc., pp. 159 ff.

inherent duality in God that is to be found the solution to many of the enigmas of existence and the key to unlock the problem of evil; at least, no better solution can be set forth than this, says Brightman.

This theodicy is thus set up at a price. God is made finite. It is a cost which, to some, may seem too great. In justification of this view it may be said: the notion of a limited God is a very old notion even in Christian orthodoxy (in terms of self-limitation); this price is less high than that required by the premise of the abstract attributes of the Aristotelian God; it affords the kind of God that satisfies a generation which is uninterested in Greek metaphysics; the implications of the Given are in metaphysical harmony with the notion of the suffering God of the simple Galilean; and finally, it is a workable and reasonable theodicy.

PESSIMISM

There are those who claim that a theodicy is impossible and choose to assert that the ills of existence outweigh the good and that, when all is said and done, the world of circumstance is fundamentally bad. Some come to this pessimistic view (aside from the temperamental factor) because of their initial metaphysical position. In this section we shall consider two cases where pessimism is metaphysically grounded, both extreme in their expression. With these before us we shall surely have a taste of about as bitter a species of pessimistic gall as is to be found in the history of Western classical thought.

The Pessimism of Schopenhauer

The case of Arthur Schopenhauer (1788-1860) is classic.[25] For him the world is fundamentally purpose-

---

[25] A classification and exposition of his metaphysics are set forth in *First Adventures,* etc., pp. 161 ff.

less, irrational, blind, surging will. From this it follows that there is no answer to the query of why we are here or to what end all this striving. We appear on the wave of blind impulse; nature asserts a monotonous round of irrational urgings in which beast and man are caught up. Life brings no unblemished satisfaction. The happy life is absurd. Why, then, continue to live and reproduce? Answer: because of the irrational will-to-live which surges through the species. Nature fools us in the strategy of propagation. Lonely souls think that through mating they shall overcome their state of unhappiness. Both sexes go through the process of ridiculously trying to charm each other, nature's trick for mating; but mating means no more than reproduction; instead of happiness it is but an exchange from one state of unhappiness to another with still more added for good measure. Sooner or later it is realized that one has been fooled.

Man's desires outreach their fulfilment; if he gets what he desires, the satisfaction is not comparable to his expectation; and, what is more, ridiculously enough, he keeps on desiring. If he no longer desires he becomes bored. We are unhappy when alone and unhappy when with others. We find ourselves unwittingly happy only in brief intervals between pains. Pleasure is negative, and it is accidental and fleeting. Life traverses paths of "red-hot coals with a few cool places here and there." Life continually teaches us the lessons of disillusionment. The intellect with its increasing knowledge adds only to pain and misery. The more we know the more we sorrow. We cannot endure thinking for too long periods; nature is fundamentally "agin'" it; irrational Will is more fundamental than intellect. The "call" to the unconscious state continually presses upon us and finally overcomes us; it is the call of nature primeval, back to the bosom of the real where the will (which never rests) can do its work without interruption.

A good part of our life is spent in sleep; we struggle to keep awake and never succeed for any length of time. Then comes the endless sleep where we are buried in those unconscious processes which have produced us. Unconsciousness is the original and natural state. All life is a struggle and a strife. Of this the animal world is exhibit *A;* and man is exhibit *B.* One preys upon the other. Dante did not have far to go to find pictorial material for his vision of hell. Sooner or later we realize that the struggle is either a comedy or a tragedy. Death and insanity are means of refuge from pain. Defeat is written across the sky. Were it not for this impulsive will-to-live man would take refuge in early self-destruction; but nature fools him, prods him with hopes that are but rationalizations. Buddhism holds out the promise of dealing squarely with reality; the doctrine of Nirvana with its surrender of all this striving to a state of will-lessness is the individual's only salvation. The less we will the less we suffer. But, this is helpful only so far as the individual is concerned; Nature still goes on committing the crime of births and deals roughly with those who survive and mocks them with dupery. In truth, this is the worst possible world!

The reader who thinks this exposition overdone may check it with the sources.[26] It may be pointed out that this pessimist was a lonely wanderer, companionless with the exception of his dog Atma. He carried memories of unhappy relations at home. He was a supreme egotist; without modesty, he claimed that only Kant and he really had done anything worth while in philosophy. Of a retiring and suspicious disposition, he fought with himself, torn by an inner struggle between restless desires unfulfilled and ideas of nobility, embittered by the long delay of professional recognition (he was intensely jealous of the popularity of his great contemporary, Hegel). And he was a bachelor. Ac-

---

[26] See *Schopenhauer Selections* (1928), edited by DeWitt H. Parker.

cording to the Jamesean expression he typified the "sick-soul." But for all that, Schopenhauer's pessimism follows logically his metaphysical premises.

The Pessimism of Von Hartmann

Another classical pessimist whose metaphysical position (an attempted synthesis of Schopenhauer and Hegel) leads to a conclusion somewhat similar is Eduard von Hartmann (1842-1906). His famous work reveals in its title his general thesis: *The Philosophy of the Unconscious.* Reality to him is an absolute spirit that appears to be essentially will, but this will works as though it were intelligent. In animal life, for example, it works instinctively as though intelligently; it works in the inorganic realm creatively and selectively as though intelligently; and yet it is an intelligence that is unconscious. The relation between will and idea Schopenhauer had likened to a strong blind man carrying on his shoulders a cripple who could see; Hartmann revises the picture as that of a subject that cannot see with its legs nor walk with its eyes (a weird figure which is supposed probably to mean that will and intelligence are bound up somehow and necessarily together and yet to be in a state of mutual incompatibility). There is purpose in the world, but it is unconscious! The unconscious becomes conscious in the evolutionary process in certain thrusts of mind. Conscious ideas then act as *an other* to the great unconscious, accentuating the strife and its futility.

If we say that the underlying subject or reality is God, then there are a number of things we should say in the light of the above. "In the beginning," *i.e.,* before time began to spin its thread, the will of the Absolute or God was potential and intelligence latent. Then (somehow) these became actual; God begins the sojourn from out of the state of potentiality and blessedness. It is the will that begins to will; it lays hold of latent intelligence. The only way by which will can become actual is by setting up its *other* or content. Intelligence thus becomes actual as *the other* of will. It is the nature of actual will to be insatiable; even intelligence as *the other* cannot satisfy. Here is the root of pain and evil. This coming to life of the will to will was a piece of absolute stupidity on the part of the Absolute which cannot be retrieved (once started) until time has spun its thread and the world run its course. Had God been mere intelligence God would never have committed the folly of having become active and creative and there would have been no world. So long as will became actual and, as such, is at the heart of being, there is a restless striving, the principle of pain and evil. Since, then, will implies a content, intelligence, an emptiness which thus comes into being, this is the only kind and the best kind of a world possible even though it spells pain and misery. That it is the best kind of a world is still further in evidence by the rôle that intelligence is to perform, *viz.*, to perform its own undoing! Let us see this possibility.

Since God is will-intelligence and will is insatiable and therefore pain and evil, God is in need of redemption. Intelligence plays the rôle of redemption, it provides the means of deliverance. It does this in the production of consciousness (a process which Hartmann calls "evolutional optimism"). Consciousness is unconscious intelligence become a more complete *other* (over against will). Conscious beings reveal to themselves and to the whole unconscious (!) how futile the whole creative process is; by realizing the vanity of the goods in life, the vanity in the hope of a future state, the vanity of the hope of happiness in a civilization-to-come, conscious beings reveal the process as one of progressive disillusionment.

Conscious beings reveal God's grand and glorious

mistake of ever having become active and creative; the more this futility is realized the more intense will desire arise and strive to attain once more the state of absolute painlessness and a return to mere potentiality (or nothingness?). As conscious beings, then, we who are caught up in this horrible drama must help the Divine (share in the suffering of Deity) to achieve the peace and painlessness of non-existence, the only redemption for God and the whole creative process. (How intelligence is to make will "see" the futility of all this striving, Hartmann does not make clear; and it is a crucial point). What is required of us, in this philosophy, then, is that we should become ambassadors of the "gospel" of futility; wherever we find a ray of hope that ray should be allowed to flicker in order, thereby, to lay bare its folly! How about the final consummation? Can we be optimistic enough with this pessimism to be certain of a return to general quiescence? Will or can the Absolute ever return to its state of bliss-in-potentiality? Answer: there can be no assured answer. Suppose, however, this is possible. How then, can there be any assurance that the process will not repeat itself and the cycle of folly be born again and again? There is no answer. Pessimism, thus, adds to pessimism.

Here, indeed, we have a philosophy of pessimism gone mad (which is only proper). Says James Ward of Hartmann: this writer "has perpetrated more absurdities than any other writer of repute I know."

Some General Remarks on Pessimism

In spite of the grim reality of evil in the world and in spite of the widespread influence (particularly in the East) of pessimism, this attitude toward the world of circumstance has not fared so well as might be expected. It magnifies the side of life which human beings have sought somehow to avoid. Like extreme optimism it is a one-sided picture; and like extreme optimism its psychological fallacy lies in the common tendency of human beings to single out (though unconsciously) certain experiences and make these typical.[27]   Whereas the truth of the matter undoubtedly lies in the recognition that for most people, though there are many hard and cruel experiences in life, there are many that are good.

In this whole matter (pessimism *vs.* optimism), the crucial question, of course, is that of comparing the evil and the good.   Hartmann undertook what he regarded as an empirical approach to the matter by setting up an accountant's sheet of the so-called evils and goods. (We are here reminded of the Catholic theologian Abelard (d. 1142) who used a similar methodology, collecting opposing Biblical passages and patristic writing in his famous *Sic et Non*, determining to draw his conclusions arithmetically by comparing all the *fors* and all the *againsts*.) His conclusions, of course, were that there are more evils than goods; and by evils he (with Schopenhauer) meant pains and by goods pleasures. For, with both, will is essentially desire and desire spells pain (for Schopenhauer pain is positive and pleasure negative; for Hartmann, both are positive).   What shall we say about such a method of comparison?   Is it sound?

To this query there are a number of counter-queries. The initial bias may be questioned.   Are all goods only those of pleasure?   The principle that pleasure is the sole good (a doctrine known as *hedonism*) seems to

---

[27] H. Höffding (1843-1931) has expressed this principle well by his term *expansion of feeling*. It is characteristic, he says, of feeling that when once aroused it tends to spread over the whole life of consciousness and to color all the elements of that psychic life. Elements of the inner state which ordinarily have nothing in common thus acquire a common character by this coloring.   Thus a single bad taste may give to one a general dismal tone and contribute to one's distorted outlook as well as make for bad logic. *See* his *The Philosophy of Religion*, (second ed., 1914), p. 94. His metaphysics is summarized in *First Adventures*, etc., pp. 282 ff.

underly this theory of the good. But, it may be asked, may there not be some positive values that are not to be had in terms of pleasure, values which Hartmann's criterion fails to take into account? Are we to be optimists or pessimists on the basis, only, of the criterion of pleasure and pain? May not the one who strikes out after pleasure be chasing down a false lead? Furthermore, is the method of arithmetic a legitimate criterion here? Can we add evils and goods even as we add apples and pears? Is it not a matter of measuring rather than of mere counting? But how are we to measure? Measurement requires a quantitative basis and evils and goods are qualitative. What then? We might reduce evils and goods to their physical and physiological counterparts and then make the comparisons. But what does such a correlation show? Evolutionary history affords the only answer. It is this: Consider pain as a subjective concomitant of disturbed physiological function. So considered, pain may be considered on a quantitative basis. If pain is a disturbance of physiological function, it belongs to the exception rather than to the rule; it is abnormal, the element that marks out life as being thwarted or in the process of extinction. Pleasure, on the other hand, then belongs on the side of the promotion of the process, *i.e.*, to normal physiological functioning. If pain had exceeded pleasures, or, in other words, if disturbed physiological functions had exceeded normal (or undisturbed) physiological functions, or, again, if the abnormal had predominated over the normal, would not the world process have been less advanced than it now is or even come to an end long before this?

Again, are Schopenhauer and Hartmann right in taking desire to mean pain? Is all desire pain? Are there not some desires that are not only pleasurable but fruitful? We may desire to become professional musicians; although we may not achieve our desire, may there not be a great deal of pleasure in *attempting* to achieve, pleasure in amateurish performance? Is there not pleasure in pursuit? We are said to be slaves of our desires. But, is this so? Do we not learn from experience, as our interests develop, *what* to desire? The two classic pessimists have identified desire with will. Is this defensible psychology? Perhaps will is but a name for the dynamic character of mental life without any specific commitment to desire; will may as well play a part in the *control* of desire.[28]

Classical pessimism abounds in reservations and inconsistencies. Consider the cases already mentioned. Job's pessimism is softened by the halo that there is meaning to suffering, hid with God; and that is, after all, for him enough. Koheleth in one breath curses and in the next blesses. The metaphysics of Schopenhauer not only led to pessimism but it pointed to a gospel of consolation and deliverance. By the rapture of esthetic contemplation, the mind goes beyond itself, unmindful of the grinding details and particulars, and the desires are quieted. This is the function of art and it is a means of salvation to the few. Art is consolation in that it takes man into the realm where desire is swallowed up; beauty is the realm of pure good. And further, by self-sacrifice, by forgetting oneself, and by living one's life for others, one is (at least temporarily) lifted out of one's own insatiable desires, one catches the peace that comes by self-abandonment and thus attains something of the bliss of quietism, Nirvana. Both scientific activity and religious asceticism, too, afford release. In other words, like the doctrine of Nirvana of Buddha which taught, not, as some have said, a state of nothingness or non-existence but a state of deliverance from need and sorrow, from birth and death, from hate and passion, Schopenhauer, too, taught personal salvation (release).

---

[28] For a fuller treatment of some such criticisms the reader is referred to James Ward, *The Realm of Ends* (second ed., 1912).

Consider Hartmann's implicit hope for a solution where pain will give way to quiescence, a doctrine, too, of deliverance. In other words, there is the subtle recognition that there may be something in the world of promise even if only of final release. Moreover, it may be observed that if pessimism did not recognize positive values there would be no point to the doctrine of pessimism itself.[29] Höffding has well remarked: "An absolute pessimism has never yet been developed either in religion or philosophy." There would be no solution to ills whatever, by way of deliverance, release, or even quiescence, in a *genuine* pessimism. Thus, even our classical exponents are not full-fledged pessimists.

So far as normal human living is concerned, both pessimism and extreme optimism are paralyzing doctrines. The one tends to make futile, efforts toward the better; the other tends to make the-world-as-it-now-is appear to be the best possible of all worlds, a view which, in the words of John Dewey, "might be regarded as the most cynical of pessimisms."[30] Whereas extreme pessimism, in other words, may deliberately mistake angels for demons, extreme optimism may well be but a peculiar type of pessimism which deliberately mistakes demons for angels.

There remain such other alternatives as meliorism and moral optimism.[31]

---

[29] The opposite has been said of Christian Science: if it did not recognize evil (if only to deny it) what is its distinguishing point?
[30] *Reconstruction in Philosophy* (1920), p. 178.
[31] *Ante,* pp. 118 ff.

CHAPTER VIII

THE SOUL IN ANCIENT AND MEDIEVAL THOUGHT

The Primitive Conception of a Ghost-Soul

Presumably the primitive notion of soul is that of a ghost-soul described by E. B. Tylor in the following way:

> It is a thin, unsubstantial human image, in its nature a sort of vapour, film, or shadow; the cause of life and thought in the individual it animates; independently possessing the personal consciousness and volition of its corporeal owner, past or present; capable of leaving the body far behind, to flash swiftly from place to place; mostly impalpable and invisible, yet also manifesting physical power, and especially appearing to men waking or asleep as a phantasm separate from the body of which it bears the likeness; continuing to exist and appear to men after the death of that body; able to enter into, possess, and act in the bodies of other men, of animals, and even of things.[1]

The origin of the notion of soul is buried in obscurity; it is safe to say, however, that early man did not set up any marked distinctions between himself and the world of which he was a part, and only gradually through a great variety of experiences were such distinctions drawn. Among the factors believed to have played into the notion of the ghost-soul are: the strange and impinging character of such marked-out experiences as sleep, trance, dreams, visions, hallucinations, memory-images; the objectification of life in contrast to dead

---

[1] *Primitive Culture* (Holt, 3d Am. ed., 1889), Vol. I., p. 429.

bodies; the peculiar tinge of will-power; and a host of other factors. The form in which the ghost-soul has been pictured has varied greatly: *e.g.*, as a kind of shadow, as the breath which seems identified with man's life, and crudely described by physical categories; the place of its habitation has varied: sometimes it has been conceived to permeate the whole body, sometimes in some vital part; more commonly it has been associated with those parts of the body which cease visibly to function with death (*e.g.*, the breath, the flowing blood, the eye), and when conceived in terms of memory-image it has been thought to reside in various places (*e.g.*, as hovering about the body of the dead, in the grave, as in the shadows and reflections on water, as abiding in far-off lands envisaged in dreams of the departed), and so on.

Professor Franz Boas offers the fruitful suggestion that the conception of the soul has followed the various manifestations of life coupled with the tendency to conceive certain attributes or qualities of that life and experience, in general, as substances. The result of this process of *objectification of qualities* makes for the notion of a concrete substance which in turn is taken to exist independently. For instance, successful hunting is conceived to be due to an independent entity or substance, *success*, which the hunter may be thought to acquire or lose as a kind of helping spirit.

The conception of the soul (ofttimes plural), may well have arisen as an objectification of many of man's noticeable qualities, constituting collectively either the man-as-he-is-as-a-whole or the man-as-he-desires-to-be. In the struggle for existence man is gradually forced to take stock of himself and so to pay attention to his qualities. It seems reasonable to suppose that the qualities would acquire a status of their own and be conceived to carry on a kind of separate and collective existence.

The Soul-Mind and Concepts of Substance

That there was a tendency to substantialize these qualities and thus make for the concept of a soul-as-an-entity becomes evident in the later conceptions which emerge in the history of the soul-concept. The effect of this substantializing process made for a more distinct separation of the soul from the body which marks the development of thought in the great tradition which came by way of Greek philosophy. Such a process of conceiving qualities collectively as a soul-substance belongs to the natural development of the concept of substance in general. Substance literally means "standing under," the permanent amidst change, the capacity for independent existence, a concept which directs itself to both the physical and mental aspects of experience.

Professor C. W. Morris in a recent study [2] points out that historic tradition thus has conceived of soul-mind as a substance. Now, the notion of substance may be either *empirical* or *metaphysical*. By an *empirical substance* is meant the notion of a *that* having qualities and relations, without which qualities and relations the *that* neither has meaning nor existence. This kind of substance has been named the *substantive*. By a *metaphysical substance* is meant the notion of a *that* which exists as an independent and unobserved substratum bearing qualities or relations that seem attached to it. As distinguished from the substantive, this metaphysical substance is termed *substance*. As now defined, it is maintained that the notion of soul that has played the major rôle in the history of thought is the substance-soul, a

---

[2] *Six Theories of Mind* (1932). The interested student should consult this important work. It gives a clear exposition and historical setting of some of the conspicuous philosophies of mind.

that which exists as a substratum in its own right independent of qualities and relations.[3]

That the substance rather than the substantive view should have loomed so large in the history of thought is accounted for, by this author, by the following considerations: the desire for the permanent; the trick of language that a constant name for a thing implies that that thing remains the same; the persistence of some quality in opposition to fluctuating and disappearing qualities; the tendency to transform practical sameness (*i.e.*, sameness for certain purposes, as a house is the same house since one lives there from day to day in spite of the fact that the house itself may have undergone many changes) into an absolute sameness; an emphasis upon some use or criterion which is relatively stable to the point of an absolute contrast with other features or purposes; the tendency to emphasize the wholeness of a thing as distinguished from its aspects or changing characters, a wholeness which is conceived as a kind of cohesive principle underlying each and every attribute.

This notion of substance, of course, makes for vagueness; for, if a thing is a substance beyond its attributes, what then is that substance? Not having in itself any attributes how can it be defined? If it is defined, is it not defined in terms of its attributes? And if so, what becomes of the substance-notion? If it cannot be defined, of what use is such a notion; is it not, then, meaningless? It is natural to expect that if soul is conceived to be such a substance, a vagueness both as to concept and definition is the result.

---

[3] Critics of Morris's classification may object to this statement by insisting that it is the substantive—rather than the substance—view which looms large in the history of thought. Such critics would incline to say that perhaps Kant is the only classic defender of the substance view. We shall, however, follow Morris's outline and thesis.

The Soul in Hebrew Thought

There are two strands of development which we should note in tracing the ancient history of the notion of soul. First, the Hebrew strand and, second, the Platonic-Aristotelian strand. With the joining of both strands in later thought we shall have the picture before us of the ancient notion which forms the background of medieval and modern Western thought.

The primitive Hebrew conception of the soul was essentially like that of the primitive conception of a ghost-soul. Two views, earlier and later, appear in the Old Testament record. In the earlier view, the soul was believed to be the seat of feeling and desire, and secondarily, the seat of intelligence. Man consists of soul and body, the view known as *dichotomy*. At death the soul leaves the body, hovering about the place of the body's burial, visiting familiar earthly scenes and then passing on (the development of later thought) to the gloomy, monotonous, and empty existence of Sheol, the underworld of darkness and desolation. (*Cf. e.g.*, the description in Is. 14:9-17.) The later view distinguishes the spirit from the soul and (with body) man thus becomes a *trichotomy*. The spirit is conceived to survive; the soul is conceived to be that of a vital principle which makes for mental life and yet which perishes with the body. The spirit returns to spirit and personal existence is swallowed up. The latter view, however, though it rivaled the former, never quite succeeded in gaining popularity.

The Soul in Plato's Thought

The importance of the Platonic-Aristotelian tradition can hardly be overestimated. The Platonic view of the soul will first be considered.

There are a number of influences in Plato's thought that should be noted. We shall but mention them. The two main influences in this direction were those of

Greek religion and the speculations of preceding philosophers.

Three periods (before the fifth century B.C.) are observed in the development of Greek religion. First, in the pre-Homeric period the conception of the ghost-soul characteristic of primitives seems to have prevailed. Secondly, in the Olympian religion depicted by the Homeric epic, the soul was conceived as a shadowy image which, after inhabiting the body, left it by way of mouth or open wound of the dying. Upon its descent into Hades it was confined shorn of its former powers and unable to haunt and mock the happiness of the living. (The Olympian religion marked a step forward by the substitution of fear of and reverence toward the gods and forces for similar attitudes toward departed souls—a parallel development noted in Hebrew thought). Thirdly, in the revival of mystic religion in the seventh and sixth centuries B.C. (and continuing down through the centuries), the soul was given a prominent rôle in schemes of personal redemption. Facing the woes of life with doctrines of personal deliverance, there were developed such cults as: that of Dionysus which set up wild dances by the practice of which the worshipers attained a state of ecstatic exaltation and mystic union with the immortal gods; the Eleusinian mysteries, a cult (adopted at Athens) which initiated its devotees into the blessed state of a future life; the cult of Apollo; and the so-called Orphic cult.

The Orphic cult particularly (developed during the sixth century B.C.) set up a well-defined theology and system of personal redemption, teaching the doctrine of a distinct entity, the soul, over against the body—a soul conceived of as an immortal being imprisoned for a time in the body, "a fugitive from god and a wanderer" —and teaching doctrines of pre-existence and reincarnation. The influence upon Plato's thought of the Orphic doctrine of the soul is widely acknowledged by students of Plato. He gave it philosophical setting and helped to establish in subsequent thought the notion of soul-as-entity, (together with the belief in pre-existence and immortality).

The speculations of preceding philosophers helped also to pave the way in this direction. Pythagoras (*c.* 580-500 B.C.)[4] is supposed to have been a disciple of the Orphic cult and to have taught the divine nature of the soul. The soul (it was taught) is imprisoned in the body, having no organic relation with that body; it is not identified with the human personality but rather an independent wanderer inhabiting now human and now animal bodies; however, it is immortal and in essence unchangeable; its ultimate destiny is that of a final return to the supernatural realm of pure souls from whence it originally came. Pythagoreanism as a religious cult taught the way of return through rites of purification and asceticism.

Other philosophical influences were: the thought of Empedocles (*c.* 490-430 B.C.) who taught that the soul leads but a temporary existence in the body and will return to a divine order, that a soul is active only in the higher reaches of thought and ecstasy; the thought of Anaxagoras (500-428 B.C.) who taught that all things are directed by a Mind (νοῦς) expressing itself in living forms as soul; and the thought of Plato's teacher, Socrates (469-399 B.C.) who gave to the soul-concept an intellectual and moral emphasis.

With this background one can see that Plato's doctrine of the soul has a history. Plato's notion of soul may be characterized as follows: intelligence is inseparable from the soul; the soul is an entity, a substance, capable of entering into and influencing the behavior

---

[4] For a brief account of Pythagoreanism, see *First Adventures,* etc., pp. 255 ff.

of the physical man; pre-existing as well as post-existing, immortal; capable of apprehending truth and the essence of reality either with or without bodily connections; the ground of personality; self-moving and the source of all motion and change; the divine element in man which is to be nurtured by reason (the doctrine of ideas) which gives the permanent in contrast to the world of feeling and sense which gives the fleeting.[5] Thinking, for Plato, is a function of the soul as are willing and feeling; yet, not all such mental activity represents that soul in its pure pristine form; only by the most correct, the purest type of thinking can that soul come to its own, and this is a process which requires much education and enlightenment and is reserved only for those who have truly caught the vision of Reality.

The Soul in Aristotle's Thought

Aristotle's conception of the soul and mind has, historically, been widely influential. All material things that manifest powers of spontaneous movement and growth, he held, are besouled. The soul is the vital principle which distinguishes an organism from inorganic things; this soul is a term covering all the peculiar characteristics of living things including mind. There are five principal expressions of the soul: vegetative, appetitive, sensitive, directive, and rational. Plants are besouled in the first sense; animals in all but the last; man expresses them all. These are not distinct souls or distinct aspects of soul; rather, they are levels of activity with the lower expression caught up in a higher unity. Soul and body are not separable (only in thought can they be separated); every living thing is both body and soul. The soul is not material; rather it is the "formal cause" which determines the form of the organism; it is the "efficient cause" producing move-

---

[5] See *ante*, pp. 76-77.

ments of the organism; it is the "final cause" of the organism, the end for the sake of which the organism exists. The body is the organism's "material cause." Aristotle's philosophy has been termed *hylomorphism*,[6] the view that matter (ὕλη) and form (μορφή) are intertwined (form in matter and matter formed).

It is in such a setting—a marked emphasis on the intimate relation of the physical and psychical, an emphasis of nature as one weave—that Aristotle's theory of soul is to be understood. The soul, he says, "is the original and fundamental ground of all our life, of our sensation, and of our reasoning. It follows therefore that the soul must be regarded as a sort of form and idea, rather than as matter and as underlying subject." [7] The soul "cannot be separated from the body: for in some cases the soul is the realization of the parts of body themselves." *And yet*, it is "perfectly conceivable that there may be some parts of it ["if it naturally admit of partition"] which are separable, and this because they are not the expression or realization of any particular body. And indeed it is further matter of doubt whether soul as the perfect realization of the body may not stand to it in the same separable relation as a sailor to his boat." [8] There appears to be in this naturalistic phase of Aristotle's thought an uncertainty as to the separability of the soul-as-reason; as for other expressions of the soul which are expressions or realizations of certain bodily organs there seems to be no doubt of the soul's inseparability from the body; but, since reason is not the realization of any particular bodily organ, the soul-as-reason appears to be unique and separable. "But with regard to reason and the contemplative power this is not yet clear, but this *seems* to be

---

[6] *Ante*, p. 78. An account of Aristotle's *Hylomorphism* is given in *First Adventures*, etc., pp. 277 ff.

[7] *Source Book in Ancient Philosophy* (Scribners, 1907), C. M. Bakewell, p. 241.

[8] *Ibid.*, p. 239.

another class of soul, and this alone is capable of existing separately, as the eternal from the perishable.[9]

Aristotle makes a distinction between creative reason and passive reason. The latter (made up of sensations, perceptions, and images) is the matter of thought; the former gives form to the latter. Creative reason, the highest function of the soul, having no bodily organ, is the separable, creative, immortal, and eternal soul. Yet, one may ask, what is such a separable soul? Does it have the character of thought which the passive reason possesses? The answer: "When it has been separated it is only that which it is essentially, and this alone is immortal and eternal (we do not remember, however, because this reason is impassive and the passive reason is perishable); and without this nothing thinks." [10] Creative reason, or "the part" of the soul that is immortal thus appears to be higher, purer, and certainly more abstract than passive reason—so much so that it is doubtful that this can imply *personal* immortality.

There has been considerable controversy over the interpretation of Aristotle. There are admitted ambiguities and inconsistencies in his thought about the soul. There is both the Platonic in him and the Aristotelian. It would be correct to say that he never moved far from the Platonic theory of soul as an immaterial substance.[11] The creative reason appears to be linked with his doctrine of pure form, the unembodied Form of Forms, which is God. This is his Platonism. On the other hand, the Aristotelianism in him lies in his emphasis upon form entwined with matter, soul entwined with organisms, and the passive reason entwined with nature. This phase of his thought—call it Aristotelian naturalism—contains suggestions hailed by modern thinkers

---

[9] *Aristotle: Selections* (Scribners, 1927), edited by W. D. Ross, p. 204.

[10] *Ibid.*, p. 215.

[11] A detailed analysis of substance as a fundamental category is given in his *Metaphysics*.

as prophetic of the modern anti-substance views of mind, of the present revolt against dualism (both ontological and epistemological) and of the modern emphasis upon the doctrine of emergence.

Passive mind appears to have appeared in the natural order as an emergent; as such it is closely linked with matter and nature in general; passive mind drawing its contents from nature directly (and thus not standing over against nature as a *sui generis* something) makes possible an affinity with such modern anti-substance views as the "process," "relational," and "functional" theories of mind; passive mind in its setting of nature gives an ancient setting to the newer doctrines of modern realists ("new" and "critical").[12]   The typically Aristotelian doctrine of mind, certain modern commentators would insist, is "that the mind is the thing when it is thought," the implication being that other doctrines of mind in Aristotle are not characteristically Aristotelian.

Religious and Philosophical Cults in the Graeco-Roman World—the Soul in Stoic Thought

Before turning aside from the Platonic-Aristotelian development we should cast a hasty glance at the disintegration of these great speculative systems, noting the character of the thought which developed with the breakdown of Greek political and social supremacy. This period takes us into the Graeco-Roman world, the immediate background wherein Christianity began its long development.   The turn now is toward the practical.   Professional thinkers cease to sit quietly and speculate; they now become ministers of salvation. The development is toward the practical problems of personal peace of mind; doctrines now reflect the thera-

---

[12] For an outline discussion of these various recent theories of soul-mind see *First Adventures*, etc., Chap XVIII.

peutic interests of troubled souls. The flood of religious and philosophical cults that swept in give one at a glance the character of the times.

Of the philosophical cults, Epicureanism, (and later) Neo-Platonism and Stoicism were prominent, the latter developing a notion of soul which came to find a place in developing Christianity. Epicureanism, as is well known, taught a more or less "don't care" attitude toward life; its motto was ἀ-ταραξία which meant: do not throw the mind into confusion. The gods do not care about men; be content with one's self and make the most of things. Stoicism, on the other hand, developed a doctrine of determinism which taught that the World-Reason, the Logos, has set everything as it is, and that one should acquiesce in whatever place one has been assigned. The motto read: ἀπάθεια *i.e.*, do not allow one's self to suffer but let one submit to one's destiny and rise above the level of complaint. The soul is an offshoot of the Divine Reason, a fine material substance, like warm air, and is closely associated with the blood which pervades the body. Mental activity is but a specialized form of this soul. The soul is substance. Just what this substance is, is not always clear —there is considerable modification of notions among the Stoics. The Stoics introduced the Greek word *pneuma* (πνεῦμα —spirit) as a kind of vital pervasive principle which is transmitted in physical generation and this spirit was conceived, on the whole, to mean more than soul (ψυχή). The relation between the two was not clearly defined. The importance of this Stoic doctrine lies chiefly in the re-introduction of a trichotomy [13] into subsequent thought. Of the various philosophical cults, Stoicism came nearest to the Christian point of view.

---

[13] *Ante,* p. 188.

The Amalgamation of Hebrew and Greek Thought at Alexandria—Philo

We return now, after this rough sketch, to show how the two traditional currents, the Hebrew and the Platonic-Aristotelian, became joined in Jewish thought and in the great Christian tradition. About the beginning of the third century B.C. there are signs of an amalgamation of Hebrew and Hellenic thought among the Jews of Alexandria in Egypt. With the passing of time, Jews in Egypt were growing up without a knowledge of the mother-tongue (Hebrew); to meet the need of acquainting the new generations with the sacred writings of their fathers there was projected and issued the so-called Septuagint or Greek version of the Hebrew books of the Old Testament. (The Septuagint was so called, it has been maintained, either because—according to tradition—it was composed by a committee of seventy Jewish scholars, or, because it was sanctioned by the Egyptian Jewish Assembly of seventy members. The Septuagint was composed during the period of about 285-130 B.C. and represents not always the most accurate type of work in translation. A number of apocryphal books written in Greek were also included in this now famous translation).

These Egyptian Jews were both in language and manners Hellenic, absorbing the ideas of that culture without altogether losing their own traditional character. That a process of amalgamation and accommodation would take place in these growing colonies between the Hebrew and the Platonic-Aristotelian tradition is only to be expected. The brilliant example of this process is that of Philo (20 B.C.-40 A.D.), the Jew who made the bold attempt to combine Hebrew theology and Greek philosophy. He belonged to the liberal school of Alexandria and is considered the forerunner of the Neo-Platonic school which achieved its concrete ex-

pression in the person of Plotinus (204-269).[14] Philo
knew his Plato well; he also knew Stoicism; the Pentateuch he knew too. The belief in the pre-existence of
souls and their unfortunate descent into human bodies
he adopted. He employed the method of allegory to
make the Hebrew Scriptures fit Greek philosophy. The
logos of the Stoics he made out to be wisdom, spirit, law,
the intermediary between a transcendent God and an
alien world—a doctrine that reappears in the Fourth
Gospel in terms of Jesus. Philo also seemed to teach
a trichotomy, taking over the Stoic *pneuma* and identifying it with the breath of the Hebrew God and the reason
of Plato and Aristotle, teaching that this spirit became
expressed in the soul of man.

Early Christian Doctrines of the Soul

If one should look in the New Testament record for
a clear exposition of human psychology one will be
doomed to disappointment. The record is blurred as
is the history of the soul-concept in previous thought.
There are passages in the Pauline writings that teach a
dichotomy; there are some passages that appear to suggest a trichotomy (*e.g.*, I. Thess. 5:23. *Cf.* also,
Hebrews: 4:12).[15] In the Gospels *psyche* and *pneuma*

---

[14] *Ante*, p. 96.
[15] Since the figure of Paul dominates Western religious thought it
might be well to turn to the utterances of some notable scholars in
their interpretation of the Pauline psychology. Professor William
McDougall in his *Body and Mind* (Methuen, fifth ed., 1920, pp. 30-31)
follows the interpretation of the noted scholar R. H. Charles: "St.
Paul's doctrine of human personality, departing in this respect from
the teachings of the other parts of the New Testament, in which soul
and spirit are not distinguished, involved a . . . trichotomy, body,
soul, and spirit. According to Prof. Charles, the Apostle adopted the
later doctrine of the Old Testament which regarded the soul 'as the
supreme function of the body quickened by the spirit. So conceived
it naturally perishes on the withdrawal of the latter. It has, therefore, no existence in the next life. And such, in fact, appears to be
the view of the Apostle. The soul, he holds, is the vital principle of
the flesh (σάρξ). Hence the epithets "fleshly" (σαρκικός) and "soul-
ish" (ψυχικός) over against "spiritual" (πνευματικός) are taken to be

are used synonymously, the former emphasizing, perhaps, more strongly the idea of individual personality. Though there has been considerable dispute as to a theory of the origin of the soul the doctrine which seems to have prevailed was that of its concreation with the body.[16]

Early Christian thought about the soul continues to mix Hebrew and Greek conceptions in various forms and in various degrees of vagueness. Clement of Alexandria (died, *circa*, 215 A.D.) follows in the footsteps of Philo, employing allegory to advantage, and attempts to make a synthesis of various schools of thought, believing that philosophy and religion are mutually contributory. The soul, he taught, is a unity with a dual origin; it is in part rational and in part irrational; the rational soul comes from God while the irrational soul has its setting in the world as a kind of animating principle. The soul begins as a blank; the senses supply knowledge to the irrational soul which in turn needs the rational soul for complete understand-

---

synonymous.' The *pneuma* or spirit comes directly from God, but, since it alone is the immortal part of man, it is not reabsorbed into the Godhead on the death of the body, as in the later Hebrew conception, and is the basis of personal immortality." He goes on to say that the Apostle does not carry through his trichotomous doctrine consistently. The noted Pauline scholar, Professor F. C. Porter, interprets the matter thus: "The present body, which does not rise, Paul calls not physical or material but psychical, a body fitted for the human soul. Soul, *psyche,* the word of honour in Plato's hope, is lowered in Paul, and made inseparable from the physical, to which in Plato it is absolutely contrasted; and the word spirit, *pneuma,* which to the Greeks was more material and less personal than *psyche,* and contained less promise and potency of immortality for man, is exalted and becomes the essential nature of the risen Christ and so of risen Christians; it becomes also . . . the expression for that present experience of the indwelling Christ. . . . It would seem that to Paul the word "body" means individual personality, and is essential in his thought to the distinction and the permanence of the separate self." "Paul's Belief in Life After Death" in *Religion and the Future Life* (Revell, 1922), edited by E. Hershey Sneath, pp. 235-236.

[16] *See* article "Soul" in *A Dictionary of Christ and the Gospels* (1917), edited by James Hastings, Vol. II. This same article points out that the traducianist hypothesis (*see ante,* p. 157) first appears in the thought of Tertullian (A.D. 200).

ing. Man differs from the animals in the possession of
a rational soul. The true end of life is to attain spiritual-
ity, a harmony of the rational soul with God—an
achievement accomplished by the aid of the Logos which
comes from God as an intermediary.[17]

Following in the footsteps of Clement comes the
prodigious figure of the Alexandrian Origen (died,
254), prince among allegorists. Everything, he taught,
is dependent upon God, the creator. The soul is united
with matter in one world; animals have souls; man has
also a spirit imparted from God. Man's soul is Reason
(νοῦς) fallen from its original glory; the soul is both
the principle of life and of degraded reason. The soul
is a kind of intermediary between flesh and pure spirit,
the cooling-off of an original fire. The soul preexisted
though there is no memory of it. Soul will continue
to go on after the death of the body in a long struggle
(æons upon æons) back to God.

Mention should be made of Claudius Galen (died
circa 200) as a representative of the medical tradition
emanating from Alexandria which combined philosophy
with scientific work. Galen made much of the relation
between mind-soul and body. His particular approach
to the problem of soul lay in a study of the emotional
life linking it up with bodily states and making the
physiology of temperaments the particular angle of that
approach. His psychology leaned strongly in the direction of a materialism. The recognition of the importance
of the nervous system and particularly the brain in the
understanding of mental life marks his approach as an
anticipation of modern physiological psychology.

The Soul in Neo-Platonism

Neo-Platonism figures prominently in the development of Christian thought by means of its influence
upon the Church fathers and particularly upon St.

---

[17] On Gnosticism, see *First Adventures,* etc., pp. 16, 72, 131.

Augustine. Plotinus [18] was concerned about the inner life; his point of departure within the Platonic conception of reality was that of an emphasis upon the life of contemplation, upon the life that will free the soul from the encumbrances of the body. The Neo-Platonic view consists of two fundamental doctrines: that of an ultimate unity, *i.e.*, metaphysical monism, and that of the emanation of plurality from unity. The Primeval Being, the One, the Infinite (strictly speaking without any attributes which would imply limitations) throws out first of all Nous, Pure Intelligence, the perfect image of the One, and the archetype of everything that exists. This, in turn, produces a World-Soul, an intermediary between Nous and the world of appearance. Individual souls of men, animals, and slumbering inorganic nature, emanate from the World-Soul; these latter become entangled with "matter" and produce strife (evil); when inclined toward the higher, *i.e.*, the fundamental unity, they will realize their true essence, and this is to be achieved by purification gained in contemplation.

Man, therefore, carries the spark of Divinity though he is held down in a realm which lies at the lower end of the scale of being. The soul is not material; its very character is immaterial, belonging to a scale of being higher than the body; it is prior to the body both in time and function; the body is in the soul rather than the soul in the body. Knowledge is the activity of the soul; organs of sense are its ministers. Desire is connected with the liver, spirit with the heart, and reason with the head. Soul and body do not mix though they cooperate.

St. Augustine's Doctrine of the Soul

Augustine's [19] doctrine of the soul as a part of his general theology and philosophy is important; his

---

[18] *Ante*, pp. 96, 156, 157, 158, 196, 197.
[19] *Ante*, pp. 155 ff.

thought helped to form later Christian orthodoxy. Influenced by Neo-Platonism, he carried over the notion of soul as an immaterial substance and emphasized its Divine origin and *sui generis* character. The soul comes from God; it is immortal although it is created. It pervades the whole body though its center of activity is the brain. The soul is not in time but time is the form through which the soul expresses itself. Soul expresses itself in seven grades of being: as life, as a sentient agent, as supporter of the life of reason, as directing itself from the world to higher values, as contemplating pure truth, as craving higher satisfactions, and as granting vision of absolute truth (a final state of ecstasy).

Medieval Scholasticism and the Re-Discovery of Aristotle

With the re-discovery of Aristotle's works (between the twelfth and thirteenth centuries), a new philosophical boom took place in Christian theology. The Church had long been (through the influence of St. Augustine) under the spell of the Platonic system of thought;[20] Aristotle's works had gone into a shadow. The doctrines of tradition seem to clothe themselves with peculiar splendor in Platonic garments; Aristotle was remembered, of course, but rather as a logician. Part of his works were known to the early medieval scholastics, but the full sweep of his metaphysics and natural philosophy did not become recognized until translations were made of Aristotle into the Latin and of Aristotle's Arabian commentators. (The Arabian philosophers had kept alive the Aristotelian tradition. Notable among this group was Averroes of Cordova, 1126-1198.) The conservative Church fought this intrusion of "heathen" philosophy, condemning Aristotle's trea-

---

[20] On Platonism and Orthodox Christian Theology, see *First Adventures,* etc., pp. 153 ff. Also, *cf.* Anselm, *ante,* pp. 80 ff.

tises on physics (1209) and his metaphysics (1215). It was a period of intense controversy.

The Soul in the Thought of Thomas Aquinas

Aquinas [21] set to work to understand Aristotle apart from the various commentators. The anti-Platonic note which he found in Aristotle struck a responsive chord with him and he set about to defend the "heathen" philosopher against the attacks of the conservative Augustinian-Platonic tradition and against misconceptions on the part of the Arabian commentators. The result of this first-hand study was a Christian Aristotle in an Aquinian dress.

Certain modifications had, of course, to be made before the Church was ready to adopt Aristotle as "her official philosopher." One such modification was the doctrine of the human soul. The logical implication of an important phase of the Aristotelian doctrine, *viz.*, that the soul is form entwined with matter, the entelechy of the body, including the soul as passive reason,[22] was a denial of personal immortality; for if the soul (including passive reason) and body are inseparably linked and the body perish, this would mean that the form too would cease to be.[23] Aquinas held to Aristotle's doctrine that the soul is the form of the body but rejected his notion of the separability of the active reason. This would have brought him to a denial of personal im-

---

[21] *Cf. ante,* pp. 76 ff., 157. On the relation of Thomas Aquinas to Arabian-Aristotelian thought, see *The Philosophy of St. Thomas Aquinas* by E. Gilson (tr. by E. Bullough and edited by G. A. Elrington, 2nd ed., 1929), p. 9 ff. and *passim.*

[22] *Ante,* pp. 192-193.

[23] The reader will recall that Aristotle taught the doctrine of immortality of the soul but found it necessary to distinguish the soul-as-creative-reason from the soul-as-passive-reason, maintaining the former to be separable, impassive, and unmixed—the Platonic note at some variance with his naturalistic emphasis. We have already pointed out that it is a question whether such an Aristotelian notion of immortality is that of *personal* immortality. *Ante,* p. 193.

mortality (as the reader plainly sees). However, Aquinas insisted upon the unitary character of the soul, declaring the whole soul to be separable.

With this revision went an emphasis upon the Platonism in Aristotle, *viz.*, the soul as an immaterial substance, and at the same time a retention of the Aristotelianism in Aristotle, *viz.*, the soul is intimately connected with nature and is the form of the body. Aquinas rebelled against the Platonic view which would hold that the soul is imprisoned in matter. Such a view carried the inference that the bodily state was one which was degrading to the soul and hence a union of soul and body was a lapse. For Aquinas, God created the world out of pure goodness, and hence the body also reflects that same goodness. The soul's connection with the body, he held, is intimate and even necessary to the fulfilment of its present function.

For Aquinas there is a hierarchy of souls: the lowest are those so intimately bound up with matter that they perform no operation beyond the qualities of mere activity and passivity, *i.e.*, without capacity to dominate matter; higher in the scale, are the souls of plants and animals, the latter revealing a form which is capable of directing matter by a certain degree of knowledge; and still higher, is the soul of man which is capable of rising above the limitations set by matter itself into those higher reaches of intellect. This peculiar quality of form at the level of intellect which reveals a certain superiority and independence of the body with which it is intimately associated, is, for Aquinas, the sure evidence of the character of separability of this soul-form and the possibility of immortality. But, in the hierarchy, there are still higher forms which reach out into the realm of pure intelligences, beings which possess neither matter nor bodies, but differing in their several modes of intelligence, an angelic hierarchy, and on and up to the Form of Forms, God.

Man's soul is related to the lower forms though higher in itself. For example, in common with the animals he has a sensitive soul; in common with the plants and animals a vegetative soul; and in common with material particles the "potency" which underlies them; yet these are not to be distinguished as separate souls; rather, the higher contains the lower (even as a pentagon contains a tetragon and a tetragon a triangle). Every stage of soul (as well as body) is *potency* to the higher and *form* to the lower stages. Lowest in the order of intellects, man's soul, is the highest in the order of material forms; the soul of man is at the cross-roads of the world of spirits and the world of matter. The soul of man, accordingly, is intimately connected with the body; it functions throughout that body. Characteristics of mental life, such as feeling, willing, thinking, are powers of that human form of forms. Animals and plants have souls, but their souls perish with their bodies; the pledge of human immortality lies in that peculiar quality of detachment which is found in the soul of man, *i.e.*, in the higher functions, exhibited only in the soul of man.

Human souls do not preexist. For Aquinas nature is linked together throughout, expressing the creative power of God and yet behaving in terms of the causal nexus. It is a double-caused nature; natural causes causing causes and yet a Supernatural Cause causing natural causes. Chopped wood, for example, is the result of the causal efficacy of the will of the wood-chopper to chop wood, and yet what is chopped is the result of the blow of the axe: two causes and yet (in a given instance) one result. Thus, the soul of man (as well as his body) has both a natural and a supernatural setting. So considered, the body may be said to grow a soul in the setting of a creative Cause. And yet, Aquinas and the scholastics were unwilling to rest the "miracle" of the human soul in its natural setting with a mere evolutionary picture; the soul of man is a little too remarkable for that. Hence, there was introduced the doctrine that the soul was specially and creatively infused into the body by God, either at the moment of conception or at a given time in the development of the embryonic body.

Another important feature of the teachings of Aquinas is his view that the soul when separated from the body after death is not whole; it needs the body which later will be joined to it in a resurrection. For man, soul without body is not the ultimate state, though it is so for the angels and for God.

The Separation of Soul and Body in Subsequent Thought

Two (among other) considerations play into the growing emphasis of the idea of the soul as an independent immaterial substance in Western thought in spite of the influence in scholastic thought of Aristotelian naturalism (close union of soul and body). First, there were all along the religious and ethical *motifs*. Christianity continued to be dramatized in terms of the redemption of the soul from its mundane connections in a world of tears and trouble—to save that soul was the paramount issue of life. To think of that soul as a substance wholly different in essence from the world of matter was but a natural corollary. The terrific struggles in adapting one's self to nature and to society continued to lead to pessimistic conclusions; the way toward optimism lay in the stress of an other-worldly order wholly unlike the present which order is envisaged by occasional illuminating insights and by the sustaining influence of the promises of a traditional revelation. The soul became more and more detached and secure in its own sphere; the substance-theory continued to hold sway in spite of a revised Aristotelianism—the soul is *sui generis*. Secondly (and later), the successful application of quantitative measurements as reflected in the development of the physical sciences helped to crowd out the soul to its "proper" place in a realm of the immeasurable—a realm which is conceived to exist in and for itself apart from the mundane and tangible sphere of bodily and temporal existence.

In Western thought, it was Descartes (1596-1650) who, in classical expression, proclaimed the philosophical divorce of soul and body, each, henceforth, to go its own way, to behave after its own manner, although continuing relations with each other which only God could understand. But, to consider Descartes, is to take us into the modern period and beyond the confines here set. We close this chapter with the reminder that the main background has been sketched of the notion of soul which continues today in orthodox Christian circles (Catholic and Protestant), in the sacred literature of the Church, in poetry, in hymns, and in the traditional, Western, religious ideology.[24]

---

[24] If the reader is interested to follow the story through the modern period beginning with Descartes and up through the various contemporary views, he will find the story continued in my *First Adventures in Philosophy,* Chapter XVIII, entitled "Recent Theories of Soul-Mind."

CHAPTER IX

HUMAN FREEDOM AND THE WORLD
OF REALITY

The question whether or not men are sufficiently free to determine and supervise the conduct of their lives and to be held in some measure responsible for their behavior is one of far-reaching theoretical and practical consequences. It is hard to imagine a more pathetic and tragic instance of disillusionment if it should turn out that this question must be answered negatively. In spite of loud voices proclaiming men to be but puppets in the world of circumstance, the history of thought and practice for the most part reveals that men have refused to take seriously such claims; though there has been a willingness on the part of critical minds to admit the theoretical difficulties in the position of freedom this has not seemed to deter men from acting as if they were in some measure free and responsible creatures, that they merit praise or censure as to their thoughts and acts. The ten commandments, the many ethical injunctions of preachers of righteousness and reform, educational programs, theories and practices of government, courts of justice and the whole field of jurisprudence, individual and social codes of behavior—all have rather consistently and insistently refused to look upon men as mere cogs in the machinery of existence. Many theologians have found in the alleged fact of human freedom the basis for the character of the good and a hopeful solution of the enigma of evil, a fact which is held to be essential to an understanding of the meaning of human life and to the hope of a heaven and the belief in a hell. Philosophers have built metaphysical edifices upon the thesis of the moral character of man which implies responsibility and freedom. The relation of a God to finite created beings has been understood in terms of the doctrine of the divine gift of freedom, the most precious and at the same time the costliest of gifts. If the testimony of practice were to decide the question, man would have no difficulty, in spite of many oppressing theoretical difficulties, in affirming that in some measure he is the captain of his soul, the master of his destiny. Unfortunately, practice is no sufficient philosophical criterion (unless one is committed to the shallowest type of pragmatic argument).

Since the problem of freedom is concerned with human psychology, we plunge at once into the psychological angle of the question.

A Psychological Account of the Nature of Will

The problem of human freedom has been called the "free will" problem; such a designation, however, is now less current since controversy over the subject has often led to exaggerated and misleading statements as to the nature of "will." "Free willists" were wont to treat "will" as a mysterious kind of force or entity which is the cause of our actions, but which in itself is *sui generis* and hence outside the causal chain of sequences; it is not man who wills, so they seemed to say, but a "will" that wills man to think and to do so and so; such a "will" was considered not only by definition "free" but also unique, a kind of supernatural gift, a specially appointed faculty of human nature.

According to the modern psychological account of the nature of the mental processes called "volitional," "will" is no longer considered a separate faculty but a name for the dynamic aspect of the intellectual life. Consider, in some detail, the conservative psychological picture.[1] Man reveals three types of activity: voluntary,

---

[1] *E.g.,* R. S. Woodworth's *Psychology* (1st ed., 1921); H. A. Carr's *Psychology* (1925).

involuntary, and automatic. In the case of voluntary activity, an act is performed in accordance with the individual's desires, wishes, and conscious needs; it is directed activity, intentional, involving knowledge and prevision. In the case of involuntary activity, an act is performed in spite of one's desires, wishes, and conscious needs; knowledge and an end-in-view may be there, but they are ineffective to promote or inhibit desired activity. In the case of automatic activity, an act is performed involving no purpose or knowledge of consequences; it is impulsive; no volitional activity is involved. When we speak of a willed act, accordingly, it refers to that kind of activity in which the intellectual factor is effective in modifying or directing the act; it is the intellectual control of an activity in terms of a cognized end.

Such a picture of the willing process is quite different from that of the older psychology and that of popular opinion. The older conception was essentially static; the present conception (under the influence of the evolutionary and genetic emphasis) is dynamic. The mind is born a going-concern "endowed" with the possibilities of acting upon its environment. When we speak of cognition we do not now mean that mind merely "recognizes" in a nonchalant way its environment; cognition implies also a stimulus to action. "Will" has its setting in this whole dynamic nature of mental life; it is peculiarly proper to speak of "will" in connection with the cognitive process especially when that process involves a stimulating influence in arousing a response that is directed to a previsioned end.

Now, any type of activity may be subject to volitional supervision. Even the heart beat may be thus influenced, although indirectly. Volitional activity is partly automatic, which is to say that an act is rarely supervised throughout by intellectual control. Volitional activity differs among individuals in respect to their intellectual differences and what is popularly known as "will power."

In the case of intellectual differences people vary greatly in what they know, to what they have been accustomed (habits, early training, environment, etc.), the way their knowledge is put together (associated), temperamental characteristics, etc. In the case of "will power" or the degree of effort, perseverance, energy, required for the attainment of an end amidst difficulties and distractions, there are wide variations among individuals; such differences are due to many factors, such as bodily health, the ability to enlist a vivid imagination to the desired end, etc. The effectiveness of volitional activity depends upon conditions of environment, intraorganic well- or ill-being, the proper enlistment of motor responses, emotions, and ideas; there may be the need of a reorganization of habits of response, further knowledge, and more adequate coordination of mind and body.

What has been popularly called "will" occurs especially when there is a consciousness of a conflict of desires or alternatives and the necessity of making a choice between them; this is voluntary activity at its sharpest. With a world of stimulation playing upon an individual there is no escape from a conflict of motives; each decision rendered and the course taken builds, for better or worse, brick and mortar into what that individual is or is to become, the construction which is referred to as character. "Will," thus, more especially refers to such responses as require effort to resolve internal conflicts of tendencies; it also refers to the external environment which offers resistance blocking effort toward a preconceived end. "Will" accordingly is not an entity nor a special kind of response; the term refers to certain relationships in which a given response may stand in regard to other responses; more specifically it is but a name for that intellectual control of activity in relation to some anticipated end, situation, or condition.

The Psychologist and the Freedom of the Will

Committed as many psychologists are to those mechanistic principles which have so successfully built up the natural sciences, much in modern psychology reflects a hard and fast determinism, *viz.*, mental laws are not different from the mechanical, physical laws of causal sequence. Without this assumption, says this group, there is no possibility of setting up a real science. When a human being behaves, he behaves according to previous conditioning factors: the nature of his inheritance and the conditions of his environment (sometimes both factors stressed, sometimes one factor stressed at the expense of the other). This methodological determinism, it is claimed, is necessary (though unproved); and certainly it is one that has brought to light many facts about human nature.

On the other hand, there are certain psychologists who, though they respect the assumption of determinism in method, insist that there is unimpeachable evidence for non-mechanistic factors in mental life which places a limit to the applicability of the physical law of causal sequence. Such psychologists move with certain biologists who have refused to sell out to the mechanistic approach.[2] A "purposive" psychologist, for example, would insist that mental life is not completely pictured in terms of the backward look but reveals a forward bent. This directive and purposive nature of mental life would seem to justify the claim of the "free willist" who asserts that man's volitional nature is an effective, initiating factor in the shaping of his thoughts and conduct. There is no special faculty here involved; it is rather the nature of mental life to intend, to realize ends though there are indeed, determining influences which

---

[2] For a discussion of mechanism, vitalism, teleology, and chance, see *First Adventures,* etc., Chaps. XVI-XVII. On behavioristic psychology see *ibid.,* pp. 230 ff.

limit to no small degree the character and possibilities of those intentions or ends. Metaphysical considerations in favor of the purpose-category as applying to the world, of course help to support the purposive psychologist; he would insist, however, that a study of mental life itself without such considerations reveals the inadequacy of mechanistic and deterministic categories. Experiments conducted by the *Gestalt* school of psychologists would be a case in point.[3]

A good many psychologists, however, would leave the question of the possibility of freedom unconsidered; their text-books are silent on the point since a consideration of such a question tends to draw them beyond their scientific-positivistic sphere toward metaphysics. Philosophers may take up the question where the psychologist leaves off. Where the psychologist has spoken in favor of a strict determinism, the philosopher will remember that it is a method that lies back of such a pronouncement and not a proved and universally applicable conclusion. He may object to scientific determinism in that it is built upon an impersonal type of causation, *i.e.*, it is not the causation which the human being experiences in himself as a free and self-determining agent. He may charge the scientific determinist who would categorically deny human freedom with having committed *the fallacy of misplaced concreteness.*[4] He may point out that present-day scientific

---

[3] Consult *Contemporary Schools of Psychology* (1931), R. S. Woodworth, Chap. IV.

[4] This fallacy consists in the error of mistaking the abstractions necessary for a scientific methodology for concrete reality. Whitehead, who has given to this fallacy this name, argues for the organic character of reality (*ante,* p. 125); if reality thus is organic then the scientific emphasis upon analysis is a case of abstractionism. To picture the Concrete in terms of the Abstract is a misplaced Concreteness; the picture has been cruelly distorted. There is no objection to the method of scientific procedure; the objection holds in making more out of it than is warranted.

determinism is less cocksure of its scheme of rigidity.[5] He may appeal to the present-day conception of law as but an expression of probable tendencies (statistical averages) and not that of necessity. The philosopher, in other words, may have much to say in criticism of the scientific dogma that would make freedom impossible; we shall find other such criticisms in the views of the men whom we shall presently discuss.

Human freedom, then, is denied by some psychologists for whom a signally successful method has become the ground for an apotheosis; the question is ignored by many, or at least, the attitude is that of non-committal so far as the science is concerned; its fact is proclaimed by others who see freedom in the very nature of mental life as somehow self-determining, self-directing, in spite of hereditary and environmental influences.

Human Freedom and the Higher Reality

When philosophers discourse on the question of human freedom they see in it not merely a psychological question of the nature of the human will nor the question of the will's freedom *per se;* they see in it the larger question of the relationship of the human being and the encompassing Reality. This is about what one would expect of a philosopher. No view is adequate for him until it finds its consistent place in terms of the whole world of reality.

The term "providence" refers to the relationship between man and the Universe, a relation which is for him, as a whole or in detail, good. When we inquire to

---

[5] He may especially wish to invoke the Principle of Indeterminacy, that uncertainty in the nature of things, as favorable to a doctrine of freedom. Yet, he will remember that the principle strictly applies to physics and should not be expected to apply necessarily to human nature. See "Objections to the Mechanistic Explanation of Physical Phenomena," in *First Adventures,* etc., pp. 340 ff.

learn what men have thought about providence, we find a great variety of views; sometimes the Factor of that providence is a personal, benevolent God, sometimes it is much less personal than the theist's conception; sometimes it is a pantheistic, impersonal Universe; sometimes providence is conceived to work in every detail, sometimes only in a general way. A doctrine of providence depends upon the kind of view that is held of the Higher Reality. Obviously, the question of human freedom is related to that of providence. On the relation of human freedom and the Higher Reality we shall find a criss-crossing of views; a wholly satisfactory classification is difficult, sometimes freedom being redefined in such a way that it appears to have lost its usual meaning.

A Three-Fold Classification of Views

Can man assert himself in a responsible way as an actor in the cosmic scene? Is he wholly free or is he wholly determined by factors beyond his control and responsibility; is he both free and not free; or is he partly free and partly not free? If we say he is wholly free we are *extreme libertarians;* if we say he is wholly determined by factors beyond his control we are *necessitarians* or *extreme determinists.* Both views are radical and may be conveniently classed together as *the first or extreme view.* If we say that he is both free and not free we have *a second or modified view.* It may conveniently be called the *aspectual* view since both freedom and determinism are affirmed, both equally true depending upon from what aspect man is viewed. This view has able defenders particularly from among the metaphysicians. If we say that he is partly free and partly determined we have *a third or modified view.* While setting great limits to man's freedom, this view asserts that there is sufficient freedom to maintain responsibility. Most apologists for man's freedom belong to this third group for reasons which will become evident later.

Three Types of Metaphysical Patterns

We may conceive of metaphysical patterns, similarly, in three ways. The first general view *tends* to be extreme. The Universe has about it a great deal of free-play. Man's fundamental nature reveals the heart of the world as spontaneous and creatively free. On such a view, the world is creatively becoming; it is in flux. There is no pre-conceived plan nor is there a definite *terminus ad quem*. The whole is plastic and unpredictable. Man reflects in his deepest nature the spontaneous and uncertainty of the Universe in which he participates; individual freedom is but a reflection of cosmic freedom with no polished-off beginning or ending. Such a view is not quite a libertarian view. There are features of determinism in it; but the deterministic features are regarded as less fundamental. Freedom here is unquestionably genuine; there is no attempt to re-define it; it is taken unmixed. There is a fearful uncertainty about the whole of Reality since this cosmic creative becoming knows no bounds; it is even non-rational. Some such view is hinted at by many interpreters of cosmic evolution. The notable exponent of metaphysical freedom and spontaneity is, of course, Bergson. On the other hand, an opposite extreme metaphysical position would be that the Universe operates in a determined or predetermined way; it wears a straitjacket; there is no swerving to the right nor to the left; whatever is, is to be. There is a Destiny that rules even the most insignificant action; every act and every thought are but the unfolding of its own rigid nature.

The second metaphysical view affirms that reality is

both free and determined depending upon from what aspect it is considered. From one point of view, man's actions are free, from another they are caught in the mesh of circumstance. Both are true, for Reality is double-faced.

The third metaphysical view offers freedom within the limits set by Reality. So many dots have been set down; it remains for the play of circumstance, for man, to draw the lines between the dots; the general pattern underlies whatever design is drawn within.

If we may take a somewhat limping analogy of the three positions it may be this: the color of a certain revolving shield is said to be all white by some and all black by others—representatives of the two opposing positions of the first general and extreme view; the shield is said to be white on the one side and black on the other—representatives of the second view; the shield is said to be gray—representatives of the third view.

With this as a skeletal background we shall consider these various views of metaphysical freedom, each of which has a bearing on the problem of human freedom. Human freedom and freedom in the world of reality in general are, we repeat, questions which interplay and cannot be wholly separated.

EXTREME EXPRESSIONS OF FREEDOM AND DETERMINISM

Extreme Libertarianism

The shield is said to be all white. The view that man is unconditionally free may be set down as *extreme libertarianism*. (Viewed on the side of metaphysics this position is called *extreme indeterminism*.) Man, it is said, experiences freedom and moral responsibility; however rigid the laws of nature may be there is one marked exception in the case of the human will: it has the power of absolute choice and is conditioned by nothing; in the causal nexus it presents an unbridgeable gap. Extreme libertarianism is on the side of caprice, chance, the wholly unpredictable so far as the human will is concerned; there is nothing that binds the will in the world outside or in the world within. Viewed in terms of motives, the unconditional freedom of the will is that of the "liberty of indifference" since no motive is held to outweigh another and so determine the will.

Defenders of this view among the philosophically discriminate are lacking; they are rather to be found among those who have not thought through the implications of such a position. On occasion one hears this view expounded in hortatory and passioned statements coming from the lips of philosophically undisciplined preachers and from writers in "success" magazines. Bent upon emphasizing man's moral responsibility or man's unlimited possibilities, extreme statements are made with reference to the unconditioned freedom of the will.

The kind of psychology which has seemed to fit an unrestrained freedom is the older faculty psychology which chisels out the will from other aspects of mental life; we have seen, however, that this is now an indefensible type of psychology.

The evident implications of the view of unconditioned freedom follow those of metaphysical caprice. Man's behavior would be chaotic, freakish, irrational, irresponsible. If previous experience did not in some measure condition man there would be no point to his education as a means to self-discipline; he would not behave because of what he has learned but in spite of it all. Character would give way to irresponsible whims. A "will" unrestrained would be a capricious and incalculable tyrant. Under such freedom man should be afraid of himself; he could not depend even upon favorable restraints; he could trust no one including himself. Moral character which depends upon an integration of motives and interests according to some defensible pattern would count for nothing. Against the indiscriminate cry "give me liberty or give me death" a sobered reflection would, in the face of such implications, raise the counter-cry: Give me death rather than such liberty. Moral codes would be quite meaningless so far as practice is concerned; paradoxical as it seems, too much freedom spells the worst kind of slavery. Unrestrained freedom joins with extreme metaphysical tychism [6] in affirming chaos.

Extreme libertarianism, moreover, is quite indefensible since it flouts the facts of experience (including moral experience). No man can do whatever he pleases. It is for our own good, no doubt, that we have limits set upon ourselves, that no one can jump out of his own skin. For better or worse we are what we are largely because of a thousand and more factors. The facts of heredity, early training, environment are written indelibly in our nervous system; a kind heaven may forgive what has gone before, but Nature (benevolently?) never forgets. A doctrine of unrestrained freedom moves against the grain of fact; it is as indefensible as it is undesirable.

St. Augustine's Doctrine of an Original, Perfect, Morally Free-Will, and Its Corruption

The doctrine of an *original* unconstrained freedom possessed by Adam (an approximation to a rather extreme statement of libertarianism in the moral sphere) coupled with the free inclination to do the right forms a part of the teaching of the Church Father, St. Augustine.[7] The Creator created "creators" whose wills were

---

[6] Tychism is a term coined by Charles Peirce meaning chance (τύχη).

[7] *Ante,* pp. 155 ff.

both wholly free and yet perfect. Adam possessed the free inclination to do right; this was an ungarnished freedom (to Augustine). Such a doctrine, though it helped to solve the question of the origin of moral evil and its relation to a good God, and though it might be envisaged when relegated to a remote past, was difficult to hold in the light of human experience. Such libertarianism (in the moral sphere) had to give way to the testimony of human experience. The drama of the prototype Adam, the temptation, the Fall, the expulsion from the Garden, and the long Exodus, is more than a mere fable; it typifies the realities of moral experience. St. Augustine had to modify his doctrine of original moral libertarianism to fit the experience of constraints in his own will. Because of the Fall, man (son of Adam) lost his power of self-determination to righteousness; he became corrupt; his will became overwhelmed in bondage to evil. Christian orthodoxy on the whole has moved with Augustine in refusing to set its stamp of approval upon any unconditioned freedom of the will in the moral sphere. Some orthodoxies have gone the whole way with Augustine and proclaimed the very opposite, *viz.*, the complete impotence of the will to will the good. In many circles, even today, a major heresy is to proclaim otherwise. In Augustine two rather extreme doctrines of free-will thus meet.

Bergson's Metaphysical Freedom

A philosophy of *extreme indeterminism* is to be had in the metaphysics of Henri Bergson (1859—)[8]. The shield of Reality, to use our former analogy, is *metaphysically* and fundamentally white. Reality is, *in its essential features*, becoming. This becoming must be caught on the wing; it cannot itself be analyzed into con-

---

[8] On the philosophy of Bergson, see *First Adventures,* etc., pp. 97 ff., 251 ff., 295, 392.

cepts. A curved line, for example, may theoretically be cut into a series of minute segments which approach straight lines or perhaps points. One might then say that the curved line consists of points or minute straight lines. This is what the determinist sees when he looks at life under the spell of concepts.

It is the major trick of the intellect to translate into its own language and then to regard this language as adequate. The fact of the matter is that a curved line is not made up of straight lines nor of points; it eludes the grasp of such cutting-ups. And so is life in its essence. It eludes the categories set up by an intellect which speaks of a series of consequents and antecedents. Scientific causality chisels out the before-after time-relation; in life, there is no such separating of past and present. The past is in the present, mental states interpenetrate. Life itself must be intuited to be grasped. It is creative and free and beyond the categories of space, position, quantity, and mechanism. The dilemma of determinism and freedom is solved not by translating freedom into a higher determinism (as some try to do) but in subjecting determinism to a deeper and more fundamental freedom.

Man is at the center of creative evolution; free-will is at the heart of consciousness. To try to whip reality into a systematic and logical structure—the ideals of science and the ways of all rational and conceptual thought—is to misrepresent and to falsify it. To understand freedom by thought is impossible; one has to intuit it and the intuition is at once the deeper understanding. A man "knows" he is free and he is free; but no science in all the world can show it, for its language is committed to determinism. The intellect begs the question for the case of determinism; free-willists must first of all show up this fallacy before they can ever hope to state their position convincingly. Not to do so is to permit the nose of the camel to come into the tent. In Bergson's own words: "All determinism will thus be refuted by experience, but every attempt to define freedom will open the way to determinism."[9] Bergson's freedom is not that of free choice; rather it is a freedom in the essence of life (a *metaphysical* freedom).

Extreme Determinism or Necessitarianism

The shield is said to be all black. Man is wholly conditioned; always are his acts the end of a causal nexus reaching back to far distant scenes; long before he appears on the stage, the machinery of existence has been spinning out its products; man is but the inevitable result of this process and so are all his acts; his consciousness of freedom is an illusion. Such is the extreme deterministic picture in barest outline. It has been drawn time and again in the history of thought; no difficulty has been found to secure adherents of the doctrine in any age, in the face of the cruelties of life, the frustrations of desires and hopes, and the distress of trying to cut against what seems to be the direction of the grain. Extreme determinism has been held by scientist and theologian, by the religious and "irreligious," by atheists, theists, and pantheists, by realists and idealists, by the unschooled, and the disciplined. A comforting doctrine it is, when one would like to be relieved of responsibility, blame, and remorse.

Scientific Determinism

This doctrine was widely held among those who fell under the spell of the optimism of the nineteenth-century mechanistic sciences and philosophy, built as they were upon the precise models of mathematics and

---

[9] *Time and Free Will* (Macmillan, 1910, tr.. by F. L. Pogson), p. 230.

physics. It was but a step to apply the mechanistic approach to biology and psychology.[10] The causal-nexus hypothesis—the royal road to knowledge—passed from hypothesis to dogma; for anyone to suggest that perhaps there were gaps in the mechanical laws of nature, including human nature, was a case of recourse to superstition and certainly a scientific anachronism. After all, is not man the product of his biological inheritance, his racial instincts, nervous system, glands—masters all of his intellect? Does not biology spin out the web for psychology?

The glorious climax of this development in psychology, of course, came with the pronouncements of extreme methodological behaviorists upon metaphysical matters. The conduct of man could be exactly predicted if we could but unfold the antecedent factors of heredity and environment. The fate of man is already determined either by his blood or by the conditioning factors of his early environment; when the intellect has developed to the point when it would be expected that it should play a part in determining the conduct of the individual, it is too late. John B. Watson, for example, speaking for the determining influences of early environment upon the whole cast of an individual's life—an environment which is thrust upon the individual and over which he is powerless to preside—says, in effect, that were he given a dozen healthy infants (assuming normal biological equipment and functioning) he could by the control of their environment make them into lawyers, artists, beggars, thiefs, regardless of any talents, tendencies, or racial inheritance.[11] Nor does one have to join the behaviorist school to argue for a social determinism.[12]

---

[10] Cf. foot-note, *ante*, p. 211.

[11] *Psychologies of 1925* (1927), edited by Carl Murchison, p. 10.

[12] We have already set forth some criticisms of scientific determinism, *ante*, pp. 211 ff.; other criticisms will occur later.

Determinism and the Higher Reality

Determinism of the scientific stripe argues for an unbroken causal nexus without an appeal to any mysterious or supernatural cause; determinism of the philosophical, religious, and theological order, generally has appealed to the larger encompassing Reality to explain the events of nature and the conduct of man.[13]   In the philosophical stress it usually goes under the name of *fatalism;* in the theological stress it usually goes under the name of *predestination.*   Fatalism pictures the Cause of causes in various ways: sometimes the all-directing reality is a vague and mysterious Fate, a Kismet or inscrutable will of Deity as in the case of Mohammedanism; sometimes it is called Fortune meaning in the Roman sense irresistible Fate, and in the Greek and popular sense Chance or Luck which operates and renders helpless human powers; sometimes it is the special function of gods or goddesses as in the case of the three famous spinners of the web of life in Hesiod, Clotho, Lachesis, and Atropos; sometimes it is Universal Reason or Necessity, as in the case of the Stoics; sometimes it goes under the notion of a Cyclic Routine as in Indian thought.   In Hebrew and in certain Christian theologies the Sovereign Will of Deity has been stressed; the will of man has become a pawn to be moved by the arbitrary (yet good) will of God.   The classical examples of this form of theological determinism are found in the predestinarian doctrines of the Protestant Reformers, especially Bucer (1491-1551), Calvin (1509-1564), and many of the later Reformed theologians (*e.g.,* the great American theologian, Jonathan Edwards, 1703-1758).

---

[13] In the metaphysical system of Spinoza (1632-1677), the Universe is conceived to operate mechanically.   Human freedom is re-interpreted to mean action which follows necessarily from one's own inner nature. This is a case where an ontology calls for a freedom that is plainly deterministic. *Cf. First Adventures,* etc., pp. 139 ff. *Cf. ante,* p. 146.

Predestination

Extreme Calvinism taught an unconditional predestination; man's deeds and destiny are not dependent upon anything he can do prior to the gift of grace.[14] God has willed those who shall attain a glorious destiny and those who shall suffer reprobation. The whole drama of salvation is conditioned by election. Back of Calvinism stands St. Augustine who taught the impotence of the human will to attain the crown by reason of the Fall of Adam and the plight of original sin. Back of St. Augustine stands the Apostle Paul whose writings declare the absolute sovereignty of God, predestination, and election. "Foreordained according to the purpose of him who worketh all things after the counsel of his will" (Ephesians 1:11); "Whom he foreordained, them he also called, and whom he called, them he also justified" (Romans 8:30); "He hath mercy on whom he will, and whom he will he hardeneth" (Romans 9:18).[15]

To believe that man is totally helpless to change or to have changed the drift of human events brings relief to an otherwise sensitive "conscience" or to an other-

---

[14] The two classic theories relating predestination to the Fall of man are: the extreme position of *supralapsarianism* which made the Fall of man a part of the Divine decree revealing the Divine attribute of punitive righteousness; the modified position of *infralapsarianism* an election by grace of those fallen by their own act into sin, a predestination subsequent to the Fall of man, God merely *permitting* the Fall.

[15] Over against such passages, Pelagians (Pelagius, *circa,* 360-420) and Arminians (Arminius, 1560-1609) who stressed the moral responsibility of man could quote such Scriptural utterances as: He "would have all men to be saved, and come to the knowledge of the truth" (I. Tim. 2:4); He is "not wishing that any should perish, but that all should come to repentance" (II Peter 3:9); "Keep yourselves in the love of God" (Jude, 21); and the Jamesean letter which stressed man's good works and brought from Luther the condemnation of being "a right strawy epistle."

It may be added that Protestant theology continued to suffer from the inconsistency of holding the two incompatible doctrines of free will and predestination. *Cf. e.g.,* Articles II and XI in the Lutheran *Formula of Concord,* inconsistencies indicated in the author's *What Is Lutheranism?* (1930), p. 294.

wise agonizing experience of remorse. Such a doctrine brings moral consciousness logically to naught and implies an immoral shift of responsibility. Rigid Calvinism has sought to rest its case upon the perfectly good will and wisdom of God in contrast to the limited perspective of man; however, to trust a higher wisdom is one thing and to mingle with that trust a disdain for the elementary insights of a moral consciousness is another. It may well be a glory that some men are consigned to hell to furnish necessary "background" to those who live on in bliss; but besides being hard on such men, it should be still harder on the finer sensibilities of those whose election has been favorable, and more particularly upon the character of a supposedly moral and responsible Deity.

Readers who have been impressed by the warnings of Bernarr MacFadden against those who are committing gradual suicide by the neglect of the simple rules of health, no doubt have been quite unimpressed if not disturbed upon hearing a certain rubber-stamp type of funeral oration. It may, on such an occasion, be an immoral assertion for the minister to repeat the entire passage from Job which runs: "The Lord gave and *the Lord hath taken away;* blessed be the name of the Lord." Knowing the deceased's way of living and then listening to a discourse which shifts responsibility wholly to God for an untimely death is pretty hard on the dullest of moral sensibilities. It would be no exaggeration to say that God has been blamed for more things of which he is undoubtedly innocent than any other actor in the great human drama.

Extreme determinism, however expressed, suffers one grave fault: men have not been able to live in accordance with its mandates either in the realm of their thinking[16] or in the realm of their conduct. It would

---

[16] On the teleological character of thinking, see *First Adventures,* etc., p. 372.

be hard to find an example of a deterministic system free from paradoxes.

FREEDOM AND DETERMINISM CONSIDERED AS ASPECTS OF REALITY

The shield is said to be both white and black. Both freedom and determinism are acknowledged, but each is confined to its special phase in the total picture. This *aspectual* view is the second of the three major *metaphysical* solutions. Reality is such, so it is maintained, that there is really no fundamental antithesis between the two views except for a difference in point of view; or, Reality is such that it admits of a parallelism. We have already indicated this second type of solution as it occurs in the metaphysics of Kant who, it will be remembered, divided the world into two: the noumenal over against the phenomenal, the one free and the other caught up in the mesh of a closely-knit causal nexus;[17] the metaphysical parallelism of Paulsen (1846-1908)[18] and the two worlds of Royce[19] may also be mentioned. Let us sample in more detail some expressions of this solution.

The Solution of Kant

The gist of the noumenal-phenomenal theory as it affects human freedom is as follows: Physically and mentally man is a part of the phenomenal world. His body obeys the laws of nature and his mental life obeys the laws of mind; his acts and his thoughts are embedded in a causal series; antecedent factors determine subsequent effects. Man in the phenomenal, scientific world

---

[17] *Ante,* pp. 85 ff., especially p. 87.
[18] On Paulsen, see *First Adventures,* etc., pp. 425 ff.
[19] *Cf. ante,* p. 104, foot-note; p. 147. On the two worlds (that of appreciation and that of description) see *First Adventures,* etc., pp. 140 ff.

is the product of heredity and environment. From this point of view it is absurd to speak of man as free, for his physical and psychical behavior is enmeshed in a mechanistic order clicking away according to the laws of regular sequence. But this is not the whole story. Man's moral consciousness asserts with overwhelming compulsion his sense of obligation. This consciousness evaluates his conduct, approving, condemning, prodding, setting judgments of value. This moral consciousness looks upon the phenomenal realm of sequential facts and pronounces judgments upon it according to standards set up by itself alone. The phenomenal realm knows nothing of such norms; but the moral consciousness does. It is this sense of ought that catches a glimpse of the other world, the real world (as over against the appearance world), the noumenal or the higher level. Man is as much a part of this realm as he is a part of the other. He is a sojourner in two realms, the one of hard and sequential facts and the other of value. The latter gives to the former a meaning; considered by the standards of scientific judgments, the realm of value seems, indeed, strange; and yet considered by the standards of value judgments it is real and, indeed, more significant.

Now, how can such two worlds be reconciled? We have here an antinomy.[20] Does the feeling of moral responsibility and freedom merely trail along after the events which take place on the level of the phenomenal? Surely, if such be the case, it would be a most ridiculous feeling both as to moral categories and to freedom. To be really free, must man not be able to control his mental activity and to initiate action? But how is this possible if the activity is enmeshed in a deterministic series? The solution of this dilemma is found in the Kantian metaphysics briefly as follows:

---

[20] *Cf. ante,* p. 124, foot-note.

In the phenomenal world, events of nature are related to one another by no discoverable link of force which is associated with our notion of cause;[21] natural events appear in this appearance world, but causes (as known by the human mind) do not appear. The appearance world of nature is a series of events into which we read the human categories among which is cause. The appearance world of nature does not of itself present order; we give order to it by the process of our thinking. The sensible world is thus shot through with our "understanding"; we "know" of no other world than that combination of sense and understanding which is the phenomenal or appearance world. What the world is beyond this appearance—*i.e.*, the noumenal world—we cannot know either by the senses alone, by the reason alone, or by both, since to know such a world implies that we should have to employ the tools of sense, of reason, or both, and this leads us back to the phenomenal world. For better or worse we cannot help it; we cannot "will" to change this world of appearance; it continues to appear necessitated by the order which we give to it. This is the world the scientist magnifies; it is the only world that we know by means of reason and sense—our tools—and it is a world of necessity and determinism.

But, we may ask, what is this world like beyond our tools of apprehension? Answer: we do not know, but we have compelling reasons to affirm what it is by the demands of the moral consciousness, by the practical reason. After all, our will is a pretty fundamental reality to us; in fact, more than our reason. Suppose we say that the phenomenal world is grounded in this super-phenomenal or noumenal world of the will or practical reason; that the world of reason-sense has

---

[21] *Cf.* David Hume's criticism of the notion that causation rests upon empirical fact. *First Adventures,* etc., pp. 346 ff. The reader should here have in mind Kant's theory of the categories of mind of which causation is one. See *ibid.,* pp. 466 ff.

its setting in this higher realm. It may be theoretically difficult to make such an assertion, but we are practically forced to do so; our moral consciousness is of such a nature that we cannot escape the assertion that the phenomenal finds its ultimate basis in the noumenal; moreover, our moral consciousness asserts the character of the noumenal; it lifts man to a higher plane; it compels us to act as though we were free in spite of the appearance of determinism. From the "outside" our acts will continue to appear mechanistic and completely conditioned; but from the "inside" we will be compelled to assert that they are the expressions of our noumenal nature, our ability to initiate action and to control our conduct so as to make for moral responsibility. Man is thus from one point of view absolutely determined; from the other point of view he is a responsible and free being. Theoretically, freedom can never be affirmed; practically, it is assured. The noumenal is a necessary postulate of the moral sense; and the noumenal is the deeper reality. He who lives by sight does not see; only he that knows by insight truly sees and understands. Knowledge is seeing through a glass darkly; faith is grasping things as they are in themselves.[22]

Thus freedom is tucked away in the noumenal realm. Kant hears men shouting their freedom even though they have been bound and gagged.

The Solution of Absolute Idealists:
Hegel, Green, Bradley

Some of the classical absolutistic idealists have maintained both freedom and determinism as aspects of Reality depending upon the point of view. Looking

---

[22] The argument is further supplemented by the famous doctrine of the "categorical imperative." The reader should link the above exposition with the moral argument for freedom as already stated, *ante,* pp. 85 ff.

at man one way he is free; looking at him in another he is completely determined. Freedom is re-interpreted as "self-determinism"; one's behavior is determined by antecedent factors and at the same time one's self, as a part of the large Self, determines what is to take place. The self as a rational being reflects the heart of the rational Whole; this freedom is not that of caprice; it is the kind of freedom that is possessed by the Absolute Spirit upon which all things and persons depend, a Spirit which is not dependent upon anything other than Itself.

Man is not free when he is driven from without nor when he acts irrationally; he is free only when he is determined from within and by rational guidance; when this rational guidance is of the kind that characterizes the Whole, *i.e.*, when and so far as man participates in this immanent guidance of the Self-Determiner is he truly free. His freedom is under the law of the whole, under the necessity of Reason. There is no other freedom than this higher Self-Determinism. Here we have the dialectic, a synthesis of both determinism and freedom; freedom is determined by a "higher" freedom which turns out to be that of the Self-Determiner of the Whole; a "higher" freedom is the truer while determinism is the partial view. This is the view, in brief, of the influential philosopher, Hegel. (1770-1831.)[23]

The Hegelian disciple, T. H. Green (1836-1882) puts it thus: freedom is to be had in the "inner self"; determinism reigns in external acts. Human behavior is determined by motive, but the self determines the motive. The self, however, is a product of circumstances and character. Viewed thus, human behavior, like all behavior in the world of events, is the necessary

---

[23] On the Hegelian dialectic, see *First Adventures,* etc., pp. 86 ff. Also, pp. 149, 502. Also, *cf., ante,* p. 104.

result of existing conditions. And yet the self is "free." How is this possible? Answer: the self as a rational being is self-determining; it has its true being in the Universal Self-Determiner upon which everything depends; so far as the self shares in the Absolute it participates in the freedom of the Absolute which is dependent upon nothing other than Itself. In one sense then the human being is determined by the causal nexus; in another sense he is free as he shares in the freedom of the Whole which is determined by nothing other than its own Self-Determination.

F. H. Bradley (1846-1924),[24] another Absolutist, is of the conviction that the dilemma between freedom and determinism is "exploded" since there is no real antithesis between the two; both are affirmed, but only as different points of view in terms of the Whole.

The Solution of Royce

So far as the individual realizes the true nature of his self, says Josiah Royce (1855-1916), he realizes his freedom, for the self reflects the World-Will which is Self-conditioning and responsible to nothing other than Itself. In realizing our true nature we have no need of the category of cause; such a category is inapplicable to the world of appreciation. The Absolute does not cause the world so far as it is regarded in itself; it just is. It is its own excuse for being; it is through and through free; nothing has conditioned it. When we rise to this perspective and apprehend its nature and unity through the unity and nature of our own self we are assured of our freedom; we must see this at a glance, in a kind of *totum simul*; when we begin to analyze and cut apart, the vision is taken from us and we see ourselves as a part of the determined world,

---

[24] *Cf. op. cit.,* p. 139.

the world as it is when describable. Our conceptual knowledge is piece-meal; but our insight is transcendental both as to concepts and as to time.

A series of chords does not *mean* to me a mere series of events (which in one sense it is). It *means* to me a symphony. The soul of the world is like such a symphony which grasps the music all at once. Of course, there are a succession of states; this is the picture furnished by the sciences, the world that is enmeshed in causal determinism. It is the finite perspective. The intuition of the self, however, reveals the higher order which is a time-transcending Whole. This is the very nature of consciousness, the reality far deeper than the world of time and space. The Self regards the world in a two-fold way: as a time series in which one event determines the next; as an eternally complete whole, the world which it chooses after its own heart. Viewed from the perspective of time as a series of exclusive presents we are creatures of the circumstance of rigid necessity. But, from the point of view of the Absolute, is not this temporal world, after all, only one of an infinite number of possible worlds, the one chosen by the Absolute? And as members of this Absolute which we apprehend through the insight of our true selves, are we not reflecting this same choice, are we not playing the drama of this higher choice in helping to make the world what the higher Self would have it to be?

You are not free to change the laws of the world which the Absolute has chosen; but you are free in the part you are playing in bringing to a realization the eternal drama which is being unfolded in time and which from the view of the eternal is the world chosen because of its worth. The Absolute sees at one glance the whole of a temporal order; it is eternal knowledge. Anything less than the Absolute cannot foresee what is to take place for this less involves the perspective not of eternity but of time. Neither God, however, nor man, can know what is to take place at any temporal moment what a free-will agent is to do. There really is no fore-knowledge; there is only the *totum simul* knowledge which the Eternal can grasp. (Royce argued for Absolutism, but never quite signed on the Absolutist's dotted line. There appears to be a distinction between God and the Absolute which makes for some difficulty of interpretation—*e.g.*, how can an Absolute choose the best possible world to play the drama of its choice and what is God's rôle in that drama? Again, does not eternalism cancel temporalism in the sense that it is super-temporal; and if super-temporal how can the Absolute see what is supposed to be included in the temporal?)

Human Freedom and God in the Thought of St. Thomas Aquinas

That man is truly free by reason of the nature of will and by reason of God's gift is emphatically asserted in the thought of Aquinas.[25] The will which is constrained is no will; to will and to be free are one and the same. If the will were determined such a will would merit neither praise nor blame. To say that man is irresponsible is to become "unphilosophical." It would amount to a violation of a "first principle." The formal essence of the will is directed toward the general good, the ultimate end, the Supreme and Universal Good. This is *its* first principle. In reality, however, the will is constantly faced with only particular goods. The particular goods are unable to satisfy the will's desire, with the result that the will remains completely free in respect to them.

The will is to be considered under two aspects: the subject of the will is the will's inner initiating movement (*cf.* Aristotle); the object of the will is the particular

---

[25] *Ante,* pp. 76 ff., 157, 202.

way in which the will acts under the influence of what is presented. As subject the will freely initiates movement both actual and potential. When one wills one's will affects not only something that is actual but something else which the will does not yet will but wills only potentially. As object the will is affected by the quality of the object which is presented. Only one object moves the will by necessity. This is the particular object apprehended by the intellect as a particular case of the good and suitable. Only one object fulfills this requirement, *viz.*, beatitude. Such a necessity affects only the determination of the act and not the initiating movement. And it amounts to saying that if the will performs its act while the intellect presents beatitude the will cannot will the contrary of beatitude. And yet the will is free to avoid thinking of the beatitude and thus is mistress even of its act.

It is interesting to observe that St. Thomas Aquinas attacked the problem (as did Royce) of the foreseeing of the temporal by the eternal. God for Aquinas is in eternity and views the temporal order as happening in a Now. As such, God foresees what the individual is going to do without compelling him so to do.[26] From the point of view of the temporal order future contingencies are uncertain though observed contingencies are certain; from the point of view of the eternal (comprising all time) future contingencies are present; from the former point of view freedom obtains although from the latter point of view events are certain. Human actions always move in the realm of the particular and the contingent; whereas the realm of the universal is unchangeable and certain, the realm of the particular is variable and uncertain. God's view is actual and as such there are no alternatives; the events which take place in the temporal order, however, are shot

---

[26] The criticism has been made that foreknowledge implies a disguised determinism. *See ante,* p. 172.

through with contingencies, with potentialities, and as such there are alternatives. The *totum simul* implies determinism (a higher freedom?); the finite perspective reveals freedom.

For the realist, Aquinas, time, contingency, and the finite are real and are not swallowed up in an eternal, necessary, and infinite order. Man's real freedom is not to be melted into a higher freedom.[27]

Some Further Compromise Solutions

The shield is neither all white, nor all black, nor both white and black. It is gray. This is the position of the third major group. It is represented by those who believe both in human freedom and determinism in a modified and mixed form. Against the second view which would speak of a higher freedom this group would maintain that such freedom is a camouflaged freedom, a subtle form of determinism. For idealists generally freedom means self-expression, *i.e.*, when the self realizes its real self as a reflection of the higher realm it is free.

To have real freedom, says this third group, one must have, at least in some measure, freedom in the world in which human beings live and move and have their being, the world of time, of matter and space, the world which idealists allow to be swallowed up by a higher, noumenal realm. Such a dichotomy of noumenal and phenomenal is an artificial make-shift. By trying to maintain both freedom and determinism such idealists end by selling the former out to the latter. Real freedom, so far as it interests human beings, must obtain in the world of here and now and not in some far-distant divine event or scene if it is to be real and genuine. The position of the extreme libertarian is of course impossible and so is the position of the radical determin-

---

[27] *Cf. ante,* pp. 220; 223, foot-note; 229 ff.

ist. Is there no compromise which will take into consideration the merits of both and at the same time avoid their demerits? More specifically, is there not a position which will save freedom from a disguised determinism implied by idealistic solutions?

Two examples will be given of the third or mixed view in which man is held to be both free and determined (partly free and partly not free) in the world of "here and now" and both free and determined in terms of the Higher Reality.

The Compromise Solution of William James

Let us consider the view of James as presented in his now famous essay entitled "The Dilemma of Determinism."[28] James shies at the word "freedom" and prefers "indeterminism" or "chance." The "hard" determinists are those who bluntly preach fatalism. The "soft" determinists are those who speak of freedom, but with reservations and evasions. For instance, a freedom which is under the bondage of a "higher" freedom is but such an evasion; frankly it is a determinism, though "soft." The issue between determinism and indeterminism must be faced in terms of implications, consequences (pragmatism); a decision for the one or the other cannot be decided on logical or theoretical grounds merely. So far as a merely theoretical demonstration of the truth of the one as over against the other, James is content to say that he is willing to go without. We do feel free and we act as if this were true. The decision between the two is a practical decision. The thesis is to show that the consequences of determinism present us with a dilemma of a sufficiently serious nature to render our decision against it and in favor of indeterminism.

---

[28] *The Will to Believe and Other Essays in Popular Philosophy* (ed. 1898, Longmans, Green), pp. 145 ff.

Free-will, says James, means nothing more than that there is novelty. Many people have a horror when the suggestion of chance is made. Really, such a horror might be legitimate if chance obtained in some absolute way. We do not contend for chance in the sense that our world might fall to pieces. The chance we mean is that loose-play which is sufficient to square with pluralism,[29] with the zest of unpredictable possibilities. The chance we mean does not entirely rule out connections with the past. One may hold that there are chance-elements in the world without at the same time denying the continuity of events. Suppose I am faced with the alternative of walking home either by way of Divinity Avenue or by Oxford Street. After the event, I look upon either alternative as continuous with the past, either one is as natural as the other. Why then shall I fear that chance destroys continuity? Chance is a term which is negative. It gives "no information about that of which it is predicated, except that it happens to be disconnected with something else." Moreover, chance is limited; it operates not in the sense that anything can happen. An indeterminist does not have to claim that any act is possible for man. He only claims that there are occasions which present alternatives and that, of these which tempt him, more than one is possible.

Determinists really worship at the altar of an unknown God when they appeal to the principle of causality. To say that uniformity rules, is a postulate, however necessary it may be to our scientific ideals. But do we not have moral natures which demand with as great a fervor the principle of indeterminism? Is one postulate or principle more objective than the other? As a matter of fact, are not both equally subjective and emotional?

---

[29] On James's pluralism, see *First Adventures*, p. 145. *Cf. ante*, pp. 110 ff.

Consider the dilemma of the determinist's position. Consider a murder. How shall it be explained? Is it the goal of cosmic history up to that point? Surely, such an answer is unthinkable. If so, or if you say that it should not have been committed, you are expressing a judgment of regret. Such a judgment says in effect that what has happened ought not to have taken place. A determinist who must deny that anything else might have taken place invites pessimism; he makes one's regret over the event of murder a regret for the universe which has made it to happen. Here is a dilemma. If we try to avoid the pessimism by affirming our judgment of regret to be in error and find some way to explain the evil (*e.g.*, in terms of a higher good) we still cannot change our judgment since the judgment of regret was determined. If the event was good then the judgment of regret was bad; if the judgment of regret was good the event (murder) was bad. However, both have been pre-determined. The deterministic view lands us in a dilemma. And we are in the quagmire of pessimism.

There is a remedy for this dilemma and that is to adopt the view-point of gnosticism or subjectivism. If we regard the world as a machine whose purpose is to make for the *knowledge* of good and evil, our own subjective *gnosis* rather than any outward good, then both the event and the regret may be good at the same time. In other words the escape from pessimism lies in looking at the goods and ills of life not as objective but as neutral materials which promote the knowledge of good and ill. Here we have a second dilemma of determinism: we must choose between the left horn of pessimism and the right horn of subjectivism. Of the two choices the latter theoretically seems the more rational. But from a practical point of view the choice of subjectivism confronts us with serious consequences which should make us pause. "Once dismiss the notion that certain duties are good in themselves, and that we are here to do them, no matter how we feel about them; once consecrate the opposite notion that our performances and our violations of duty are for a common purpose, the attainment of subjective knowledge and feeling, and that the deepening of these is the chief end of our lives —and at what point on the downward slope are we to stop?" In theological matters such a subjective view has resulted in antinomianism (no longer subject to law); in literature, romanticism; in practical life, sentimentality or sensualism.

The escape from the dilemma of determinism is a practical one. The call of duty remains. There is work to be done. No matter how we feel, no matter what the theoretical difficulties are, no matter whether we succeed or fail, somehow we must perform our tasks; to leave them undone spells perdition. The philosophy of pluralism which permits of both good and bad in the world as objectively real and the implication of chance is far better to follow than the dilemmas offered by determinism. Whatever theory we adopt there are difficulties. But the free-willist who respects the demands of the moral consciousness which in turn presents the world as vulnerable and human beings as responsible has a view that is less repugnant and irrational than the determinist. I for one, says James, will not call the Brockton murder, a good necessitated by the Universe; my moral sense revolts from loyalty to such a Whole; there are some instinctive reactions I will not tamper with. A world with a chance in it of being good even if that chance never comes to pass is better than a world with no chance at all.

If man is free and plays a responsible part in the drama of possibilities and risks, how shall we conceive of a Divine Providence in relation to this liberty and uncertainty? The answer comes in the analogy of the two players at chess: the one God, the expert, and the other the finite player, the novice. God knows all *possible* moves which confront the other though he cannot foresee any one actual move; he is able to counter any move the other makes. The finite player faces critical and actual decisions; and whatever decisions he makes God can bring ultimate victory for himself since he knows how eventually to checkmate the novice's king. The details of the game are blank, but the possibilities are laid down. The element of chance comes into play. God does not know how the game will be played; the moves of the player will determine which of the possibilities become realized; not until the very last will God know the course that has been followed. All along, however, the novice is playing a losing battle; no matter how zig-zag the course, the expert will know how to win.[30] Freedom there is, since the drama is being realized from moment to moment and possibilities are open for the individual; he really plays his own part. But determinism there is since that freedom is bounded by possibilities laid out and is being matched by a higher wisdom. James argues for human freedom, the reader will see, on a pragmatic and a moral basis.

The Compromise Solution of James Ward

Another case of an attempted compromise between freedom and determinism is the view of James Ward (1843-1925).[31] The determinist and indeterminist, says Ward, are both right in what they affirm and wrong in what they deny. It is quite possible that a person's volitions have causes though these causes are free. A volition in one sense may be determined; and in other it is undetermined.

Consider the notion of causation. The source and

---

[30] On this analogy, see the essay by Luther A. Weigle in *Contemporary American Theology* (1933), edited by Vergilius Ferm, Vol. II, p. 319.

[31] *See* his *The Realm of Ends* (1912, 2d ed.), Lectures XIII and XIV. A résumé of his metaphysics is given in *First Adventures,* etc., pp. 176 ff.

primary meaning of causation is to be had in our own inner experience. This kind of causation is termed "efficient causation." An "effect" is the result of such activity; without an efficient there is no effect. Just how a determining or efficient cause produces its effect is difficult to show since to show it necessitates the cutting up of the process into simpler elements. In the case of physical causation, the cause is a motion and therefore a consequent on a preceding motion and so on back in an infinite regress. So far as experienced causation goes we cannot go back thus indefinitely without violating our experience; we experience efficient causation and this appears to be unanalyzable further; in the thought of Aristotle it is simply the beginner of motion, not itself motion.

Efficient causation is used in two senses: *transeunt* and *immanent*. Consider an example: the sun shines. By this we may mean the sun's shining is resolved into molecular motion; it is the result of antecedent mass and motions. We look for antecedent connections. The sun as an inanimate object is regarded as inert, as incapable of changing itself. The sun's shining is thus resolved into a series of transeunt causes. However, we may mean that the shining is to the sun as breathing is to a living man, the one interlocked with the other, the causal relation is in the inherent activity or nature. Here we regard the sun as an animate body and speak of its activity as immanent. Indeed, this latter meaning is metaphorical, *i.e.*, we treat the sun as if it were alive. There is still another kind of causation: *final* cause, the reason for a thing's acting, its purpose, end. The natural sciences do not consider this type of causation. The causation which the human being as a conative subject experiences is immanent efficiency and purposiveness; the kind of causation that is implied in the case of inanimate things is neither immanent efficiency nor purposiveness.

241

When causality is used in the sciences the idea of necessary connection according to law, or natural uniformity, is meant. What is meant by this necessary connection according to law? It is not a logical necessity that is implied: such causation does not rest on intuitive certainty, nor is it demonstrative; nor is it perceived. Indeed, we perceive a *post hoc* and then proceed to assert a *propter hoc*, frequently on the strength of a single instance. But this procedure is an anthropomorphic venture: we read into the situation by analogy what we find in our own experience. The popular conception of transeunt causation is anthropomorphic. The more completely thought reflects upon immediate experience the more does the notion of causality imply the connection of *efficiens* and *effectum* which is *real* necessity. Conversely, the less the notion of causality reflects immediate experience the less does it imply such real necessity. The direction of modern thought in this matter is to stress the latter conception, *i.e.*, no real necessity.

The scientific concept of causality does, then, not involve the kind of necessities described above as efficient and real; its necessity is simply the postulate of uniformity; this is to say that *scientific* knowledge is possible only upon the assumption that events actually take place with strict uniformity and regularity. Such scientific knowledge is expressed, accordingly, in terms of general *propositions* concerning matters in the world of fact. This is its methodology. Now, the one theory of the universe which fits this program of approach and would, if it were true, justify it, is the mechanistic theory of the world. The methodology then passes easily into an ontological dogma; the initial supposition of uniformity (methodology) often surreptitiously masquerades as a metaphysical principle and thus freedom is supposed to be ever refuted.

Now, says Ward, there is a great deal of muddled

thinking going on with reference to the nature of causal determinism. The above analysis plainly shows that causal determination may mean a number of things. I may use the word determinism and may mean not what you mean. I may mean self-direction, efficient and immanent causation; you may mean merely uniformity without efficient causation or self-direction or purpose; and so on. To say that an event has been determined raises the question of the nature of that determination. Two forms of determinism stand out and their difference lies deep; self-determination and determination. The one implies categories of worth, personality, ends; it is teleological. The other implies the categories of mechanism; it rests upon the supposition of uniformity, law; this is the kind of determinism that is meant by our scientific descriptions of nature. In the case of human behavior we find self-determinism; a human being experiences self-direction; he does not appeal to a law of uniformity to describe his acts; he points ahead to what he intends, the values involved for him and thus gives reasons for his conduct.

Self-determination obtains not only in the case of self-conscious, rational, and moral beings; it obtains wherever there is in nature spontaneity and individual activity. When the scientist applies his *concept* of uniformity he deals with constant quantities, with inert entities; he rules out spontaneities, and the notion of guidance or ends. The scientific conception of necessity, in other words, worships at the shrine of a *concept* which is incapable of paying homage to a greater god, fact. For does not nature reveal ends, spontaneity, individuality, directions toward, and the like, as facts? *Prima facie* at least there is no doubt that there is such guidance as every moment of every living thing is an instance of it. Nature is teleological, a "realm of ends."

In the case of human conduct the determinist may

say that such conduct reveals the law of uniformity. Do not our habits and even our deliberate activities reveal such rigid uniformity? We may grant that they do, answers Ward; but for all that there remain two forms of determination and each is altogether different from the other. Though human agents do decide alike, each is nevertheless conscious of his own self-determination, of his own purpose and his effort to pursue his own end; he doesn't feel that his determination is wholly a push from behind; he feels the pull from ahead. And what is more, though in like situations there frequently appears like reactions on the part of agents, the fact of the matter is that there are individual variations. One cannot predict with that nicety—so close to the heart of the scientist—just what the individual's action may be even though we grant that there is a natural law which works on the average.[32]

---

[32] This position reminds us of the contention of Professor W. H. Sheldon (of Yale) that "No event perfectly manifests obedience to the universals of science, the 'laws of Nature.'" No perfect case of the law of uniformity has ever been found. "There is no empirical guarantee whatever that . . . the same cause always produces the same effect." Indeed, nearly; but not exactly.

Sheldon's view may be taken as an instance of the third major solution, a compromise between freedom and determinism. Nature, he says, seems to give equal opportunity to all possible combinations of events. Nature has a tendency to spread; it behaves like the water coming from a garden hose: there is direction in the current (law) but there is also a spreading, spraying (variations). Conditions which remain quite the same will make for a corresponding accuracy of prediction; but as a matter of fact conditions do not repeat themselves identically; there are new combinations, new situations, further causes, further complexities. Where conditions remain largely undetermined we tend not to see the chance-element playing into events; nevertheless, it is there. The world is full of a vast number or combination of causes and independent causal series; they are independent of things which are external to one another. The freedom of the individual entity lies in the particular way it behaves or reacts; each entity has its own nature. At any given moment there are numberless possibilities in the way of reacting, alternatives of behavior. A perfect knowledge of everything that happened in the past would not permit an infallible prediction of what a thing is to be, since new combinations, new conditions might bring the entity to show another aspect of its nature not heretofore revealed. These differences may be however slight. Not even the entity would "know" of its possibilities since its

Every event, says Ward, which moves on the level of guidance and control is a new beginning, and no mechanical system is able to take it into account. A human individual is just such an event. The categories applicable to a human individual are efficiency, spontaneity, purpose, worth, self-determination. As such they lie outside the commitments of the scientific method of approach. To describe man as the end of a train of causal antecedents is to deny the reality of the self and the immediate experience of that self. There is this subjective factor in experience; to deny this is to explain that experience away. Man is, then, a free agent, a *natura naturans;* he has his setting in a world where there is spontaneous activity, the kind that initiates new beginnings (epigenesis) and secures future ends. At the same time he experiences *natura naturata,* the world of law and order, which in a pluralistic world is being creatively achieved.

As to the relation of human freedom and the Higher

---

nature could not be known until all possible ways of reacting had taken place.

The determinists have made their point; it is the fact that "all that happens is subject to the law that the same conditions give the same results." The indeterminists are right when they insist that the nature of a thing is itself an ultimate fact and that in a given situation it reacts as it does. "One and the same reaction of a given body to a given force acting upon it may be regarded as free, or determined, or both." The reaction is determined when the reaction is but an individual event while the nature of the body is a permanent character. The reaction is free when the reaction is identically the nature of the body. Both are the same yet distinct; it is this sameness-in-difference which makes for the truth of both freedom and determination. Reality is ultimately dyadic.

Human freedom is but a special case of this fundamental principle of duality. See *Strife of Systems and Productive Duality* (Harvard, 1918), pp. 239 ff.; 481 ff.

A more recent comment on his position is that he now holds that freedom and determinism are not reconcilable *in any one instance.* Professor Sheldon still would maintain the "gray" position: freedom here (always within limits) and necessity there. On the inorganic level, freedom is chance; on the organic and mental, freedom is self-direction; there are, however, always necessary laws limiting the range of chance and free-will. On the general metaphysical position of Sheldon, see *First Adventures,* etc., p. 289.

Reality, Ward's solution is similar to that of James. God has created creators; their nature is partly his doing and partly their doing. There are total possibilities, but within these are undetermined eventualities. Man's freedom or self-determinism reflects the self-limitation of that God as does the whole realm of ends at work in the pluralistic world.

CHAPTER X

RECONSIDERING PRAYER

A consideration of the question of freedom moves easily into a philosophy of prayer. In a few pages we shall outline such a philosophy in the framework of a belief in a God. There are real intellectual difficulties involved in prayer. But there are intellectual difficulties about everything. The question is whether these difficulties are insurmountable.

Difficulties in Prayer

The major reason why people break with prayer is the fact of unanswered prayer. We all have experienced this first step to doubt. The more modern reason which adds reason to reason why many break with prayer is the inconsistency which apparently is involved in respect to natural law. If God sets up natural laws should they then be broken? Moreover, why should God stay the natural processes in behalf of our puerile wishes and fancies? Thus this second reason goes into the third without even crossing a line: who are we that Deity should care to carry on such particular negotiations— little specks in a world immeasurable in time and extent. It is preposterous to ask the presiding officer of such a gigantic establishment to fix things for us. We should overcome our feelings of self-importance; the major premise of ourselves, our importance, is untenable. There is a fourth reason. Some people claim to have had answers to their prayers. But we can account for their explanation in other ways. They are mistaken. We all rationalize; we all mistake coincident events for purposes; we are all prone to commit the pathetic fallacy;[1] and there are a thousand explanations to anything. There is a fifth reason. Many people have such ideas of God that the question is begged from the start. God cannot answer prayer because God is such that prayer cannot be answered. This last reason carries right on to atheism.

Meeting the Difficulties

The easiest way to meet a difficulty, of course, is to look the other way. This may not be the right solution but it is one solution. Let us give up prayer. But, suppose it is not so easy for us so to do. There is still within us something of the old emotional ties which prevents scoffing. May we not keep the values though we must deny the fact? Some modern apologists, considering the difficulties, now advise us that we need not throw up the idea and practice; we need only reconsider the whole thing. Surely there is the value of autosuggestion. Even though God has his back turned or is unable to do anything for the children of men, at least they can do something for themselves by the proper kind of imagination. No one will dispute this side to the case. If such a reconsideration is insufficient, let one not stop with that. Let one think of prayer not as petition but as fellowship, communication: a sort of "Top of the morning to You, God." We can at least say "hello," pay our respects to God, even though we cannot expect anything in return. After all, should we not at least be friendly and give our greetings? We can praise if we cannot ask. So, forget asking; rise to that higher level of comradeship. Is this not a more lofty conception of prayer? But there is still another reconsideration. Let one think of prayer as lying outside the pale of reason; one just cannot talk about it;

---

[1] This fallacy (a natural tendency) consists in imputing motives and purposings where such may not apply.

prayer belongs to the heart and reason knows nothing about it. Pascal was right. Let reason be anathema!

Negative Reconsiderations

The above ways of meeting the difficulties may well be called negative reconsiderations. We term them negative, since, so far as an adequate philosophy of prayer is concerned, they are not really helpful. If one is to reconsider prayer as a sort of mental gymnastics *only* (autosuggestion) this is self-defeating. It will not be long before the fact discovered brings to naught the value. If God is only the reflection in the mirror it will not be long before those so engaged will be looking the other way and ceasing their incantations. It is a curious but nevertheless real fact that one cannot continue to be religious with a psychologist of religion measuring the pulse, heart-beat, and noting the stimulus-response bond. If one is to reconsider prayer as mere fellowship and not petition this is a negation. For the heart has been taken out of the thing. Prayer is not prayer without petition. If our sophistication tells us that we should get over the "gimmie" stage and just be kind o' friendly with God, moments of exasperation and despair, periods of frustration and defeat, will find us calling on God in violence to theory.

If prayer does not mean asking for something the word is already stripped of its characteristic connotation. If we are to reconsider prayer as beyond the pale of thought, we can only say that such a view involves either dogmatism or self-inconsistency; dogmatism, because nothing can be said; inconsistency, because if an attempt is made to validate it to anyone reason must be employed. If it be said that so-called answers to prayer can be explained in other ways, we must, in all fairness, remind ourselves that this does not apply to prayer only. We can always posit more than one explanation about anything. The consideration is justified as a caution; it is not justified as a refutation.

Positive Reconsiderations

Intellectual difficulties involved in real prayer mean that the whole question must be reconsidered. We cannot go back; perhaps we can go forward. We cannot stay where we are; the muddled state cannot continue. The negative reconsiderations (above outlined) are symptomatic of the middle-ground muddled state. It would, perhaps, be better to acknowledge philosophical defeat rather than to adopt measures ineffective. Are the difficulties, however, insurmountable? Perhaps they are not. It may well be that even the reconsiderations ought to be reconsidered; it may well be that there should be an attempt, in all candidness, to see how difficult the difficulties really are. There are at least five positive reconsiderations.

In the first place, real prayer (petition) involves a belief in a God. You assume somebody in the asking. Prayer does not prove God; but God is involved in praying. Perhaps the first major operation in overcoming the difficulties is a reconsideration of the notion of God. If a conception of God is inadequate or unreasonable or not vital, prayer will suffer. This is not the place to reconsider God. There is needed only to point out the very real possibility that either atheism or agnosticism (perhaps unexpressed), or a faulty God-concept is the real reason why belief in prayer is broken.

Secondly, effective prayer involves a belief in a *God-as-Is*. This is only a crude way of saying that the God involved in many prayers may not be the real God; if so, such prayers are idolatrous. Though not all of man's thought (including a God-concept) is necessarily wishful, some of it may well be. Wishful thinking needs watching at every corner; the God-concept needs such watching as does any other. We must be sure when we are asking for something that we are addressing ourselves to the right party. Some perfectly well-intentioned prayers to God may be directed to an idol or a devil. Not only is *the fact* of God involved in effective prayer but *the character* of God as well: that is, *God-as-Is*. Some people break with prayer just because they have already been broken by idolatry. They fail to consider the possible *qualities* of Deity.

The question of the power of Deity to comply with our petitions has found a stumbling block in our modern emphasis upon natural law. But this difficulty is not insurmountable. Natural law is only a name for order. This may mean that either God must obey order as something higher or else that order is a function of the establishment ordained by him, over which he presides. In the first instance natural law is God and what we call God is not God; in the second instance natural law may be a revelation of an attribute of God's fundamental character. There is no legitimate reason why, if God works in an orderly manner, there is not a real possibility of answers falling into line with God's orderly processes and purposes. God could answer them in a way *consistent with that order*.[2] To ask for an upset of orderly processes may be asking for a change in Deity's character: a petition which asks that God refrain from being God. Moreover, it should never be forgotten that the conception of natural law is a workable hypothesis, a hope that things are intelligible, a premise to knowledge. To treat natural law as a Necessity, a Super-Decree which God and man must obey as one submits before a Tyrant may be idolatry; from the natural scientific view-point, such a treatment involves

---

[2] On this point, *e.g., see* Macintosh, *ante,* pp. 167 ff.

the fallacy of making an Entity out of a name, of raising the abstract to the stature of the concrete (a fallacy known as *the reification of abstractions*).

Third, effective prayer involves Number One: the party of the first part. This means that the petitioner must consider himself, his attitude, his purpose, his desire. He may be insignificant according to the measuring-standards of geologic time and light-years, but he must believe himself to have qualitative possibilities which far outstrip such standards. Else praying has come to naught before it has begun. A major premise of effective prayer is a sense of worth. (Even in a big world a tiny thing may become significant.) Again, he may well ask himself whether he is really a part of what he asks? Again, is he *asking* or is he *demanding?* If he asks he is praying; if he demands he is assuming Deity's prerogative or he is playing the rôle of the magician. The magician's attitude is coercion; the praying man's attitude is petition. Again, he may well ask himself whether he is using words as proxies, substitutes for the attitude; or whether he is using words as symbols, however poor, of that attitude? Do we not need to be reminded that a look, a glance, may be far deeper symbols of meaning and desire than the usual modicum of formal expression? Effective prayer involves the petitioner and his attitude; not somebody else's idea of him, nor words; it involves beseeching not compelling.

Fourth, effective prayer involves Number Two: the party of the second part. This means that a consideration must be had for the other side's attitude, purpose, desire. The reason why many prayers may be ineffective is perhaps because the desire is wholly us-ward. If God is good enough and great enough, the answer might well be entrusted to him. Even common courtesy requires consideration for the other side to the matter. The question is: whose desires should be underscored, ours or God's? This is but to say that there is good common sense in the petition of Jesus: Thy will be done. Were everybody to have their will done, not only would God be in a predicament but the world itself would become chaotic. Effective prayer requires that an attempt be made to consider what may be the desire of God in the matter at hand. There may be ways of learning this. Some degree of patience and self-discipline may be required in this as in all learning.

Fifth, effective prayer involves Number Three: the contact of both parties. Something may be born in prayer that may not have been born otherwise. It is not enough to make the contact, but one must look for results. The results, to be effective, must emerge from both parties. There may well be some things we never would get without a prayerful attitude; there may well be some things God would never get without such an approach; what emerges may be the really significant thing. Here is a book before me. I am asked to read it. Three items are involved: myself, the author, and the resulting contact. I cannot get all I should get out of it without a certain attitude. The book may have something to give if I approach it in that attitude. The result could never have been without the book and me; I may find that with my own growing insights coupled with the wisdom contained in that book something distinctly additive and new may emerge which will carry both me and the author beyond our separate limitations. Thus there is a third item involved in effective prayer. Perhaps the reason why we say our prayers are unanswered is because they *seem* to be unanswered. Perhaps the prayer has been incipiently answered but we have let our attitude slip so that we have committed its abortion. We failed because we did not continue. We read the book and let it go at that.

Further Considerations

It was a word of wisdom on the part of a contemporary theologian who, when approached by an earnest skeptic, advised him in the matter of prayer to begin where he was. The trouble in this matter with many is, perhaps, that they try to begin far up the ladder without taking each rung as it comes. Few are where the saints were. It is no disgrace to be a doubting Thomas; even such a Thomas may pray effectively if he recognizes himself for what he actually is. It was also a word of wisdom on the part of another who advises that we have to earn the right to pray even as we have to earn the right to question. It may be well on occasion to beg, but it is something else to remain a beggar. There is some ordinary common sense about this growing in wisdom and grace even in the matter of prayer. There is no harm in asking for a million dollars providing one has earned the right to ask it, being willing to take the consequences that may be expected to follow from such a gift. There is nothing wrong in asking for anything under the sun providing one can employ the gift in a way which would satisfy the Giver (implying as this does the *character* of the Giver). It hardly need be said that most frequently the best prayers (those which have been more real) are the ones which have not been spelled out in words nor have seen the light of public utterance. This does not mean that prayer is beyond a reasonable account; it only means that real and effective prayers are intimately private before they are public.

There appears, then, to be nothing insurmountable about the intellectual difficulties in real prayer. Crooked ways need to be made straight here as anywhere else. The twentieth century critical mind has given up looking for evidence by way of proof; there is nothing under the sun that can be proved (or disproved). It is content with reasonable possibilities. It must admit that real and effective prayer is just another one of man's genuinely promising possibilities.

CHAPTER XI

HUMAN IMMORTALITY

Kinds of Immortality

The term immortality has a number of meanings. At the outset of this discussion, therefore, the reader is cautioned against taking over the term from writers without noting precisely what is meant. While the term generally is taken to mean the survival and indefinite continuation of personal consciousness after the experience of death, for some immortality has no such meaning. We do well to suggest the different kinds of immortality that have been pictured and to distinguish some other concepts which have been closely related.

George Eliot (Mary Ann Evans Cross, 1819-1880) in her well-known poem, "O May I Join the Choir Invisible," conceives of immortality in terms of influence. One is immortal as one lives again in the thoughts of others or as one has left some legacy of blessing which others may enjoy.

O MAY I JOIN THE CHOIR INVISIBLE

George Eliot

O may I join the choir invisible
Of those immortal dead who live again
In minds made better by their presence: live
In pulses stirr'd to generosity,
In deeds of daring rectitude, in scorn
For miserable aims that end with self,
In thoughts sublime that pierce the night like stars,
And with their mild persistence urge man's search
To vaster issues.
      So to live is heaven:

To make undying music in the world,
Breathing as beauteous order that controls
With growing sway the growing life of man.
So we inherit that sweet purity
For which we struggled, fail'd, and agoniz'd
With widening retrospect that bred despair.
Rebellious flesh that would not be subdued,
A vicious parent shaming still its child,
Poor anxious penitence, is quick dissolv'd;
Its discords, quench'd by meeting harmonies,
Die in the large and charitable air.
And all our rarer, better, truer self,
That sobb'd religiously in yearning song,
That watch'd to ease the burthen of the world,
Laboriously tracing what must be,
And what may yet be better—saw within
A worthier image for the sanctuary,
And shap'd it forth before the multitude,
Divinely human, raising worship so
To higher reverence more mix'd with love,—
That better self shall live till human Time
Shall fold its eyelids, and the human sky
Be gather'd like a scroll within the tomb
Unread forever.
        This is life to come,
Which martyr'd men have made more glorious
For us who strive to follow. May I reach
That purest heaven, be to other souls
The cup of strength in some great agony,
Enkindle generous ardor, feed pure love,
Beget the smiles that have no cruelty,
Be the sweet presence of a good diffus'd,
And in diffusion ever more intense!
So shall I join the choir invisible
Whose music is the gladness of the world.[1]

George Santayana (1863—) similarly speaks of that double immortality which consists in being a part of the eternal while one lives in the realm of the ideal and, after death, in continuing to live by the influence that one has brought to bear upon those who follow

---

[1] *Types of Poetry* (Ginn, 1927), H. J. Hall, p. 213.

as they become identified with one in the same realm of the ideal.[2] Münsterberg (1863-1916)[3] speaks of eternal life in terms of eternal values which are beyond time; immortality is taken to mean not personal survival but the fact that one stands for timeless values: *an immortality of value.*

Besides this *social* immortality or *immortality of influence* there are those who speak of immortality in terms only of one's descendants. This kind of immortality is more explicitly stated as *biological* or *plasmal.* Then there are those who would hold that immortality means a reabsorption by Nature of the elements of the body—what one might call *chemical immortality.*

What has been termed *immortality of absorption* is the kind of immortality visualized by extreme mystics, by extreme absolute idealists, and frequently by those who have become enraptured in art. The reader will see in this group a common ontological position of extreme numerical monism: the extreme mystic loses his identity in his beatific experience of oneness with the All[4] and the extreme absolute idealist tends to minimize the importance of the individual and the reality of time in his vision of the whole and of the eternal. Eternal life becomes a present experience. Death is interpreted to be the expansion of the self into the Whole. The esthetic experience also tends to a similar conclusion in the loss of the individual self in contemplation of the beautiful: a monism of the affectivistic, idealistic order.[5] The experience of beauty brings release from individuality; the part finds its reality in the whole.

Those who hold to the continuance of individual life after death, *i.e., personal immortality,* remark that such

---

[2] *Reason in Religion* (1913), p. 273. *Cf., ante,* pp. 119, 133, foot-notes.
[3] *The Eternal Life* (1906). *Cf., ante,* p. 144, foot-note.
[4] *Ante,* pp. 95 ff. On the implications of extreme ontological monism, see *First Adventures,* etc., pp. 124 ff.
[5] On affectivistic idealism see *op. cit.,* pp. 156 ff.

conceptions of immortality—those of social influence and absorption—are most inadequate. If immortality is to mean the loss of individuality it is an immortality without significant meaning. For what is it to a drop to become a part of the ocean? Indeed, the drop, in a sense, may be there but it is no longer sufficiently identified with what it was; so far as the drop is concerned it might just as well have perished. As to the doctrine of social or biological influence, it is asked: how can we be assured that people will go on blessing us for having lived, however helpful to others our lives may have been? True, there may be some whose names will be remembered long after death. But how few these are! There may be an Abraham Lincoln to be remembered in each February and other greater heroes; but how about those whose lives were less conspicuous and yet who may have in their own smaller sphere rendered comparable services and bequeathed valuable legacies?

How many of us remember the names and deeds of our great grandfathers? We may have to thank them for plasmal gifts; but how about this kind of immortality if the family tree becomes barren? Suppose the earth cools off and life can continue here no longer, what then becomes of immortality? What does George Eliot's noble thought offer? At most: but an endless succession of souls, each one but a link in a chain which never is complete, each a means and never an end. It may be beautiful and well that one hands over to the next generation something of value—but is it enough that sacrifice and toil shall constitute the whole story?[6] Does not the individual have a value *per se* which makes any doctrine of means fundamentally superficial? George Eliot's vision may be lofty—but does it not render life quite irrational? Moreover, if, as those who

---

[6] *Cf.* Kant, *ante,* pp. 88 ff.

hold to an *ideal immortality* claim, the ideal remains eternal, would not these ideals continue to exist independently and eternally in their realm, apart from the existence or non-existence of human individuals? Is not an immortality envisaged as beyond or above that of experienced time an abstraction? Does it not imply a metaphysical view quite divorced from the experience of duration, radically different from the world of time and space?

Strictly speaking (and it is a paradox), immortality would seem to imply an existence encompassing all time, both pre-existence and post-existence. The temporal, in the only way extreme absolutists could recognize it, is included within the eternal so that from the ultimate point of view human beings always have existed and always will exist, in some sense. This is eternal life, but it is a life which, from the present existential and temporal point of view, is quite beyond significant meaning. When immortality is thought of by one who has not risen to such metaphysical heights it is an immortality which does not cancel finite and temporal existence but includes and prolongs it indefinitely. Whatever may be the theory of the origin of the individual the doctrine of personal immortality insists that the person persists and the continuation implies the reality of the kind of time which experience teaches.

SOME MODERN DIFFICULTIES IN THE BELIEF IN PERSONAL IMMORTALITY

The Loss of Reality-Feeling

A characteristic feature of our age is the breakdown in the vitality of many traditional beliefs associated with religion. In comparison with the generations which have preceded, our age, for example, appears less concerned about the importance of the doctrine of personal immortality. A number of factors have made for this change: the impact of the spirit of scientific caution, the notion of evolution, the growing recognition of the dependence of mind upon body, the revolt from authoritarian bases as grounds for belief, the loss of trust in the older arguments for God and immortality, the growing confidence in the world, and the turning away from supernatural interests (*e.g.*, humanism, positivism, naturalism), the expressions of pessimism issuing from high places affirming that life under any form is not desirable, the loss of a reality-feeling for the traditional soul and its outright denial by many contemporary psychological schools, reactions against crude notions of immortality by those who believed in it— *e.g.*, doctrines of endless punishment to be meted out to those who disagreed with a given orthodoxy, crude and revolting pictures of hell (*cf.* Dante's *Inferno*), crude pictures of heaven, unethical notions of God, etc.— and a host of factors too numerous to list here.

Questionnaires circulated among selected groups of contemporaries have revealed some surprising results: many respondents have frankly admitted that the doctrine of personal survival did not interest them; some went even further in asserting that the prospect of Death was to them a welcome gospel.[7] Many monographs on the subject of immortality reveal a shift of interest: there is less debate on the question "Is life after death possible?" and more concern over the question "Is it desirable?" The religious spirit, so it has come to be more widely proclaimed, is not lessened by the increasing lack of interest or doubt concerning the existence of a God and the possibility of survival. One may, with the Hebrews of old, be religiously minded without

---

[7] *E.g.*, see *The Belief in God and Immortality* (1916, 1921), J. H. Leuba, especially Part II.

belief in survival. One's happiness, one's ethical life, need not thereby be affected.

Reasons for such a startling increase in the lack of vital concern for personal survival by contemporaries of fame, beginning in the nineteenth and continuing in the twentieth centuries (especially prior to the World War) have, undoubtedly, been many (as above indicated). One factor, however, is conspicuous, and because of its psychological character, it should be noted. It has to do with what Professor J. B. Pratt has, with so much illumination, called *the principle of reality-feeling*.[8]

The principle is very simple: that with which one is engrossed in from day to day, that which carries with it vivid and concrete significance to the imagination, tends to become real; and, conversely, that which claims little or no attention, which has for the mind no concrete imagery, tends to become unreal. A plumber, for instance, will have a great reality-feeling for sewer pipes, plumbers' tools, and such like; whereas to a musician such things are as if they did not exist. A student's world of reality is quite unreal to a ditch-digger; and, conversely, the merits and demerits of picks and shovels will be quite unreal to the student. A surgeon will look at a patient with a different kind of reality-feeling from that of the clergyman; the one will see chemical reactions, muscles, blood, tissues; the other qualities of the human spirit which are intangible, significant, eternal. Now, the existence of God, the survival of the human spirit, tend (other things being equal) to take on a reality-feeling to those who think continually of them, especially so if there is adequate imagery; such themes become quite unreal to those who do not.

_____
[8] *The Religious Consciousness* (1920), pp. 238 ff.

Natural scientists who are accustomed to think only of material things, to deal only with the measurable, in short, who focus their attention upon the quantitative rather than the qualitative aspects of life, will have a high degree of reality-feeling for such things and a correspondingly low reality-feeling for the immeasurable, intangible, the qualitative. That there should be a loss of vital concern over the question of immortality and like questions is not due so much to intellectual difficulties, to the difficulties in logical proofs; rather, such a loss is a reflection of the age in which we live: an age which has turned away from the intangibles to the tangibles, one which has witnessed an amazing growth of physical technique, an emphasis upon experimental, quantitative methods, laboratory sciences, and like disciplines.

Even funeral customs of Western Christians, so Pratt observes, reflect our tendency to focalize our attention upon the tangible. One thinks of the departed as out there in the cemetery; we think we honor the dead by glamorous floral tributes, expensive caskets, steel worm-proof containers, and what not; we honor the dead by the number of carriages in the funeral train. We concentrate, in short, upon the physical. Our reality-feeling has become confined to things compatible with the senses. Whereas, what really ought to obtain (if Christians took their hope seriously) is less concentration upon things of the flesh and more upon the reality of the spirit. The Hindu with his method of quick disposal of the body (*e.g.*, by cremation) has a decided psychological advantage: he is left free to concentrate upon the things of the spirit by the removal of physical suggestions and, consequently, is more consistent in his practice with his faith. It is not surprising, then, to find contemporary belief in personal survival at low ebb; our matter-of-fact civilization—so influenced by the rapid rise and expansion of the physical sciences and techniques—has made the world of spirit seem quite unreal; and further, there is no longer any concrete imagery—now that the older pictures have become obsolete—with which we can grasp a continued existence, now that we are so carnally minded.[9]

The Reality-Feeling Principle Further Considered

So many conceptions have been held as to the nature of continued existence that it is impossible even to enumerate them. C. Lamont in his recent book, *Issues of Immortality* (Holt, 1932)[10], sets forth three factors which go to make up the *psychological* reality of the belief in continued existence. If belief in personal immortality is to mean anything of significance to the ordinary individual, says Lamont, that idea must be emotionally efficacious, imaginatively real, and intellectually acceptable. By the first factor is meant the ability of the idea to awaken an emotional response of whatever character. By the second is meant the ability to imagine in some concrete way the future state—the second contributing to the first since the unimaginable can have no emotional power. By the third is meant the ability of that idea to carry an intellectual appeal with what goes to make up one's total intellectual outlook. For primitives undoubtedly the latter criterion was less significant; for the man of the modern age of critical intellectual discernment it is of great consequence.

Now, ideas of personal immortality have varied greatly inasmuch as what makes for emotional appeal, what is imaginatively real, and what is intellectually

---

[9] There are signs in the contemporary sky of this "materialistic" emphasis waning. The present vogue of appealing to esthetic feelings (rather than to mere utility) is such a sign. And there are more.

[10] A selected bibliography on immortality is given in this book, pp. 185 ff. Readers should acquaint themselves with the well-known series of Ingersoll Lectures on Immortality (given at Harvard) published by the Harvard University Press.

acceptable vary with culture and experience. For some the picture of the future life consists of great detail, even to the kind of food to be consumed, the pleasures to be anticipated, the dangers to be confronted, the games to be played, animals to be hunted; for others the picture is but sketchily outlined; for all, however, who take their belief seriously, something has to be imagined, something has to call out their emotional response and something has to square with and give aid to their general intellectual interpretation of life. Otherwise, the idea is barren.

Relatively few people—says Lamont—will have a vital belief in an immortality where only ideals persist since few can have such a belief with any emotional feeling, with any real imagination or with any intellectual satisfaction. A bodyless existence is quite beyond the imagination of most of us. Hence, when immortality is spoken of by the great masses it is not the aristocratic type represented by those who can make much of pure forms or pure ideas—rather it is in terms of bodily existence. It is accordingly no accident, psychologically, that bound up with the idea of personal immortality have been the notion of resurrection, scenes drawn from the earthly state, and anthropomorphic ideologies in general. Many modern liberals have followed the Platonic scheme of setting forth an immortality of pure spirit, having difficulties with the notion of bodily survival; but they have set up their notion quite at the expense of real significance to the great masses who know themselves not as pure spirits but as spirits linked with bodies.

Modern liberals appear to furnish no adequate picture of immortality; the conception of personal immortality that many of them offer is as hazy as the deacon's definition of God: a kind of purplish oblong blur. The Aristotelian insistence upon the intimate union of soul and body may have difficulties for a doctrine of immortality, but it has one advantage: such a doctrine can at least be visualized somewhat concretely, it can be made to appeal to the imagination of the average person. We know individuals only as mind-bodies; the notion of separation of mind (or soul) from body and its continued existence apart from any kind of body, for most people not only is one which is nigh impossible to visualize but is one which makes continued *individual* existence quite meaningless. St. Thomas puts it thus: "The human soul," he said, "is immortal: so that it survives the body after its separation from it. It is also manifest from what has been stated that the soul is united to the body naturally: since it is by its essence the form of the body: wherefore it is unnatural for the soul to be without the body. Now nothing unnatural can last forever: and consequently the soul will not remain forever without the body. Therefore, since the soul is immortal, it must needs be reunited to the body: and this is to rise again. Hence the immortality of the soul would seem to demand the future resurrection of the body."[11]

Conservatives in religious circles have been characteristically Aristotelian in their picture of personal immortality. The Christian doctrine of immortality has been historically linked with a doctrine of resurrection. The Apostles' Creed in its developed form states that the body will rise; Catholicism has been explicit on this point. Conservative Protestants and Fundamentalists hold to bodily resurrection. Theosophists, Spiritualists, Swedenborgians, Russellites, Seventh Day Adventists, and other cults, in their insistence upon personal immortality of soul *and* body, have been accused of being materialistic in their spiritualism, but they have had the advantage of clarity of doctrine; for most folk such an immortality has been one which

---

[11] Quoted by Lamont, p. 32. *Cf., ante,* pp. 202 ff.

measures up to the three criteria above suggested. Personal immortality in terms of body and soul is something that can be imagined; an immortality of spirit without body remains intangible, vague, and imaginatively unreal to the average mind.

The tendency of modern liberal religion and the teaching of men with metaphysical interests concerning the nature of life after death to idealize it out of all contact with what can be for most people imaginatively real, emotionally significant, and intellectually acceptable, has been induced very largely by difficulties concerning bodily resurrection. The result is that with an immortality tucked away beyond categories of this world, there is nothing concrete to which the idea can be attached; gradually it is left to float in a kind of shadowy nowhere. It seems to make no difference; it is so unlike what is now experienced that it might just as well not be. Liberals may be convincing in the possibility of immortality, but of what use is a life of spaceless, time-inclusive, motionless, bodyless existence? Pure spirit reads well on paper, but what, after all, is it vividly and concretely?

The thesis that ideas of immortality reflect social cultures is now accepted as commonplace. A people's notion of heaven is, whatever else it may be, a reflection of themselves: a picture of desires which have been frustrated here and their imaginative fulfilment there. Hell, too, reflects men's desires: evils unpunished here, but punished there, the desire for justice, and so on.[12] In a matter-of-fact kind of civilization which is ours today, with reality-feeling centered upon tangibles, it is no surprise to find conceptions of immortality, which some are trying desperately to depict, vague, emotionally uninspiring, and intellectually unreal to the common herd. If former cultures had conceptions of a

---

[12] The psychological-social approach to religious ideology is illuminating. On this approach in general, see *First Adventures,* etc., pp. 63 ff.

life to come altogether too anthropomorphic for our critical age, our day is being presented with conceptions so non-anthropomorphic in character as to be psychologically unreal to the masses. Lamont's point, the reader will see, is to disclose the dilemma of modern religious liberalism on the question of immortality.

The Problem of the Resurrection

It ought to be evident that the belief in personal immortality is independent of a belief or disbelief in a resurrection. Christians, historically considered, however, have associated the two almost inseparably. The resurrection of the body has meant that in some future time life will return again to the disintegrated body and the latter will be reconstructed. The doctrine probably came into Christianity from Persian thought by way of Judaism. A certain obscurity has attended the doctrine; sometimes the concept has meant a literal physical resurrection, the reconstruction of flesh and blood; sometimes it has meant the renewal or refashioning of the body (which lends itself again to various interpretations, some of which are somewhat removed from older and cruder associations).

The doctrine of the immortality of the soul is characteristically Greek and the thought has been that the body has been kept under control by some internal motive power other than itself. The two doctrines were fused in historic Christianity, though the fusion meant considerable revision from their original meanings. Paul helped greatly to fuse these rather distinct notions.[13] The theories as to the condition of the departed during the interim between death and the resurrection have varied greatly; the doctrine of Purgatory, or condition of cleansing, probation, and final preparation before beginning the purer life, has been

---

[13] *See ante,* p. 197, foot-note.

one of the orthodox beliefs of a large part of Christendom.[14]

The traditional Christian belief in the resurrection of Jesus has played a major part in the belief in personal immortality: Jesus' rising from the dead is held to be the one great instance, or empirical proof, of individual survival. For centuries it was the one chief argument in the Western world. It is now well known that doubts have been raised, with increasing force, as to the validity of this emphasis; accordingly, it becomes necessary to recognize what are considered the indisputable difficulties connected with this belief and how the modern Christian apologist goes about to meet them.

Western Christian thought long dominated by a sincere trust in the traditional confidence that since Jesus arose from the dead there is now irrefutable proof of personal immortality, has now become unsettled by the problems raised by historical criticism. No longer is it felt by many that the center of gravity on the question of personal immortality lies in the traditional claim; that there is an explicit historical demonstration of such a survival, claimed by Christians, is now cruelly questioned. Let us look into the *pros* and *cons* of this question.

Historical criticism[15] has coldly examined the sources of the tradition. Psychological explanations have tended to minimize the unique importance and interpretation given to certain alleged happenings, reducing what had been called miracle by an earlier generation to the great body of natural laws.[16] Re-interpretations of what was

---

[14] The doctrine of Purgatory, when stripped of some of its historically allied features, is one which may be defended on a highly reasonable basis.

[15] *Cf.*, p. 149, foot-note.

[16] The term "miracle" may be (and is) used in two senses: to refer to an event which involves the upsetting of natural laws (by intervention), and to an event which is incomprehensible. In the latter sense, a miracle is relative to a context of understanding, ceasing to be when that context is superseded.

said to have happened have taken from tradition much of what was awe-inspiring. The realization that there is a long period of oral tradition between the alleged events and the written record of them has made for caution in trusting the record. A generation passing stories from lip to lip can easily add and subtract and modify. The Oriental mind is not given to exactitude in expression; it is enough if it employ poetry and symbols. The great impression made by the personality of Jesus made exaggeration normal. The traditional dates of the records, authorships, and other literary questions are not beyond dispute. Tradition in itself cannot be trusted. There were no historical critics then; no careful records were made; parchments are fragmentary, extant manuscripts late, and there are indisputable evidences of emendations and interpolations in the record. Psychologically considered, the phenomena of the alleged appearances of Jesus may be matched by other claims in human experience; they are similar to what goes under the name of spiritualism, a modern religious cult.

That Jesus did come from the grave, appeared, and gave *quasi*-physical demonstrations of his survival has been supported by Christian apologists in a number of ways. The chief historical argument has centered on the story of the empty sepulcher. Considerations which have weakened this claim are many and serious: the legendary element between the event and its record; lack of detail in our knowledge of what became of the body; the traditional stories as to the finding of the empty tomb do not harmonize; Paul made no use of this as an argument; the belief in an empty tomb by the disciples must not be taken without the qualification of the human frailty to err and the possibility of social and collective suggestion and even of hallucination; the burden of proof rests upon those who claim that the body did not disintegrate. That Jesus actually appeared as a reanimated dead body though miraculously transformed presents chemical difficulties: what became of the atomic elements that composed his terrestrial body? That such a body arose and disappeared in the clouds and ascended toward heaven may well fit a Ptolemaic universe, but hardly a Copernican. Moreover, there is no close correspondence between the appearances recorded in the gospels and those referred to by Paul. A conservative psychology has a much simpler way of explaining the alleged events than that recorded by tradition. May not a subconscious repression suddenly released explain what seemed to be a miracle and this in turn confirmed a faith and a hope? The fact that many were convinced reminds us only of the laws of social suggestion. Was it not an age of legends? Resurrection stories were not uncommon.

In the face of such difficulties modern apologists who recognize them as such, have generally resorted to a different type of apology. It is now said: does not the belief of the disciples in the resurrection of Jesus rest rather upon a haunting religious conviction of a life to come, and was not this the chief *motif* behind the traditional stories? Did not Jesus himself teach personal survival, and were not the disciples moved to a deep-seated belief in it even before the crucifixion? They may have had their doubts, but was not personal survival a deep conviction in spite of them? Is not the real value of the resurrection stories religious and moral rather than any *quasi*-physical emphasis or demonstration? Was it not natural that such a conviction be transformed to what would be real to the imagination? Could such a man of power who had worked wonders among them be overcome by death? Was not defeat for him unbelievable? As to the theory that Jesus' body was kept in hiding by Joseph of Aramathea, does this not present serious psychological difficulties?

A characteristic modern apology points to the gloom

and frustration which came over the little band during and following the crucifixion. Peter is the representative. How account for the tremendous transformation which came over him (and others) soon after? From out of an unpromising, timid, and fearful group there came a movement which saw cowards transformed into heroes and martyrs. Forty days after his death Jesus had more power than he ever had during his ministry over the minds and hearts of men. Peter preaching on the streets of Jerusalem was not the same man. From discouragement and defeat there came an amazing conviction that Jesus was alive and that whatever befell his disciples they were victorious in his resurrection. Something changed despair into confidence, doubts into convictions. Is there any cause adequate to this amazing transformation other than that something of deep and momentous significance had happened? Did not Jesus somehow certify his unique divinity and mission to them?

However true or false the details may be into which their explanations were clothed, surely there must be a cause adequate to the effect. That Jesus somehow proved his power over death is the unity and reality that underly the conflicting stories. The full explanation as to what actually happened is lacking, but the fact is clear; and for Christians who have never asked that faith be surrendered to material demonstration—a lesson taught and emphasized in his own ministry—this is evidence enough to reinforce the belief in human survival. Moreover, the nineteenth century fashion of denying the possibility of "miracles" is an out-moded way of speaking in the twentieth. There is nothing "impossible" in the traditional belief of the survival of Jesus, in the reputed demonstrations nor in the doctrine of the resurrection; first-rate men in the various sciences no longer speak of impossibilities but of probabilities. And the tradition, though difficult to "prove," is not, in certain of its elements, without a high degree of probability.

The Relation of the Mind-Body Problem to Belief in Personal Immortality

One of the chief obstacles against belief in personal immortality is the inability of many to conceive how personal consciousness could continue apart from the brain and the nervous system. We know of no consciousness without brain; harm to the latter spells ruin to the former. Is not then the fate of the individual bound up with the fate of the brain? If the latter disintegrates will not the former? Such questions bring up the whole problem of the mind-body relation.[17]

Suppose we grant the dependence of mind upon brain structure and function; could we then say that the survival of consciousness might be possible apart from the fate of the brain? Could we still say with Longfellow:

> Dust thou art, to dust returnest
> Was not spoken of the soul.

Two answers have been given in favor of the possibility of personal survival even though dependence of mind upon brain is granted. The first: It is true that our present experience shows that psychic life is intimately dependent upon the physical. But, the limitations of a present experience do not make for the impossibility of another type of experience. In the course of evolution the body has taken the lead; before mind appears there is a long development of the physical structures which have made it possible. As the evolutionary process moves on, however, mind gradually wins a certain amount of independence over the body; the

---

[17] For a discussion of this important philosophical problem, see *First Adventures,* etc., Chap. XIX.

course seems to indicate that mind is destined to win its complete freedom from a long partnership and strike out on its own. Although, from present experience, we cannot say that this freedom has been completely achieved, yet there are strong indications of this direction of human evolution. May, then, there not be in this development a strong suggestion that mind, under circumstances made favorable by a Reality which has produced it, could carry on its own existence apart from the body in a kind of momentum acquired here and now? Belief in the separate existence of a mind is no greater a strain on the imagination than a belief in the existence of a God (who is not pictured in terms of physical limitations).

A second consideration is that made famous by William James.[18] Suppose, he says, we grant that thought is a function of the brain, that mind is functionally dependent upon physiological structure and processes—all that a natural science can claim. Are we, then, compelled to affirm that the destruction of the physical means the destruction of the psychical? By no means. For, consider the notion of functional dependence. When one says that A is functionally dependent upon B, one might mean that B has produced A. If so, we have a definite kind of functional dependence, that of *productive* function. On such a basis, if A's continued function depends upon B's continuing to produce A, then the continued existence of A apart from B is denied. If B dies, A dies. But functional dependence does not necessarily mean productive function. It may mean something else. The firing of a gun (A) depends, let us say, upon the pull of a trigger (B): no trigger-pull, no firing. Here we have a functional dependence that signifies not that A is produced by B in the sense of creating or engendering; rather, B

---

[18] *Human Immortality* (2nd ed. 1899). Ingersoll Lecture.

is the means of release: the relation is that of *releasing* or *permissive* function. The light (*A*) which has passed through a prism (*B*) is functionally dependent upon the prism: no prism, no *such* light. Here we have a functional dependence that signifies not that *A* is produced by *B* in the sense of creating or engendering; rather, *B* is the means of transmitting light: the relation is that of *transmissive* function. So far as saying, then, that mind is functionally dependent upon brain, there is in this statement nothing that compels us to say that the relation is *necessarily* that of productive function; to say that such a statement implies *productive* function is to go into the realm of the metaphysical and, strictly speaking, quite beyond the province of natural science. One may affirm that mind is dependent upon brain, and hold, at the same time, to the permissive or transmissive type of functional dependence.

Let us add our own illustration: a musician may be dependent upon a violin for violin music; destruction of the violin (in general) will destroy violin music; but this is not to say that the musician may not take up some other instrument and express the music that within him lies. No doubt, there will be a different expression; but that is quite different from saying that further expression is impossible. It may well be that the brain is an instrument upon which the mind plays; a poor instrument (*e.g.*, injury to brain, etc.) gives poor music; the destruction of the instrument means the cease of *that kind* of expression. And yet, how on *scientific* grounds, can we be certain that there will be no other instrument through which the mind may further express itself? Scientific facts cannot as such deny the possibility of the permissive or transmissive types of functional dependence.[19] The doctrine, then, which some physiological psychologists have set up,

---

[19] *Cf.* the analogy of the relation of a coat to a nail-on-the-wall suggested by Bergson. See *First Adventures,* etc., pp. 431 ff.

viz., that mind is a *product* of a developing nervous system because of its functional dependence upon that nervous system, is a dogma based upon a metaphysical and scientifically unwarranted assumption. The immortality of mind is still an open possibility.

The Silence of the Dead

We hear it said: why, if personal immortality is a fact, is there no breaking through the veil to give us such an assurance? There are some who claim that there is such direct communication, *e.g.*, those of the spiritualist cult. (We shall consider this claim under a separate heading). Grant for the moment that there is no voice nor sign from the other side. Does this preclude the possibility of life beyond? And further —how about those who, having been reported dead, return to life with nothing to say in regard to a life on the other side?[20] Should they not be able to bear a testimony if there is another life? Is it not of great significance when they testify that their experience was that of a deep sleep beyond the pale of self-consciousness of which they have no memory?

Now, undoubtedly, all this *may* be of significance to a belief or disbelief in personal immortality. But to say that there is no after-life because the dead are silent, because there is no affirmative testimony concerning it from those who are reported to have crossed and re-crossed the line, is to offer no demonstrable proof against the possibility of personal immortality. Immortality may be still highly possible. For consider: it may well be that the state into which the departed have entered is so unlike that of the present space-time world that communication becomes difficult if not nigh impossible; or, in the case of one "who has come back," it

---

[20] We pass by the possible counter-claim that "reported dead" is not synonymous with the fact. It is a matter of dispute just when the condition of death may be said to have come to the body.

may well be that memory under the present limited circumstances cannot bridge the gap between the two states. Or, it is still possible to say, granting that the immediate state after death is that of deep and unconscious sleep, that there is an *eventual* re-awakening and continuation of conscious existence. The human mind when bound up with material instruments (brain and nervous system) may function in such a limited way as to make it impossible for it to grasp, hold, and transpose conditions so unlike those of the present.

ARGUMENTS IN FAVOR OF PERSONAL IMMORTALITY

It may be stated very frankly, at the outset, that there are no fully worked out proofs for personal survival. This, of course, is not a startling statement to a philosopher; we are accustomed, by this time, not to be too disappointed in our failure to arrive at "proofs"; it is enough if we can attain to reasonable conclusions, to what may seem to be the higher probabilities. And all this, of course, is not peculiar to philosophy; it is characteristic of all human endeavor, including the "facts" and theories of the various sciences.[21] A classification of some of the outstanding types of arguments follows.

An Analytic Type of Argument

In the celebrated dialogue *Phaedo* where the problem of immortality comes in for serious discussion Plato uses as an argument what he calls the "law of contraries." Everything which possesses an opposite is generated only from its opposite. "I mean such things as good and evil, just and unjust—and there are innumerable other opposites which are generated out of opposites. . . . Anything which becomes greater must become greater after being less. . . . That which becomes

---

[21] *Cf., ante,* p. 254.

less must have been once greater and then have become less. . . . And the weaker is generated from the stronger, and the swifter from the slower. . . . And the worse is from the better, and the more just is from the more unjust. . . . Well, and is there not an opposite of life, as sleep is the opposite of waking? . . . Is not death opposed to life? . . . And they are generated one from the other? . . . Then here is a new way by which we arrive at the conclusion that the living come from the dead, just as the dead come from the living; and this, if true, affords a most certain proof that the souls of the dead exist in some place out of which they come again." [22] All things pass in rhythmic process—there is pre-existence and there is post-existence.

In the *Republic* [23] the analytic type of argument appears as follows: We find in almost everything an inherent evil or disease. Nothing can destroy a thing unless this inherent evil. The soul has its evils, such as injustice, intemperance, etc. But these evils do not destroy the soul as disease destroys the body. It is unreasonable to suppose that a thing which cannot be destroyed from within by its own corruption can be destroyed by some external evil. Bad food cannot destroy the body without communication of that bad food to within. Destruction must come from within. No bodily evil can infect the soul for no one can prove that even death makes a man more unholy or unjust. Therefore, since the soul cannot be destroyed by evils, inherent or external, it must exist forever and so be immortal.[24] Immortality is thus arrived at by assuming the difference in kind of soul and body; a different kind of fate, accordingly, awaits each.

The analytic type of argument represented by Plato

---

[22] *Plato: Selections* (Scribners, 1927), edited by R. Demos, pp. 165-168.
[23] *Plato: The Republic* (1928), edited by C. M. Bakewell, pp. 409 ff.
[24] This argument involves, it is clear, the fallacy of *petitio principii*.

has been characterized as "fantastic," "unconvincing," "verbal," "play on words," and too closely bound with a definite metaphysics to convince anyone unwilling to subscribe to initial premises and to a certain theory of reality.[25]

The Emotional Type of Argument

Here we have an appeal to the feelings. How fruitless is life if there is no personal survival! Though there are difficulties in the way of belief there is a demand of the heart that cannot easily be dissuaded. Consider the folly of a man set to work to build for himself a house and finds that however he tries he cannot complete it; the folly of a world in which is found the yearnings to make possibilities actual and which yearnings are ever incompletely realized. The intellect may cry out "vanity of vanities! all is vanity" and not without good reasons; and yet man's deepest nature continues to assert that his hopes for a fuller life are not mocking him. *Le coeur a ses raisons que la raison ne connaît pas.* (Pascal).

Dr. Minot Simons pictures the emotional basis of belief which has been so widespread and common: "Hosts of people experience a strange illumination which comes when they are brought personally close to the meaning of death in the loss of some one dear to them, whose vigor of life and whose strong, lovely, and noble qualities of character have made a deep impression upon them. Before they had such an experience they may have been complacently skeptical about immortality, but now, to imagine the end of such vital and significant qualities is quite impossible. . . . The whole country had such a spiritual experience in the death of Lincoln. He was killed on a Good Friday

---

[25] For an exposition of Plato's several arguments see *The Idea of Immortality* (1922), A. Seth Pringle-Pattison, pp. 44 ff.

evening. On the following Easter Sunday morning there was a mighty incoming tide of faith that such a personality could not have an end. . . . In the Great War the whole world had such an experience with death on a vast unprecedented scale." [26]

We have learned not to discount the significance of the life of feeling in coming to terms with Reality (*e.g.*, the mystics in general, Bergson) and therefore it would seem to be an act of unwisdom to suggest that there is no value to this general approach. Human hopes may, indeed, be as significant as any other class of data. And yet, standing alone, the emotional appeal is hardly an argument. Frequently the emotional approach is closely allied to the moral arguments and it is fitting then to go on and discuss their general nature.

The Moral Argument

A classical statement of the moral type of argument for belief in personal immortality is that presented by Kant and already given on preceding pages.[27] His argument should be reviewed in this connection.

The moral argument which, for contemporary religious thought, has become one of the major arguments, has generally been linked with a theistic world-view. If God is good and God is sufficiently powerful, how can such a God allow the values (potential or actual) bound up with individuals to become forever lost? The very character of such a God is at stake in the question of personal immortality. The world would be irrational if, after having brought into being human beings who aspire against so many almost overwhelming odds to achieve higher values, it should dash them into nothingness. Would a Raphael have the patience and courage to paint if he knew that his painting upon completion

---

[26] Quoted in Lamont's *Issues of Immortality,* pp. 92-93.
[27] *Ante,* pp. 85 ff.

would some day be dashed to pieces? Are not the great moral seers of mankind persuaded that somehow—even though society shall not persist—those who labor for great moral ends labor not in vain? Would God be any less than a human father who would not that any of his children should perish? How solve the problem of evil unless there be a continued existence where shall obtain appropriate rewards and readjustments and further opportunities? Do not reason and justice demand that somehow there are further chapters to be written which will give moral meaning to human suffering and struggle? It has been said that if we should all become extinct we would never know the difference; to which it is replied: but would not a God know? And if God be morally good and sufficiently powerful how could he endure a memory of the tragedies of human existence without doing something about them? What object is there in the evolutionary process culminating in man unless there be moral ends reaching out beyond a present existence?

True, the moral argument has been set down in ways that have been offensive to finer moral sensibilities. The doctrine of *conditional* immortality as stated by certain theologians is a case in point. The alleged arbitrary election and condemnation on the part of God was a doctrine proclaimed in a moral setting but one which was pivoted on a moral enigma.[28] The widespread belief that men have but one chance to "get to heaven" regardless of their opportunities has made for a kind of conditional immortality morally questionable.[29] The doctrine of conditional immortality, however, can be defended on the basis that personal immortality is not a necessary free-for-all-birthright but a condition to be achieved by those worthy (in terms of adequate opportunity); the harsh statement of the notion has brought

---

[28] *See ante,* pp. 223 ff.
[29] On the moral necessity for further opportunity, *see ante,* pp. 166 ff.

it into disrepute in modern thought. Properly stated, the notion is defensible.

Someone may suggest: is it not a sufficiently adequate doctrine, from a moral point of view, to hold that individuals toil and sacrifice for those who come after, regardless of their own fate? To which the reply is: Yes, if the doctrine of means, morally considered, is greater than a doctrine of ends. But is it? Which is more moral: I treat You as a means or I treat You as an end? The latter, of course. Now, if the world is grounded in a Reality of the highest type, morally considered, any doctrine which, no matter how high sounding, fails to give to the individual the highest moral consideration—*i.e.*, to treat him as an end and not merely a means—is by that token less moral. If one should think that there is no point to the survival of some people then the answer comes: we do not know what possibilities are bound up with individuals. The seeming worthlessness of some people may be due to a mote in the eye of him who passes judgment. If I have no use for a person it does not follow that the Universe has no use for him.

The moral argument has been given a practical emphasis by William James who would put it thus: All things considered, it is better to believe in personal survival than not. The argument follows closely the pragmatic approach which we have already considered in another connection.[30]

An Idealistic Approach

As we have already indicated, certain forms of modern idealism have by their very metaphysics guaranteed immortality. We refer here, of course, to Absolute Idealism. The argument naturally has an appeal only to those committed to that kind of metaphysics. If

---

[30] *Cf., ante,* pp. 110 ff.

everything is a part of the great All nothing can perish if the All is eternal. Just how *personal* immortality can be taught on this basis is hard to see, as already indicated.

Royce [31] tried hard to overcome this difficulty and did it, as he thought, by declaring that individuals in the-here-and-now are not really individuals (in the fullest sense) but only individuals in the becoming. We are on the way to become individuals. The great All which is the one truly complete Individual, will not allow finite individuals to be swallowed up but will bring them to a fuller realization of their individuality; immortality will be achieved by the dropping of the rôle of the finite and a larger place will be attained with the Infinite.[32] Unending time thus is required for the individual to realize fully his individuality.

The Empirical Approach

There are four groups which would claim a place under this heading: the mystics who assert that they have a direct experience of unending existence in certain glorious experiences; those who hold to what is known as the historical form of the empirical argument, *viz.*, the resurrection of Jesus; modern Spiritualists and some Psychical Researchers; and those who ground their claim in religious experience.

Extreme mystics have asserted that they have come to terms with the nature of Reality; in their experience of that reality the time-lessness of real existence, the loss of the limitations of the finite, have come to them with overwhelming force. Life eternal does not mean a continuation in time but rather the quality of timelessness and of finite-transcending. There is here no argument. It is an experience. It is difficult to conceive how the individual can be saved on this basis from being swal-

---

[31] *Cf., ante,* p. 147, foot-note. Also, *cf., ante,* p. 231.
[32] *The Conception of Immortality* (1899). Ingersoll Lecture.

lowed up in the eternal. For extreme mystics, he is swallowed up.[33] Individuality is something to be overcome. In losing one's self one finds himself: even as one becomes engrossed in one's work one becomes identified with it; one ceases to be something apart from; one merges one's self into it. This is the fuller life and this is life eternal. One moves from the poverty of isolation to the enrichment of absorption.

All this, of course, is beautiful and ennobling. But, how about the individual? What becomes of *him*? Is he worth something *as such* or is he but a means to something else? Is not the unity which swallows up difference in the mystic ideal less an ideal than a unity which resolves clashing differences and yet preserves distinctions?

The second type of empirical argument we have already considered.[34]

The third, the claim of modern Spiritualists and of some Psychical Researchers, is one that offers alleged "proof" of survival and thus merits a respectful hearing. It is quite beyond the limitations of this exposition to go into detail in the matter of what these people claim or claimed to have accomplished. A summary exposition, however, seems called for before we give an evaluation.

Modern Spiritualism and the S.P.R.

The contemporary religious cult known as spiritualism [35] is supposed to date back to the mysterious rap-

---

[33] *Cf., ante,* p. 257.

[34] *Ante,* pp. 267 ff.

[35] For a comprehensive and fair treatment of the spiritualists' cult see *The Drama of Life after Death* (1932), by G. Lawton. Also see *The Confusion of Tongues* (1928), by C. W. Ferguson, Chap. II; *Modern Religious Cults and Movements* (1923), by G. G. Atkins, Chap. X. For various estimates of Psychic Research see *The Case For and Against Psychical Belief* (1927), edited by Carl Murchison. An essay entitled "The Good and Evil in Spiritualism" by Lily Dougall in *Immortality* (1922), by B. H. Streeter and others, is recommended.

pings that were heard in a little cottage in Hydesville, New York, in 1848. The Fox sisters were the instruments of peculiar noises which were supposed to be communications from departed spirits. Their later confession that these noises came by means of agile toes did not deter the movement which in a credulous age had already gained considerable momentum through reports of other strange occurrences. Unaccountable phenomena have long interested the human race and there are always those who are ready to draw hasty and mystifying deductions. Emanuel Swedenborg (1688-1772) had visions of the New Jerusalem, an alleged contact with the spirit world.

Hydesville is but another chapter in the long history of human interest in occult phenomena. The Fox house is said to have been haunted; mysterious noises were supposed to have taken place before the Foxes had taken up their residence there. The parents of the children had become mystified by the apparent control of their daughters over the noises; they seemed to carry on conversation with a spirit world; answers came back "yes" or "no" as the number of taps indicated. Neighbors came to witness. The fire of enthusiasm and superstition spread. The children became saints. A cult was born; Hydesville became the mecca of a large following. Other mediums sprang up overnight. It is given to some, it was widely heralded, to communicate with the departed; it is given to a few chosen to act as mediums for conversation. Seances were arranged; people believed. Belief in personal survival was no longer a belief; it was now a demonstration. People could come and taste and see. The amazing information at the command of mediums, demonstrations of a queer physical sort, proved too formidable to deny with the wave of the hand. Names of departed friends, unknown to the medium, but known to members of a group, were announced by the medium in the trance-state; circumstances known only to some visitors would be alluded to—all this was sufficient demonstration, beyond a doubt, of the communication of mediums with the spirit-world and of first-hand contact with that host of encompassing witnesses round about. A definite religion and theology arose about these strange phenomena; a definite set of interpretations given to them is the answer of the religious cult known as spiritualism.

Now, such phenomena need not be surrounded by the kind of interpretations which the spiritualists have set forth. They may be interpreted in other ways. A desire for a critical investigation of the validity of the facts upon which spiritualism has given its interpretation and of other possible interpretations and of alleged claims gave rise to the Society for Psychical Research, founded in 1882. In other words, spiritualism as a religious cult is not to be confused with the S.P.R.

Two classes of phenomena have been studied by the S.P.R. (members of which have been and are men of high standing, *e.g.*, William Barrett, F. W. H. Myers, Henry Sidgwick, James Hyslop, Frank Podmore, Tennyson, Oliver Lodge, A. J. Balfour, W. Crookes, Ruskin, G. S. Hall, William James, and others): First, physical phenomena, such as strange noises, music, luminous appearances, automatic writing, table-tipping, movement of objects without any apparent physical cause, rappings, etc.; and secondly, psychical phenomena such as alleged supernormal communications, clairvoyance, hypnotism, trance-states, impersonations, etc. Now what are the results of such careful investigators into such strange phenomena? Let us summarize.

Some mediums are found to be honest; others (and many) are practicing deceit. (Houdini, the magician, for example, thought that all the physical performances of mediums were clever tricks and could be duplicated by any competent magician). That some mediums do possess extraordinary knowledge seems to be allowed by the evidence. That all psychic phenomena are the result of collective hallucination or hypnosis is highly improbable. Strange psychical and physical phenomena do occur. Some of these may be accounted for on the basis of known natural causes. It becomes the duty of the scientific investigator to follow the naturalistic attack if he shall attain understanding—*i.e.*, to look for natural causes; it is his duty to remember the law of parsimony.[36] Much can thus be explained. And yet, when all is said and done, there are certain exhibitions of mediums which as yet do not seem to fit in with what is known about natural laws. What and how shall such residua be explained?

It may be the part of greater wisdom to reserve judgment until more is known rather than to rush immediately to the category of the supernatural as explanation or to acknowledge the spiritualists' explanation that such phenomena are evidences of contacts with the spirit or supernormal world. For instance, the extraordinary knowledge of mediums may be catalogued as but an instance of telepathy (communication other than through usual channels) as yet so little understood but which seems to be confirmed by experience. Certain information may not be acquired consciously nor come by way of the known senses.[37] Perhaps the subconscious mind is at work taking photographs and that this is the source of information. Cases where people are thinking of the same thing at the same time and without the usual means of communication are not uncommon. Perhaps there are certain people so constituted that they are gifted to a high degree with the ability to commune with others, outside the usual manner of contact. Perhaps certain

---

[36] Entities must not be multiplied beyond necessity.

[37] Perhaps we are possessors of more senses than we now realize. *See* the highly suggestive article by Professor E. D. Starbuck, entitled "The Intimate Senses as Sources of Wisdom" in *The Journal of Religion,* Vol. I. No. 2, March, 1921.

mediums are such rare psycho-physical beings. Who knows the powers of the subconscious mind? Perhaps those who consult mediums find themselves credulous by their reading specific applications into general statements of the medium.[38] Perhaps there is the element of coincidence which is not uncommon in human experience.

What, then, about the strange physical phenomena that go to make up the performances of certain famous mediums? J. Malcolm Bird, who was sent out under the auspices of the *Scientific American* in 1922 to investigate certain celebrated European mediums, gives the following summary opinion of physical phenomena which occur during the medium's trance-states: "Of all the physical phenomena which I have witnessed, there are many for whose fraudulent production, under the given conditions, I can without serious difficulty see a way. There are many more for whose production by fraud I can still see a way, but only with serious difficulty—that is to say, so far as I can see, to account for them in this fashion one would have to make assumptions so far-fetched that the question would arise whether they were not more objectionable than the outright hypothesis that some psychic force was at work. And finally there are many for whose fraudulent production, under the given conditions, I can conceive *no possible way*. It is understood that I do not know all there is to know about fraud and sleight of hand. But making due allowance for this, it is my best judgment that, of physical manifestations which baffled me altogether or forced me to make objectionable assumptions in the effort to explain them as due to fraud, I have

---

[38] Fortune-tellers, as a professional class, know this subtle art. Somebody is to come into your life next August. Look out for a dark and handsome. Such generalized statements which may be specifically applied by anyone may easily carry a personal reference and ring with a prophetic note.

seen enough to establish a good degree of probability that some of them were genuine psychic phenomena." [39] In other words, Bird's conclusions suggest that there are facts not-yet-explained which Psychic Research has uncovered, elements which include strange physical happenings. This represents the best conservative opinion.

There are those who rush to the spiritualists' hypothesis, *viz.*, that mediums are in contact with spirits. Is such an explanation legitimate? Our answer is that it is a legitimate hypothesis; but an hypothesis it remains. There are other legitimate and possible explanations; what remains unexplained may some day be explained in terms of natural sequence; it is the duty of scientific caution to look for natural sequences; it is well to avoid a pre-mature jumping to supernatural solutions.

Granting that there is a strange power of mind not yet understood, power over other minds and power over matter, this does not lead one necessarily into the one explanation upon which spiritualists have insisted. There are other doors open. Bird, for example, suggests that in the seances which he witnessed he was unable to find anything that had occurred that was "in the least degree demonstrative of survival and communication and activity on the physical plane by deceased humans." On the other hand, with certain exceptions, he admits that he found nothing in his experiences with mediums which would indicate strong evidence against the spirit hypothesis. But he concludes: "Bringing all my experience together, I regard the probabilities . . . as overwhelmingly in favor of some other explanation for whatever psychic phenomena, subjective and objective alike, may occur."

It has been said that inasmuch as the messages sup-

---

[39] *My Psychic Adventures* (Scientific American, 1924), pp. 304-305. This book will be found useful to the reader unacquainted with the work of mediums. It is extremely cautious; the records are from one who has tried to carry scientific caution with him in a first-hand investigation.

posedly coming from across the border are of the nature of trivialities and often reveal low culture, this is enough to discredit the spiritualists' interpretation. Would departed spirits concern themselves with such twaddle as the mediums bring forth? To which the spiritualists reply: it is not to be expected that the departed spirits reach at one jump the highest sphere of existence; they begin where they leave off in this world; they still have the concerns that they had. Further, it is said against the spiritualists that their view is discredited by the methods involved in securing alleged communications; for consider, the medium after a seance becomes, temporarily at least, a nervous wreck. Could it be possible that, to effect communication, a good and powerful God would have to resort to an indirect method which draws so heavily upon the nervous energies of women-mediums and that *this* is to be taken as the demonstrative means to prove the reality of personal survival? Why must such demonstrations take place in the dark? To which it is retorted: it is not so strange that there are certain ways of doing certain things in ordinary life; why should it be strange that there are certain ways of communication with the supernatural? Is it not reasonable to suppose that a person endowed with certain sensitivities (which in human beings come by way of the nervous system) should be peculiarly fitted for this kind of work? And as for darkness in the room at the time of seance: is it not proper that there should be excluded certain elements of distraction (light, *e.g.*, may well be a distraction in meditation and concentration) when one has come apart to commune with the higher world?

Again, it is said against the spiritualists who claim men of scientific distinction as supporting their contention, that such a claim has another side: if a man achieves distinction in one field, this is no basis for contending that he is competent to judge in another. Sir Oliver Lodge may indeed be an eminent scientist who at the same time supports the claim that there is real spirit-communication; but Oliver Lodge in one field is not necessarily the same man in another. To which there comes the retort: Oliver Lodge did not come to his belief in the demonstration of personal survival without the scientific caution to which his mind is accustomed.

And again, why, ask the spiritualists, should not those who have passed on give us demonstrative evidence of their being alive; has not Christianity all down through the ages held it as a firm conviction that the sting of death has been withdrawn and that there are hosts of witnesses all about? Is it not glorious to have the assurance that there are about us unseen companions who have our welfare continually before them? Why all this doubt and unbelief when there have been so many evidences of the re-crossing of the bar in well attested communications? To which some Christians may say: we agree that there ought to be some *assurance* for such a comforting belief; but we are not seeking for the *kind* of assurance (evidence) which Spiritualists seem to demand.

The Claim of Religious Experience

The basis for an empirical assurance of personal survival is to be had in religious experience of the highest order. This is a claim that has been widely proclaimed. More specifically stated, it is held that in religious experience at its best there is given an immediate perception of God, a Divine Factor, and that this experience is an empirical grounding for assurance of personal immortality. Professor Macintosh, for example, has this to say: "The person of adequate religious experience and logical reflection can say, 'I know God, and I know he will not let me die; whatever may befall this instrument which I use temporarily (my body of flesh and blood), my real self will survive.' " This is an affirmation which is not only "practically imperative" and "theoretically permissible" but it is one which "we can now affirm as religiously certain." [40]

The assurance of personal survival is here given not in terms of a mystical awareness of that condition but as a certainty which, in that it issues directly from an experience of God, is empirically grounded. To know God, it is claimed, is to know that one is eternal. The assurance of immortality is thus held to be bound up with a religious experience that is adequate; a lack of this experience would mean the loss of that certainty. This was the kind of assurance, it is asserted, that the Founder of Christianity possessed; and it was the kind of assurance (rather than the assurance that comes from any outward demonstrations) that turned first-century skeptics and cowards into Christian believers and heroes.

Some Summary Considerations

Belief in personal immortality, it would seem, rests pretty much upon one's theory of the Universe (*e.g.,* whether there is a God that is sufficiently powerful to make it possible and sufficiently moral to bring moral meaning to human existence).[41] Belief in personal immortality, too, is not confined to one type of argument: it would seem to rest upon accumulative considerations and insights. Professor W. W. Fenn offered the following fruitful suggestion: Some of our beliefs, he said, have causes; others have reasons. The deeper the subject the more do our beliefs concerning it depend upon causes (psychological) rather than upon reasons

---

[40] *Theology as an Empirical Science* (Macmillan, 1919), p. 205. The reader must understand this in terms of Macintosh's moral optimism and religious realism which have already been set forth, *ante,* pp. 115 ff.

[41] This is not to say, however, that it is impossible to believe in personal immortality without believing in a God. J. M. E. McTaggart, for example, held to such a belief on purely theoretical grounds, but had no belief in a God.

(logical). Beliefs which are due to causes rather than reasons are apt to be truer since they fit into a more general frame of reference rather than in isolated intellectual processes. Immortality is a theme which lies below the surface of things and nearest the deepest springs of thought and conduct. Any estimate of it, accordingly, should be presented in accordance with a *general* view-point and not by a single logical argument. One's general slant on life—perhaps, one's unuttered metaphysics—accordingly, is determinative.[42]

To those who would say that personal immortality is a selfish belief, it can be replied: was it selfish on the part of Plato to have had a concern over the survival of Socrates (*cf.* the *Phaedo*)? Without doubt there have been selfish considerations bound up with notions of personal immortality; but this is not to say that the belief is thereby discredited. There may, indeed, be a moral worth in individuality that would make it morally imperative that individuals should survive. Suppose, it has been suggested, one had an option between survival and ultimate extinction: could one morally consent to annihilation? This, of course, is to be answered only by first considering the worth of personalities: whether they are ends in themselves or mere means.

Even though a life has been a failure—in terms of higher standards—may not such a life still have potential values which ought to come to their realization eventually? Even though belief in personal immortality remains a postulate (however necessary to a rational and morally meaningful human existence) it is not an indifferent postulate; it is one that does make a difference. This does not mean that a disbelief in personal survival would necessarily make for an unethical type of living; rather such a disbelief would vitally affect the moral *meaning* of existence. In the scale of postu-

---

[42] *Immortality and Theism* (1921). Ingersoll Lecture.

lates belief in life-after-death does not rank low. Even though it may not be demonstrable it is quite highly probable. There is nothing in the way of scientific investigations nor in logical argument to disprove it.

There is something to be said for the rather universal desire and hope of a continued life after death. Man's desires and hopes are not to be summarily discounted. Dean Emeritus Charles R. Brown re-states an old argument: [43] every desire that is normal, widespread, and persistent has a corresponding satisfaction. For hunger, nature has answered back with food; for breathing, air; for knowledge, a cosmos which permits intelligence to have its play; for sex, its opposite; etc. No matter how a desire arose (whether implanted by a Creator or called out by the environment) the complementary relation of demand and supply holds. Nature has not set up a fool's paradise; nature does not call up desires to mock them. Organisms do not normally and persistently respond to fictitious and imaginary forms; in the long run, they respond to what is real. The desire to live is one among many desires; and in the higher reaches of natural evolution, with its crowning achievement of man, there are corresponding higher desires. There has emerged a desire for a life—not merely of length—that is fuller and richer and morally significant. Can it be that such a desire alone remains to mock man when in the course of evolution there have been adequate "answerings back" to fundamental needs? If so, then there is an irrationality about the whole drama of evolution. And a word more: in the course of evolution, mind has shown an ever-increasing tendency to free itself from physical control, to live a life of its own. (*Cf. e.g.*, telepathy). This tendency toward independence and autonomy strongly suggests the possibility of mind's becoming entirely liberated from present

---

[43] *Living Again* (1920). Ingersoll Lecture.

limitations and to continue a life of its own, independently free.[44]   That it is difficult for us to imagine in representation what such a condition would be—apart from bodily connections—cannot be gainsaid.   That it makes for a loss of reality-feeling is true where one's vision is of the earth earthy; that a reality-feeling for such an existence could be cultivated (*e.g.*, by discernment of the nature of our inner selves) is not without possibilities.

It is well, occasionally, to be reminded of the wisdom suggested in Shakespeare's *Hamlet*:

> There are more things in heaven and earth, Horatio,
> Than are dreamt of in your philosophy.

---

[44] On this point, the tendency of mind to transcend its physical setting and limitations, *see* the section on "Sheldon's Defence of the Soul" (Professor W. H. Sheldon of Yale) in *First Adventures,* etc., pp. 407 ff.

APPENDIX

A SELECTED LIST OF READINGS

A. General Works

I. DICTIONARIES

Encyclopedia of Religion and Ethics, 12 volumes (Scribners).
Encyclopedia of the Social Sciences, 15 volumes (Macmillan).
A Dictionary of Religion and Ethics (1921), S. Mathews and G. B.
    Smith, editors.
Dictionary of Philosophy and Psychology (1901), 3 volumes, J. M.
    Baldwin, editor.

II. MAGAZINES

The Journal of Religion, S. J. Case, editor. University of Chicago
    Press.
The Hibbert Journal (a Quarterly Review of Religion, Theology,
    and Philosophy), L. P. Jacks, editor. London: Constable.
    Boston: Leroy Phillips.
The International Journal of Ethics, T. V. Smith, editor. University
    of Chicago Press.
The London Quarterly Review, J. Telford, editor. London:
    Epworth Press.
The Christian Century (a Journal of Religion), C. C. Morrison,
    editor. Chicago: Willet, Clark Co.
Christendom (a Quarterly Journal), C. C. Morrison, editor. Chi-
    cago: Willet, Clark Co.
Religion in Life (a Christian Quarterly), J. W. Langdale, editor.
    New York: Abingdon Press.
The Personalist (a Quarterly Journal of Philosophy, Theology, and
    Literature), R. T. Flewelling, editor. The University of
    Southern California.

III. PSYCHOLOGY OF RELIGION

The Psychology of Religion (1899), E. D. Starbuck.
The Varieties of Religious Experience (1902), William James.

295

FIRST CHAPTERS IN RELIGIOUS PHILOSOPHY

The Psychology of Religious Experience (1910), E. S. Ames.
Psychology of the Religious Life (1911), G. M. Stratton.
A Psychological Study of Religion (1912), James H. Leuba.
The Psychology of Religion (1916), G. A. Coe.
The Religious Consciousness (1920), J. B. Pratt.
An Introduction to the Psychology of Religion (1923), R. H.
  Thouless.
The Psychology of Religion (1924), W. B. Selbie.
Introduction to the Psychology of Religion (1926), F. S. Hickman.
A Short Psychology of Religion (1927), G. J. Jordan.
The Psychology of Religion (1927), C. C. Josey.
An Approach to the Psychology of Religion (1927), J. C. Flower.
Recent Religious Psychology (1928), A. R. Uren.
The Psychology of Religious Adjustment (1929), E. S. Conklin.
The Psychology of Religious Awakening (1929), E. T. Clark.
A Psychological Approach to Theology (1931), W. M. Horton.
Normative Psychology of Religion (1935), H. N. Wieman and R.
  W. Wieman.
Psychology and the Promethean Will (1936), W. H. Sheldon.

The Psychology of Religious Sects (1912), H. C. McComas.
Psychology and Folk-Lore (1920), R. R. Marett.
The Belief in God and Immortality (2nd ed., 1921), James H.
  Leuba.
The Psychological and Ethical Aspects of Mormon Group Life
  (1922), E. E. Erickson.
Psychology and the Christian Life (1922), T. W. Pym.
Miracles and the New Psychology (1922), E. R. Micklem.
Primitive Mentality (tr. by L. A. Clare, 1923), L. Levy-Bruhl.
Christianity and Autosuggestion (1923), C. H. and C. E. Brooks.
Christianity and Psychology (1923), F. R. Barry.
Recent Psychology and the Christian Religion (1923), C. E. Hudson.
The Psychology of Religious Mysticism (1925), J. H. Leuba.
More Psychology and the Christian Life (1925), T. W. Pym.
Conversion: Christian and Non-Christian (1925), A. C. Under-
  wood.
The Psychology of the Methodist Revival (1926), S. G. Dimond.
Speaking With Tongues (1927), G. B. Cutten.
The Religious Attitude: A Psychological Study of its Differentiation
  (1927), A. S. Woodburne.
God or Man? (1933), James H. Leuba.
The Return to Religion (1936), H. C. Link.

IV. PHILOSOPHY OF RELIGION

Modern Theories of Religion (1910), E. S. Waterhouse.

The Philosophy of Religion (2nd ed., tr. by B. E. Meyer, 1914), Harald Höffding.

The Philosophy of Religion (1914), G. Galloway.

Outlines of a Philosophy of Religion (no date), A. Sabatier.

Problems of Religion (1916), Durant Drake.

Theology As An Empirical Science (1919), D. C. Macintosh.

A Student's Philosophy of Religion (1922, rev. ed., 1935), W. K. Wright.

The Philosophy of Religion (1924), D. M. Edwards.

The Reasonableness of Christianity (1925), D. C. Macintosh.

Religious Experience and Scientific Method (1926), H. N. Wieman.

The Wrestle of Religion with Truth (1927), H. N. Wieman.

The Interpretation of Religion (1928), John Baillie.

"Philosophy of Religion," E. Leroux in *Philosophy Today* (1928), edited by E. L. Schaub.

"Interpretations of Religion," E. L. Schaub in *op. cit.*

Religion (1929), E. S. Ames.

Christianity and Philosophy (1932), D. M. Edwards.

The Meaning and Truth of Religion (1933), E. W. Lyman.

The Two Sources of Morality and Religion (transl. ed., 1935), H. Bergson.

American Philosophies of Religion (1936), H. N. Wieman and B. E. Meland. _____

What Is Religion? (1907), W. Bousset.

The Sources of Religious Insight (1912, 1914), Josiah Royce.

The Problem of Christianity (2 vols., 1913, 1914), Josiah Royce.

The Meaning of God in Human Experience (1916), W. E. Hocking.

The Reign of Religion in Contemporary Philosophy (1920), S. Radhakrishnan.

Christianity in its Modern Expression (1921), G. B. Foster. Edited by D. C. Macintosh.

Present Tendencies in Religious Thought (1924), A. C. Knudson.

Essays and Addresses on the Philosophy of Religion (2nd series, 1926), F. Hügel.

Religion in the Making (1926), A. N. Whitehead.

The Science of Religion (1927), L. G. Rohrbaugh.

The Pilgrimage of Buddhism and a Buddhist Pilgrimage (1928), J. B. Pratt.

Religious Thought in the Last Quarter-Century (1928), edited by G. B. Smith.

Current Christian Thinking (1928), G. B. Smith.
Methods of Private Religious Living (1929), H. N. Wieman.
Belief Unbound (1930), W. P. Montague.
The Issues of Life (1931), H. N. Wieman.
Religious Realism (1931), edited by D. C. Macintosh.
The Pilgrimage of Faith (1931), D. C. Macintosh.
Contemporary American Theology. Theological Autobiographies.
   Vol. I (1932); Vol. II (1933). Edited by Vergilius Ferm.
Realistic Theology (1934), W. M. Horton.
A Common Faith (1934), John Dewey.
God and the Common Life (1935), R. L. Calhoun.
Present Theological Tendencies (1936), E. E. Aubrey.
Contemporary English Theology (1936), W. M. Horton.

A History of the Warfare of Science with Theology (1896), 2 vols.,
   A. D. White.
Christian Thought to the Reformation (1911), H. B. Workman.
Protestant Thought Before Kant (reprint, 1922), A. C. McGiffert.
An Outline of the History of Christian Thought Since Kant (1911),
   E. C. Moore.
The Rise of Modern Religious Ideas (1915), A. C. McGiffert.
A History of the Christian Church (1918), W. Walker.
The Story of Religions in America (1930), W. W. Sweet.
A History of Christian Thought, Vol. I (1932); Vol. II (1933);
   A. C. McGiffert.

Problems That Perplex (1923), J. W. G. Ward.
Religious Perplexities (1923), L. P. Jacks.
The Christian Doctrine of Health (1923), L. Dougall.
What Is Modernism? (1924), Leighton Parks.
Adventurous Religion (1926), H. E. Fosdick.
Does Civilization Need Religion? (1927), R. Niebuhr.
Conflicts in Religious Thought (1929), Georgia Harkness.
Beliefs That Matter (1929), W. A. Brown.
Pathways to Certainty (1930), W. A. Brown.
The New Freedom in the Natural Order (1931), C. F. Wishart.
What Can We Believe? (1933), J. G. Gilkey.
The Social Gospel and the Christian Cultus (1933), C. C. Morrison.
Speaking of Religion (1935), Bruce Curry.
The Church at Work in the Modern World (1935), edited by W.
   C. Bower.
Philosophy and Faith (1936), Dorothy M. Emmet.
The Testimony of the Soul (1936), Rufus Jones.

The Resources of Religion (1936), Georgia Harkness.
The Short Bible (1933), edited by E. J. Goodspeed and J. M. P. Smith.
The Unknown Bible (1926), C. H. Moehlman.
The Literature of the Old Testament in Its Historical Development (1924), J. A. Bewer.
The Literature of the New Testament (1932), E. F. Scott.

B. LITERATURE RELATIVE TO CHAPTER TOPICS

For a more complete list consult references given in the text (including footnotes) of each chapter.

For a list of readings of philosophical works, more general in character, consult the Appendix to the author's *First Adventures in Philosophy* (1936).

CHAPTER I. ENTANGLED RELIGIOUS EXPRESSIONS

Elements of the Science of Religion (1897, 2 vols.), C. P. Tiele.
In Tune With the Infinite (1897), R. W. Trine.
The Making of Religion (1898), A. Lang.
The Native Tribes of Central Australia (1899), B. Spencer and F. J. Gillen.
Lectures on the Origin and Growth of Religion (1901), M. Müller.
Magic and Religion (1901), A. Lang.
The Study of Religion (1901), M. Jastrow.
The Varieties of Religious Experience, A Study in Human Nature (1902), William James.
Religions of Primitive Peoples (1905), D. G. Brinton.
Folkways (1906), W. G. Sumner.
The Threshold of Religion (1909), R. R. Marett.
Native Tribes of South-east Australia, A. W. Howitt.
Primitive Traits in Religious Revivals (1910), F. M. Davenport.
The Psychology of Religious Experience (1910), E. S. Ames.
The Development of Religion (1910), Irving King.
Primitive Culture (5th ed., 1913, 2 vols.), E. B. Tylor.
Elements of Folk Psychology (tr. by E. L. Schaub, 1916), Wilhelm Wundt.
The History of Religions (1918), E. W. Hopkins.
The Greek View of Life (13th ed., 1920), G. L. Dickinson.
Pagan and Christian Creeds (1920), E. Carpenter.
Accepting the Universe (1920), John Burroughs.

Modern Religious Cults and Movements (1923), G. G. Atkins.
The Origin and Evolution of Religion (1923), E. W. Hopkins.
The Golden Bough (abridged ed., 1923), J. G. Frazer.
The Birth and Growth of Religion (1924), G. F. Moore.
Yoga as Philosophy and Religion (1924), S. Dasgupta.
The World's Living Religions (1924), R. E. Hume.
The Religion of Yesterday and To-Morrow (1925), Kirsopp Lake.
The Idea of the Holy (tr. by J. W. Harvey, 3rd imp., 1925),
    Rudolf Otto.
The Elementary Forms of the Religious Life (tr., reprint, 1926),
    E. Durkheim.
The Worship of Nature (1926), J. G. Frazer.
Humanist Sermons (1927), edited by C. W. Reese.
The Hindu View of Life (1927), S. Radhakrishnan.
The Confusion of Tongues (1928), C. W. Ferguson.
The Quest of the Ages (1929), A. E. Haydon.
Experience With the Supernatural in Early Christian Times (1929),
    S. J. Case.
Tongues of Fire, "A Bible of Sacred Scriptures of the Pagan World"
    (1929), compiled by Grace H. Turnbull.
On the Religious Frontier, "From an Outpost of Ethical Religion"
    (1931), P. Chubb.
The Religion of Man (1931), R. Tagore.
Religion in Various Cultures (1932), H. L. Friess and H. W.
    Schneider.
"The Dark Side of Religion," Morris R. Cohen. Essay in *Religion
    Today* (1933), edited by A. L. Swift, pp. 75 ff.
Varieties of American Religion (1936), edited by C. S. Braden.
Living Religions and Modern Thought (1936), A. G. Widgery.

CHAPTER II. MISTAKEN NOTIONS

On Definitions:

"Definitions of Religion and Critical Comments," Appendix in *A
    Psychological Study of Religion* (1912), James H. Leuba.
"The Definition of Religion: A Symposium" in *The Journal of
    Religion*, Vol. VII, Nos. 2 and 3, March and May, 1927. E.
    S. Brightman, D. Drake, A. E. Haydon, R. E. Hume, E. S.
    Ames, and H. N. Wieman.
"The Recovery of the Religious Sentiment," W. K. Wright. Vol.
    II, pp. 341 ff., in *Contemporary American Theology* (1933),
    edited by Vergilius Ferm.
Also Consult Readings listed under "General Works."

CHAPTER III. DEFINITIONS

"Scientific Naturalism: A Platform for the Church Historian," Vergilius Ferm, in *The Journal of Religion*, Vol. XIV, No. 4, October, 1934.
"Religion, Theology, and Philosophy," Chapter III in *First Adventures in Philosophy* (1936), Vergilius Ferm.

CHAPTER IV. TRADITIONAL ARGUMENTS FOR BELIEF IN GOD

The Evolution of Theology in the Greek Philosophers (2 vols., 1904), E. Caird.
The Idea of God: Historical, Critical, Constructive (1922), C. A. Beckwith.
The God of the Early Christians (1924), A. C. McGiffert.
Kant's Philosophy of Religion (1926), C. C. J. Webb.
Religion Within the Limits of Reason Alone, I. Kant. Edited by T. M. Greene and H. Hudson.
Also Consult Readings listed under "General Works."

CHAPTER V. CONTEMPORARY ARGUMENTS FOR BELIEF IN GOD

Theism (1887, 1902), Borden P. Bowne.
Christian Mysticism (1899, 3rd ed., 1913), W. R. Inge.
Mysticism (1913), E. Underhill.
The Meaning of God in Human Experience (1916), W. E. Hocking.
The Experience of God in Modern Life (1918), E. W. Lyman.
God and Personality (1919), C. C. J. Webb.
The Idea of God in the Light of Recent Philosophy (2nd rev. ed., 1920), A. S. Pringle-Pattison.
At One With the Invisible (1921), edited by E. H. Sneath.
What and Where Is God? (1921), R. L. Swain.
Recent Theistic Discussion (1921), W. L. Davidson.
"Religious Apriorism," A. C. Knudson in *Studies in Philosophy and Theology* (1922), edited by E. C. Wilm.
Fundamental Ends of Life: What Men Want (1924), Rufus Jones.
Moral Values and the Idea of God (3rd ed., 1924), W. R. Sorley.
Religious Values (1925), E. S. Brightman.

The Reasonableness of Christianity (1925), D. C. Macintosh.
Religion in the Philosophy of William James (1926), J. S. Bixler.
Reality (1926), B. H. Streeter.
The Christlike God (1927), F. J. McConnell.
Hindu Mysticism (1927), S. Dasgupta.
My Idea of God (1927), edited by J. F. Newton.
New Studies in Mystical Religion (1927), Rufus Jones.
The Word of God and the Word of Man (tr. by D. Horton, 1928),
    Karl Barth.
Studies in Christian Philosophy (2nd ed., 1928), W. R. Matthews.
The Theology of Crisis (1929), H. E. Brunner.
The Doctrine of God (1930, 2nd imp. 1934), A. C. Knudson.
Belief Unbound (1930), W. P. Montague.
Philosophical Theology, Vol. II, "The World, the Soul, and God"
    (1930), F. R. Tennant.
Theism and the Modern Mood (1930), W. M. Horton.
The Finding of God (1931), E. S. Brightman.
The Growth of the Idea of God (1931), Shailer Mathews.
"God and Emergent Evolution," W. K. Wright in *Religious Realism*
    (1931), edited by D. C. Macintosh.
The Natural and the Supernatural (1931), J. W. Oman.
Contemporary Philosophy and Thomistic Principles (1932), R. G.
    Bandas.
"The Ontological Argument in Royce and Others," W. E. Hocking.
    Essay IV in *Contemporary Idealism in America* (1932), edited
    by C. Barrett.
"God and Cosmic Structure," J. E. Boodin. Essay IX in *op. cit.*
Is There a God? "Conversations," by Wieman, Macintosh, and Otto
    (1932), edited by C. C. Morrison.
"Theology as Group Belief," Shailer Mathews in *Contemporary
    American Theology*, Vol. II (1933), edited by Vergilius Ferm.
Christianity and Personality (1936), J. W. Buckham.
Also Consult Readings listed under "General Works."

CHAPTER VI. CURRENT THEORIES OF VALUE

A Study in the Logic of Value (1929), Mary E. Clarke.
"God and Value," H. N. Wieman in *Religious Realism* (1931),
    edited by D. C. Macintosh.
"The Concept of Supreme Value," Chap. III in *Normative Psy-
    chology of Religion* (1935), H. N. Wieman and R. W.
    Wieman.

CHAPTER VII. EVIL, THEODICY, AND PESSIMISM

Studies in Good and Evil (1898), Josiah Royce.
The Mystery of Pain (1905), James Hinton.
The Theory of Good and Evil (2 vols., 1907, 2nd ed., 1924), H. Rashdall.
Human Nature and Its Remaking (1918), W. E. Hocking.
God in a World at War (1918), D. C. Macintosh.
The Disease and Remedy of Sin (no date), W. M. Mackay.
Human Nature and the Social Order (1922), G. H. Cooley.
The Christian Idea of Sin and Original Sin in the Light of Modern Knowledge (1922), E. J. Bicknell.
The Doctrine of Sin (1922), R. S. Moxon.
Psychology and Morals (1926), J. A. Hadfield.
God and Pain (1927), G. Stewart.
The Problem of Evil (1931), R. A. Tsanoff.
Belief Unbound (1930), W. P. Montague.
The Art of Ministering to the Sick (1936), R. C. Cabot and R. L. Dicks. Chap. VII, "Pain"; Chap. VIII, "Evil."
Also Consult Readings listed under "General Works."

CHAPTER VIII. THE SOUL IN ANCIENT AND MEDIEVAL THOUGHT

A History of Psychology, "Ancient and Patristic" (1912), G. S. Brett.
The Idea of the Soul (1924), J. Laird.
First Adventures in Philosophy (1936), Vergilius Ferm. Chap. XVIII, "Recent Theories of Soul-Mind."
Also Consult Readings listed under "General Works."

CHAPTER IX. HUMAN FREEDOM AND THE WORLD OF REALITY

A System of Ethics (1899), Bk. II, Chap. IV, F. Paulsen.
Time and Free Will (1910), H. Bergson.
The Problem of Freedom (1911), G. H. Palmer.
Free Will and Human Responsibility (1912), H. H. Horne.
The Unique Status of Man (The Freewill Problem in the Light of Modern Scientific Developments, 1928), H. W. Carr.
The Freedom of Man (1935), A. H. Compton.
First Adventures in Philosophy (1936), Vergilius Ferm. Chap.

XVI, "Readings from Nature: Mechanism and Vitalism";
Chap. XVII, "Readings from Nature: Chance and Purpose."
Also Consult Readings listed under "General Works."

CHAPTER X. RECONSIDERING PRAYER

The Meaning of Prayer (1915), H. E. Fosdick.
"The Psychology of Power," Essay III, J. A. Hadfield, in *The Spirit* (1919, 1922), Streeter and others.
The Philosophy of Prayer (1922), C. K. Mahoney.
The Psychology of Prayer (1923), K. R. Stolz.
In Defence of Christian Prayer (1925), E. J. Bicknell.
The Life of Prayer in a World of Science (1927), W. A. Brown. Consult the Bibliography in this volume.
Methods of Private Religious Living (1929), H. N. Wieman.
Prayer (tr. and edited by S. McComb, 1932), Friedrich Heiler.
"Prayer," Chap. VII in *Normative Psychology of Religion* (1935), H. N. Wieman and R. W. Wieman.

CHAPTER XI. HUMAN IMMORTALITY

Is Immortality Desirable? (1909), G. L. Dickinson.
The Christian Hope (1912), W. A. Brown.
The Assurance of Immortality (1913), H. E. Fosdick.
Metempsychosis (1914), G. F. Moore.
Pagan Ideas of Immortality during the Early Roman Empire (1918), C. H. Moore.
The Idea of Immortality (1919), G. Galloway.
Greek Hero Cults and Ideas of Immortality (1921), L. R. Farnell.
The Belief in God and Immortality (2nd ed., 1921), James H. Leuba.
Religion and The Future Life (1922), edited by E. Hershey Sneath.
Immortality (1922), B. H. Streeter and others.
The Idea of Immortality (1922), A. Seth Pringle-Pattison.
Immortality (1924), edited by J. Marchant.
A Living Universe (1924), L. P. Jacks.
Immortality in Post-Kantian Idealism (1925), E. S. Brightman.
Spiritual Values and Eternal Life (1927), H. E. Fosdick.
The Meaning of Selfhood and Faith in Immortality (1928), E. W. Lyman.
Why I Believe in Personal Immortality (1929), Oliver Lodge.
Pagan Regeneration (1929), H. R. Willoughby.
Phantom Walls (1930), Oliver Lodge.

APPENDIX

Theism and the Present Mood (1931), J. S. Bixler.
Immortality and the Cosmic Process (1933), Shailer Mathews.
And the Life Everlasting (1933), John Baillie.
Indian Conceptions of Immortality (1934), W. E. Clark.
The Chances of Surviving Death (1934), W. P. Montague.
The Illusion of Immortality (1935), C. Lamont.
Forty Years of Psychic Research (1936), H. Garland.
First Adventures in Philosophy (1936), Vergilius Ferm.   Chap.
    XIX, "The Relation of Mind and Body."
Also Consult Readings listed under "General Works."

INDEX

(The Appendix to this book is not indexed)

Abelard, 180.
absolute idealism, *see* idealism, metaphysical.
absolutism, 98-100, 104.
absolutistic theory of value, *see* value.
abstractionism, 212.
Adam, 156, 157, 218, 219.
Adventists, Seventh Day, 265.
agnosticism, 75, 107, 170, 250, 254.
Alexander VI, Pope, 9.
Alexander, S., 170.
Alexandria, 77, 196 ff., 199.
allegorism, 197, 199.
Allis, C., 31.
Almagro, 31.
Ames, E. S., 48, 49, 59.
Amos, 150.
analytic type of argument for personal immortality, *see* immortality, personal.
Anaxagoras, 190.
angels, 203, 205.
Anselm, 80, 81, 82, 97, 201.
anthropomorphism, 171, 242, 264, 267. *See* fallacy.
antinomianism, 239.
antinomies, Kantian, 124, 227.
apathy, as attitude, 118.
apathy, 195.
apocryphal books, 196.
Apollo, cult of, 189.
apologetics, 126, 170; and the resurrection, 268 ff.
Apostles' Creed, 265.
appreciative view of value, *see* value.
a priori, moral, 92, 102.
a priorism, 117; *see* religious, *a priorism*.
Aquinas, Thomas, 78 ff., 80; and the "Medieval Synthesis," 76 ff.; his three explanations of evil, 157-158; on the soul, 202 ff.; and human freedom and God, 233 ff.; on immortality and resurrection, 265.
Arabian philosophers, 201, 202.
Araucanian Indians, 31 ff.

argument from opposites, *see* analytic type of argument.
Aristotle, 76-78, 82, 135, 157, 171, 174, 197, 233; Aristotelianism, 75, 79, 80, 188, 194, 196, 264, 265; on the soul, 191 ff.; Aristotelianism of, 193, 194, 202, 203, 205; Platonism in, 193, 202, 203; rediscovery of, 201, 202; creative *vs.* passive reason, 192-194, 202 ff.; Christian Aristotle, 202; on God, 203.
Arminius, Arminians, 224.
art, 257; Schopenhauer on, 182. *See* esthetic experience.
asceticism, 182, 190.
aspectual view, the, 214, 226 ff., 229 ff., 235.
atheism, 30, 52, 62, 70, 75, 115, 163, 170, 221, 248, 250.
Atkins, G. G., 283.
Attis, the god-lover, 14 ff.
attitudes toward life, 118.
Augustine, St., and Augustinianism, 79, 155-158, 224; on the soul, 200-201; on freedom and determinism, 218-219.
Australian bushmen, 52.
authoritarianism, 260.
autosuggestion, *see* prayer.
Averroes, 201.
axiology, the term, 143.

Bacon, 83.
Baillie, John, 108 ff.
Bakewell, C. M., 192, 277.
Balfour, A. J., 285.
Baptist preacher, pioneer, 19 ff.
Barnes, H. E., 170.
Barrett, Wm., 285.
Barry, F. R., 160.
beatitude, 234.
behaviorism, 137, 211, 222.
Bergson, H., 215, 279; on metaphysical freedom, 219-221; on the mind-body relation, 274.
Berkeley, G., 104.
best of possible worlds, 162, 164, 169, 178.

Bible, the, 149, 224, *see* Old Testament; New Testament.
biblical criticism, *see* criticism, biblical; historical criticism.
Bicknell, E. J., 160.
biocentric — psychocentric theory of value, *see* value.
Bird, J. M., 287 ff.
Boas, F., 185.
Boehme, J., 96.
body and mind, *see* mind and body; dependence of mind upon brain.
Bower, Jacob, pioneer Baptist preacher, 19 ff.; 24.
Bradley, F. H., and freedom, 229, 231.
brain, *see* mind and body; dependence of mind upon brain.
Brightman, E. S., theodicy of, 164; 170 ff.
Brogan, A. P., 131, 132.
Brown, C. R., 293.
Brown, W., 160.
Brown, W. A., 51.
Bucer, 223.
Buddhism, 10, 46, 52, 53, 176, 182.

Caird, E., 104.
Caird, J., 104.
Calvin, J., 223.
Calvinism, extreme, 224, 225.
carpenter theory, 83 ff.
Carr, H. A., 208.
categorical imperative, 86, 87, 91, 229; three necessary postulates of, 87 ff.
categories of mind, 228.
Catholicism, 80, 206, 265; contemporary, 78, 79; mystics, 96; missionaries, 31 ff.; traditional views of sin and evil, 155 ff. *See* Aquinas.
causation, 231; and Hume, 228; types of, 204; kinds of, efficient, physical, transeunt, immanent, final, 240 ff.; cause, efficient, 191; impersonal type, 212; final, 192.
chance, 147, 165, 166, 211, 217, 223, 230, 236, 237, 239, 240, 244, 245.
character and freedom, 217, 218. *See* moral responsibility; freedom.
Charles, R. H., 197.

chess-player analogy, 239-240.
children and Puritanism, *see* Puritanism and children.
Christianity, 46, 71, 145, 153 ff., 169, 170, 196, 199, 201, 205, 206, 219, 223; early doctrines of soul, 197 ff.; and Platonism, 201; and Stoicism, 195; and spiritualism, 290; and immortality, 265, 291; and resurrection, 267 ff. *See* Jesus.
Christian-Jewish tradition, 147, 148 ff.
Christian Science, 53, 146, 183.
Christology, 79.
Cicero, 101.
Clement of Alexandria, 198, 199.
Clotho, Lachesis, Atropos, 223.
Coe, G. A., 169.
Cohen, M. R., 49, 170.
coincidence, 247, 287.
communication with spirits, 283 ff., 285 ff. *See* spiritualism.
communion, 16, 17.
concretion, principle of, 125.
Confucianism, 46.
conservatism in religion, *see* religious conservatism; Fundamentalism.
Contemporary American Philosophy, 143, 169.
Contemporary American Theology, 51, 96, 124, 126, 240.
conversion, 16 ff.; 19 ff.; 28.
Cook, E. F., 26 ff.
Copernican universe, 270.
cosmological argument, 76, 79, 80, 82, 83, 85, 91, 124, 126.
creation, *see* God, self-limitation.
critical monism, *see* knowledge.
criticism, biblical, 149; lower and higher, 149. *See* historical criticism.
Critique of Practical Reason, 87.
Critique of Pure Reason, 87.
Crookes, W., 285.
cult, the, of the vague, 33 ff.
cults, *see* religious cults; mystery cults; *Magna Mater;* Todas, the; Lough Derg; Peyote cult.
cursives, the, 149.
cyclic routine, 223.

Dante, 176, 260.
Darrow, C., 170.

Davenport, F. M., 11 ff.
dead, the, silence of, and possibility of immortality, 275, 276.
death, 257, 260, 277, 279; value of, 169.
Deists, eighteenth century, 101.
Demos, R., 277.
Denck, H., 96.
dependence of mind upon brain, kinds of, 273 ff.; and possibility of personal immortality 272 ff.
Descartes, R., 80-82, 206.
determinism, 165, 228, 230-233, 235; meanings of, 243; disguised, 172, 234, 236; extreme, 214, 221; hard and soft, 236; scientific, 221 ff.; methodological, 211-213, 221 ff., 241 ff.; and metaphysics, 215, 223; and self determinism, 243-245; in Koheleth, 153; in Stoicism, 195; Sheldon's view, 244, 245; and theodicy, 165 ff.; dilemma of, 172, 236 ff.; criticism of, 220, 225, 226; *vs.* freedom, 220, 224; and freedom both affirmed, 214-216; and freedom as aspects of reality, 214, 226 ff.; and freedom, aspectual view, 235. *See* predestination; freedom; mechanism; causation.
Devil, the, 82, 93, 147, 163, 173; worship of, 31 ff.
Dewey, John, 147, 170, 183.
dialectic Hegelian, 230; of Hocking, 98, 99.
dichotomy, 188, 197.
Dionysus cult, 189.
dogmatism, 97, 249.
Dougall, Lily, 283.
dualism, metaphysical, 147, 164; and evil, 156.
duality, principle of, 245.
Dubs, H. H., 141.
Dunkards, the, 19 ff.
dyadic principle, 245.
dysteleologies, 29, 85, 155, 173.

early environment, influence of, 222.
Eaton, H. O., 143.
Ecclesiastes, *see* Koheleth.
Edwards, Jonathan, 25, 223.
Ehrenfels, C. von, 143.
election, 224, 225, 280.

elective theory of value, *see* value.
Eleusinian cult, 189.
Elihu, 152.
Eliot, George, 255, 256, 258.
emanation, 200.
Emerson, R. W., 29, 53, 96.
emotional type of argument for personal immortality, *see* immortality, personal.
Empedocles, 190.
empiricism, religious, 115 ff., 126. *See* religious realism; intuitionism; mysticism; perception, religious; knowledge.
English school of psychologists, 159 ff.
Enoch, 147.
Epicureanism, 153, 195.
epistemology, *see* knowledge.
esthetic experience, and immortality, 257; feelings, 263.
Ethical Culture, 53.
ethics and ethical life, *see* God; immortality; religion; virtue; *summum bonum;* moral consciousness; moral responsibility; freedom; *a priori,* moral.
Evil, Chap. VII, 95, 127, 128, 174 ff., 178 ff., 207, 219, 276, 277; origin of, 156-158, 162, 178; classification of, 145 ff.; physical and natural, 146, 165 ff.; moral, 146, 168, 169; metaphysical, 146, 147; as value, 139 ff., 141 ff.; as negative interest, 146; as imperfection, 162; as differentiation, 157; as a lack, 156, 158; as illusion, 146; as insoluble, 147; traditional Catholic views of, 155 ff.; and sex, 156; and immortality, 277, 280; mitigation of, 167 ff.; *vs.* good, 276 ff.; and good, relative, 135 ff.; as contrast to good, 157; and the higher good, 146, 147, 162. *See* dysteleologies; theodicy; good, the; pessimism; pain; suffering, human.
evolution, 36, 181, 209, 215, 260, 272, 273; creative, 220; and theodicy, 162, 163, 165 ff., 167; and immortality, 280, 293.
expansion of feeling, *see* fallacy.
expression, free, 160.
Ezekiel, 150.

faculty psychology, 4, 38, 211, 217.
faith, 77-79, 90, 107, 108 ff., 117, 120, 126; in justification of, 111 ff.; ladder of James, 114. *See* proof *vs.* possibility.
Fall, the, 147, 156, 157, 219, 224.
fallacy of analogy, 242; of anthropomorphism, 242; of begging the question, 81, 277; of intellect, 220, 221; of misplaced concreteness, 212; pathetic, 247, 248; *post hoc ergo propter hoc*, 242; psychological, expansion of feeling, 180; rationalization, 247; re-ification of abstractions, 61, 252; wishful thinking, 250, 251.
fatalism, 223.
fear, *see* religious attitude and fear.
feeling, expansion of, psychological fallacy, 180; and intellect, 279, 291, 292.
Fenn, W. W., on personal immortality, 291, 292.
Ferguson, C. W., 283.
Fichte, 173.
finiteness of God, *see* God.
First Adventures in Philosophy, 75, 76, 78, 80, 85, 86, 96, 99, 104, 110, 113, 117, 124, 126, 139, 144, 146, 173, 174, 180, 190, 192, 194, 199, 201, 206, 211, 213, 219, 223, 225, 226, 228, 230, 237, 240, 245, 257, 266, 272, 274, 294.
"first principle," 233.
Fleming, S., 25, 26.
Flower, J. C., 18.
foreknowledge, 232, 233; criticism of, 234; a disguised determinism, 172.
Formula of Concord, inconsistency in, 224.
Fortune, 223.
fortune tellers, 287.
Fourth Gospel, the, 197.
Fox, G., 96.
Fox sisters, the, 284.
freedom, human and the world of reality, Chap. IX, 120, 124, 125, 164-169, 172, 273, 293, 294; three-fold classification of views, 214 ff.; Eastern *vs.* Western thought of, 156; re-interpreted, 223; the freedom of the will, 208 ff., 237; and modern psychology, 211 ff.; moral argument for, 236 ff.; and character, 217, 218; compromise solutions, 214, 216, 235 ff., 240 ff., 244 ff.; "higher," 230, 231, 235, 236, 245-246; *vs.* determinism, 220, 224; and higher determinism, 220; and determinism both affirmed, 214-216; and determinism as aspects of reality, 214, 226 ff., 229 ff.; and determinism, aspectual view, 235; and metaphysics, 213 ff., 215-216, 226 ff.; and metaphysical idealism, 235; and absolute idealism, 229 ff.; Kant on, 87, 88; Augustine on, 218-219; in the thought of Aquinas, 233 ff.; Bergson's metaphysical, 219-221; and Hegel, 229, 230; and T. H. Green, 229-231; and Royce, 231 ff.; and Bradley, 229, 231; and James Ward, 240 ff.; and William James, 236 ff.; Sheldon's view, 244, 245. *See* libertarianism; indeterminism.
Freud, S., 170.
Fundamentalism, 53, 265.
funeral customs, 262; sermons, 225.

Galen, C., 199.
Gaunilo, 80, 81.
Gestalt, psychology, 212.
Gilson, E., 202.
"given," the doctrine of, 172 ff.
Glacier National Park, episode, 26 ff.
Gnosticism, 199.
gnosticism, James's, 238.
God, definition of, 52 ff., 61-63, 69 ff.; difficulties of definition, 56; deacon's definition, 264; traditional arguments for belief in, Chap. IV, 126, 260; lack of argument for in Western Christian thought, 75; contemporary arguments for belief in, Chap. V, 261; existence as axiomatic, 101; argument from religious experience, 94 ff.; and the mystic claim, 95 ff.; and value-argument and Ritschlianism, 104 ff.; moral-religious-faith

argument, 108 ff.; the religious *"a priori"* argument, 100 ff.; existence, pragmatic argument, 110 ff.; favors life of feeling, 115; moral optimism—religious empiricism argument, 115 ff.; inadequate notions of, 260; traditional attributes, 171; contemporary substitute gods, 170 ff.; character involved in possibility of immortality, 279; as finite, 147, 164, 171 ff.; self-limitation of, 163, 169, 174, 246; *vs.* the absolute, 233; interference with natural law, 166 ff., 247, 251; and the mitigation of evils, 167 ff.; power and goodness, 163 ff.; as suffering, 151, 154, 155, 174, 179; as struggling, 164; in need of redemption, 178 ff.; inadequate conceptions of, and prayer, 250; and personal immortality, 291; and metaphysics, 75; and metaphysical idealism, 103, 104; belief in, and ethical conduct, 260; of Aristotle, 203; traditional Aristotelian conception, 171 ff., 174; in the thought of Aquinas, 233 ff.; James's conception of, 114, 115; Wieman's conception of, 125, 126. *See,* teleological argument; cosmological argument; ontological argument; moral argument; theism; deism; pantheism; religion; religious.

good, the, 127, 128, 145, 276; as value, 139 ff., 141 ff.; *vs.* evil, 276 ff.; and evil relative, 135 ff.

gospel of futility, 179.

Gospels, the, and the soul, 197, 198.

grace, 156, 224.

Graeco-Roman world, religious and philosophical cults, 194 ff.

Greek religion, 189.

Greek thought, 75, 77 ff., 149, 154-156, 174, 186, 188 ff., 191 ff., 194 ff., 196 ff., 198 ff., 223, 267; amalgamation with Hebrew, 196 ff.

Green, T. H., and freedom, 229-231.

Green, T. M., 87.

Habakkuk, 151.

Hades, 189.

Hadfield, J. A., 160.

Hall, G. S., 285.

Hall, H. J., 256.

Hamlet, 294.

happiness, 89 ff., 175, 179 ff., 261; *see* pleasure; optimism.

Harris, W. T., 104.

Hastings, J., 198.

Haydon, A. E., 48, 119, 147.

heaven, 260; a psychological reflection, 266.

Hebrews, 75; thought, 148 ff., 189, 198, 223; amalgamation with Greek, 196 ff.; and soul, 188; on suffering, 150 ff.; and personal immortality, 260, 261. *See* Judaism.

hedonism, 180 ff.

Hegel, G. W. F., 39, 41, 47, 65, 96, 104, 105, 176, 177; and freedom, 229, 230.

hell, 25, 26, 31 ff., 207, 225, 260, 266.

Hesiod, 223.

higher criticism, *see* criticism, biblical; historical criticism.

Hilaria, day of, 15.

Hinduism, 96, 223, 262.

historical criticism, 266; and the resurrection, 268 ff.; and literary criticism, 149.

Hobhouse, L. T., 161.

Hocking, W. E., 97 ff., 104, 117, 161.

Höffding, H., 170, 180, 183.

Holmes, J. H., 164.

holy, the idea of, 101 ff.

Homer, 189.

Horton, W. M., 160.

Hosea, 150.

Houdini, 285.

Hudson, C. E., 160.

humanism, 96, 147, 260; extreme, 52, 119; religious, 26 ff., 50, 51, 53.

human suffering, *see* suffering, human.

Hume, D., 228.

Hume, R. E., 52.

Huxley, Julian, 170.

Hydesville, N. Y., 284.

hylomorphism of Aristotle, 192.

Hyslop, J., 285.

idealism, metaphysical, 97 ff., 99, 100, 103, 104, 110, 117, 146, 147, 221; contemporary, 104; and freedom, 229 ff., 235; and immortality, 281, 282; affectivistic, 257; Platonic, 76; absolute, 147; and freedom, 229 ff.; and immortality, 257, 259, 281, 282.

idolatry, 250, 251. *See* God, contemporary substitute gods.

ignorance, 166, 167.

immortality, human, Chap. XI, 163, 189-191, 197, 199, 201; kinds of, 255 ff.; double, 256; chemical, 257, 258; biological or plasmal, 257, 258; of absorption, 257, 258, 283; social, 257, 258; of value, 257, 258; of influence, 255 ff., 258; ideal, 256, 257, 259, 264; Christian, 265; and æsthetic experience, 257; and absolute idealism, 257, 259; and scientific approach, 273 ff.; and culture, 266; and human suffering, 280; and individuality, 255-259, 283; in Hebrew thought, 150, 152, 153, 260, 261; in Old Testament, 188, 197; in early Greek religion, 189; possibility of in Aristotle, 192, 193; in Paul, 197, 198; Kant on, 88 ff.

immortality, personal, 120, 166, 167, 198, 202-204; ideas of, 263 ff.; criticism of other views, 257 ff.; arguments in favor, 276-294; and the moral argument, 279 ff., 292; emotional type of argument, 278, 279; analytic type of argument, 276 ff.; widespread hope of, argument from, 293; and the empirical proofs, 282 ff.; and religious experience, 282; empirical assurance of from religious experience, 290 ff.; historical form of the empirical proof, 268, 282; summary considerations in favor of, 291 ff.; and crude notions, 260; modern difficulties in belief in, 259-276; 262, 263; questionnaires on, 260 ff.; is it desirable?, 260; is it desirable for all?, 280, 281, 292; can extinction be morally justified?, 280, 292; is it selfish?,

292; can the mind survive the brain?, 272 ff.; and the mind-body problem, 272 ff.; three factors which make for psychological reality of, 263 ff.; and the principle of reality-feeling, 259, 261 ff., 263 ff., 294; and irrationality of the universe, 293; and rational universe, 258; and values, 279 ff., 292; and God, 291; and the character of God, 279 ff.; conditional, 280, 281; and the doctrine of means *vs.* ends, 281, 283, 292; and evil, 280; and evolution, 293; and further opportunity, 280 (*see* Kant); and the finite individual, 283; and metaphysical idealism, 281, 282; and extreme mysticism, 282, 283; and the ethical life, 260, 261, 292; and communication, 275; and spiritualism, 283 ff., 288 ff.; and the silence of the dead, 275, 276; and resurrection, 267; and Jesus, 291; and Christianity, 291; Royce on, 282; Fenn on, 291, 292; C. R. Brown on, 293; Macintosh on, 290, 291. *See* resurrection; Psychical Research, Society of.

immutability, 171, 172.

impassibility, 171, 173.

impotence of will, 224. *See* original sin; freedom.

indefinability of value, *see* value.

indeterminacy, principle of, and human freedom, 213.

indeterminism, 216, 236, 245. *See* libertarianism; freedom.

Indians, the, *see* Winnebago, the; Araucanian, the.

infinite regress, 82, 124.

infinity *vs.* finity, 124.

infralapsarianism, 224.

Ingersoll lectures, 263.

instincts, 159-161; defined, 160-161; modifiability of, 161; religious, *see* religious instinct.

intellect and feeling, 279, 291, 292. *See* reason, inadequacy of; knowledge.

interest, as value, *see* value; negative, evil, 146.

intrinsic values, *see* value.

intuition and intuitionism, 77, 91, 97-100, 103, 105, 107, 110, 121, 122, 126, 134, 220, 241, 242; older, 101. *See* Knowledge; mysticism.
inversion, religious, 24, 66.
Irenaeus of Lyons, 149.
Isaiah of Jerusalem, 150.
Isaiah—Second, of the Exile, 151.

Jainism, 52.
James, St., 42, 224.
James, William, ix, 53 ff., 63, 116, 118, 124, 127, 147, 173, 177, 246, 285; pragmatic argument for God's existence, 110 ff.; on skepticism, 113; faith-ladder, 114; will to believe, 120; meliorism, 118 ff.; and freedom, 236 ff.; chess-player, analogy of, 172; on mind's continued existence apart from brain, 273 ff.; and personal immortality, 281.
Jamnia, council of, 149.
Jefferson, H. B., 147.
Jeremiah, 150.
Jesus, 71, 75, 149, 174, 197, 198; and human suffering, 151, 153-155; and prayer, 253; and personal immortality, 291; and the resurrection, 268 ff.; his resurrection, 282. *See* Christianity.
Jewish thought, 148 ff. *See* Hebrew thought; Judaism.
Job, 29, 151, 152, 225; pessimism in, inconsistent, 182.
John, St., 96.
Jonah, 140.
Jones, Rufus, 95, 96.
Joseph of Aramathea, 270.
Judaism, 46, 75, 147, 148, 267. *See* Jewish thought; Hebrew thought.
justice, 152.

Kant, I., 43-45, 51, 80-83, 85-94, 100-102, 104, 105, 108, 124, 126, 176, 226, 258; and the three classical arguments for the existence of God, 79 ff.; his constructive view of God's existence, 85 ff.; an appraisal of, 91 ff.; and the substance view, 187; asserting both freedom and determinism, 226-229; and the

moral argument for personal immortality, 279.
Khayyam, Omar, 153.
Kismet, 223.
knowledge, Greek conceptions of, 77; Aquinas on, 78 ff.; Kantian theory of, 86, 228, 229; subjective and objective idealism, 103, 104; and feeling, 98, 99; intimate senses, 286; religious, 77 ff.; religious empiricism, 115 ff., 118, 120 ff.; critical monism, 117, 120 ff. *See totum simul; a priorism;* religious *a priorism;* subconscious; intuition and intuitionism; mysticism; revelation; reason, inadequacy of; intellect and feeling.
Koheleth, 151-153; and pessimism, 182.

Laird, John, 129 ff., 133 ff.
Lamont, C., 263 ff., 279.
laughter, 30; religious significance, 59.
law, natural, 244, 245, 268; and theodicy, 165 ff.; and prayer, 247, 251, 253; present-day conception of, 213; statistical, 244, 245.
Laws, the, 76, 82.
Lawton, G., 283.
legends, 270.
Leibniz, G. W., theodicy of, 161-162.
Leuba, J. H., 260.
liberalism, religious, *see* religious liberalism.
libertarianism, extreme, 214, 216 ff., 235. *See* freedom.
liberty of indifference, 217.
Lincoln, A., 278-279.
Lodge, Oliver, 285, 289, 290.
logic, mathematical or symbolic, 35.
logos, 197, 199, 200; Stoic, 195.
Longfellow, 272.
Lotze, R. H., 105.
Lough Derg, 8 ff.
lower criticism, *see* historical criticism; criticism, biblical.
Luck, 223.
Luther and Lutheranism, 135, 224.

MacFadden, B., 225.
Macintosh, D. C., 139, 251; argument for God, 115 ff.; theodicy

of, 164 ff.; and personal immortality, 290, 291.
Mackay, W. M., 160.
Mackenzie, D. A., 10.
magic, 252.
Magna Mater, cult of, 14 ff.
Mahavira, 52.
Mani, 156.
Manichaeism, 156.
Martin, E. D., 170.
Martineau, J., 39.
Massoretes, the, 149; Massoretic text, 149.
materialism, 199, 262, 263, 265, 266.
mathematics, modern and infinity, 124.
McDougall, W., 160, 197.
McTaggart, J. M. E., 135, 291.
mechanism, 84, 85, 211, 213, 220, 222, 223, 226-229, 242, 243, 245; Kant on, 87.
"Medieval Synthesis," the, 76 ff.
mediums, *see* seances.
Meinong, A., 143.
meliorism, 118 ff., 183.
memory, 276, 280.
Messiah, the, 151.
metaphysics, 107, 109, 117, 119, 124-126, 200, 207, 217, 218; and determinism, 223; and human freedom, 213 ff.; and freedom—three types of, 215-216; and value, 140 ff., 143, 144; and pessimism, 174 ff., 177 ff., 182; and theodicy, *see* theodicy; of Kant, 226; of Hegel, Green, Bradley, 229 ff.; of Royce, 231 ff.; of Aquinas, 233 ff.; of James, Wm., 236 ff.; of Ward, 240 ff.; of Sheldon, 244 ff.
Methodism, 155.
Micah, 150.
Micklem, E. R., 160.
Miles, Sir Owayne, 9.
Milton, 147.
mind and body, 260, 276; and belief in personal immortality, 272 ff. *See* dependence of mind upon brain.
mind, freedom from matter, 293, 294.
mind, philosophies of, 186.
miracle, 166, 271; defined in two senses, 268.

Modernism, 53. *See* religious liberalism.
Mohammedanism, 46, 223.
Moore, G. E., 132-135.
moral argument, 108 ff., 117, 126; Kant's, 85 ff.; and appraisal of Kant's, 91 ff.; for immortality, 279 ff., 292.
moral consciousness and freedom, 236 ff. *See* moral responsibility.
moral disease *vs.* sin, 161. *See* original sin.
moral optimism, 115 ff., 118 ff., 168, 183, 291; phases of, 122, 123; and religious empiricism mutually contributory, 123 ff.
moral responsibility, 167, 169, 208, 216, 225, 227.
Morris, C. W., 186, 187.
Moxon, R. S., 156, 160.
Münsterberg, H., 144, 257.
Murchison, C., 222, 283.
Myers, F. W. H., 285.
mystery, 65; cults, 14, 189. *See* cults; religious cults; mysticism.
mysticism, 95 ff.; 100, 102, 105, 107, 110, 116, 117, 126, 144, 279; negative *vs.* affirmative types, 95 ff.; extreme, 52, 97, 257, extravagant claims, 95; on immortality, 282, 283; cults, 189; Oriental, 75, 77 ff.; Christian, 96; and the ontological argument, 97 ff.; 200. *See* Neo-Platonism; intuition.
mysterium tremendum, 41, 42, 49, 101 ff.
myths and theology, 27 ff.

natura naturans vs. natura naturata, 245.
naturalism, 119, 147, 260, 286, 288; of Aristotle, 192-194, 202, 205.
natural law, *see* law, natural.
natural sciences and causation, 241 ff.; and the reality-feeling, principle, 262.
natural selection, 85, 118.
Natural Theology, 83.
necessitarianism, 243. *See* determinism.
Neo-Platonism, 75-77, 96, 156, 158, 195-197, 201; and soul, 199 ff.
New Jerusalem, 284.

new realism, *see* realism, new.
New Testament, 147, 149, 224; on
the soul, 197.
Newton, J. F., 53, 164.
Nietzsche, F., 28.
Nirvana, 176, 182.
numinous, 102, 122.

objectification of qualities, 185.
occult phenomena, 284. *See*
seances.
Old Testament, 149; and the soul,
188, 197; on immortality, 197.
See Hebrews; Judaism.
omnipotence, 171, 172.
omniscience, 171, 172.
ontological argument, 80 ff., 85,
103, 117, 120, 126; two forms
of, 80; Hocking's revision of,
97 ff.; Macintosh on, 120 ff.
optimism, 118, 148, 158, 179, 180,
183, 205; "evolutional," 178;
vs. pessimism, 180, 183. *See*
moral optimism; meliorism;
pessimism.
options, kinds of, 112 ff.
order, in nature, 251. *See* law,
natural.
Oriental thought, 179, 269.
Origen, 199.
original sin, 156, 157, 219, 224;
reinterpreted, 158 ff. *See* freedom.
Orphic cult, 189 ff.
Otto, Rudolph, 41 ff., 49, 101, 102.

pain, 146, 148, 152, 168, 175, 178,
180, 181; *vs.* desire, 181. *See*
evil; suffering, human.
Paley, 83, 84.
Palmer, G. H., 135, 169.
pantheism, 52, 62, 75, 95, 100, 104,
140, 214, 221; and absolute idealism, 104.
parallelism, 226.
Parker, DeWitt, 141, 176.
parsimony, law of, 45, 46, 286.
Pascal, 96, 249, 278.
pathetic fallacy, *see* fallacy.
Patrick, St., 7 ff.
Patripassians, 155.
Paul, St., 96, 140, 197; psychology,
197, 198; and predestination,
224; on the soul, 267; on immortality, 197, 198; and Jesus'
resurrection, 269, 270.

Paulsen, F., 226.
Peirce, C., 218.
Pelagius, and Pelagians, 224.
Pentateuch, the, 197.
perception, religious, 122 ff.; *see*
knowledge; intuition; religious
realism; empiricism, religious.
Perry, Charner M., 141.
Perry, R. B., 124, 130, 131, 133,
135, 144, 146; relational theory
of value, 137 ff., 141.
Persian thought, 267.
pessimism, Chap. VII, 28 ff., 118,
119, 148, 164, 174 ff., 177 ff.,
205, 238, 260; radical, 179; general remarks on, 179 ff.; and
metaphysics, 182; *vs.* optimism,
180, 183; inconsistency in, 183;
of Koheleth, 182; of Job, 182.
See Schopenhauer; Von Hartmann; optimism.
Peter, St., 271.
petitio principii, 277. *See* fallacy,
of begging the question.
Peyote Cult, 16 ff.
Phaedo, the, 276, 277, 292.
Phelps, Wm. L., 5.
Philo, 196-198.
philosophy, and religion, *see* religion. *See* value; metaphysics.
Plato, 35, 68, 82, 83, 135, 188-191,
197,292; influences in his thought,
188 ff.; proof for God's existence, 76; on the soul, 188 ff.,
190-191, 193; and immortality,
276-278; *vs.* Paul, 198; Platonism, 75, 79, 188 ff., 193, 194,
196, 197, 200-203, 264-266;
Platonism and Orthodox Christianity, 201.
pleasure, 175, 180, 181. *See* pain;
happiness; hedonism.
Plotinus, 96, 197, 200. *See* Neo-
Platonism.
pluralism, metaphysical, 147;
James's, 237, 239; Ward's, 245,
246.
Podmore, F., 285.
Porter, F. C., 198.
positivism, 64, 119, 147, 260.
post hoc ergo propter hoc, 242.
pragmatism, 107, 110 ff., 119, 126,
208, 236, 240, 281; critique of
pragmatic argument for God's
existence, 116 ff.

Pratt, J. B., 40, 111, 261, 262.
prayer, reconsideration of, Chap. X; difficulties in, 247-248, 254; a negative way of meeting difficulties of, 248 ff.; five positive ways of meeting difficulties of, 250 ff.; real or petition, 249, 250, 252, 254; as fellowship, 248, 249; unanswered, 247, 252, 253; alleged answers, 247-249; and human insignificance, 247, 252; and autosuggestion, 248, 249; and natural law, 247, 251; and human attitudes, 252-254; and reason, 248-249; and magic, 252; and formal expression, 252, 254; and idea of God, 248-251; and idolatry, 250, 251; and emergence, 253. *See* God.
predestination, 156, 172, 223, 224 ff. *See* determinism.
prediction, scientific, 244, 245.
pre-existence, 189-191, 197, 199, 204, 259, 277.
primary qualities, *see* qualities.
principle of indeterminacy, *see* indeterminacy, principle of.
Pringle-Pattison, Seth, 278.
proof *vs.* possibility, 254, 271, 272, 276.
prophetic writings, 150 ff., 154.
Protestant thought, 206, 223, 224, 265; orthodoxy, 79, 219.
providence, 213, 214.
Psychical Research, Society of (S. P. R.), 282, 283, 285 ff.
psychology, faculty, *see* faculty psychology; Kant's, 92; physiological, 199; of religion, 266. *See* English school of psychologists; Gestalt, psychology; soul; schools of psychology.
Ptolemaic universe, 270.
punishment, 150-153, 157, 224, 260.
purgatory, 267, 268.
Purgatory, St. Patrick's, 7 ff.
Puritanism, New England, 24 ff.; and children, 24 ff.
Pym, T. W., 160.
Pythagoras and Pythagoreanism, 190.

Quakers, the, 53, 96, 97.
qualities, primary, 121, 133, 139; secondary, 121, 133, 139; tertiary, 122, 133.

Raphael, 279.
rationalization, 247.
Rave, John, 16 ff.
realism, metaphysical, Platonic, 68, 76, 81.
realism, new, 137, 139; and critical, 194. *See* knowledge.
realism, religious, of Macintosh, 115 ff. *See* religious realism.
reality-feeling, principle of, 259; 261 ff.
reason, inadequacy of, 278, 279, 291, 292. *See* intellect and feeling; mysticism; revelation; fallacy, of intellect.
Reese, C. W., 30.
Reformation, the, 96.
reification of abstractions, *see* fallacy.
Reinach, S., 50.
reincarnation, 189. *See* preexistence.
relational theory of value, *see* value.
relativity of values, *see* value.
religion, definitions and conceptions of; problem of definition, ix; criteria for defensible definitions, 55 ff.; adequate definition of, 37; mistaken notions of, Chap. II, 55, 56, 61, 62; "narrow conceptions" of, 46, 47, 55; "broad conceptions" of, 47 ff., 55; confusion of descriptive and normative definitions, 49 ff., 54-56; etymology of, 55; inadequacy of etymological approach, 36; psychological errors of, 38 ff., 55; further psychological errors, 44 ff.; as the expression of intellect, 38 ff.; as the expression of feeling, 39 ff.; as expression of will, 42 ff.; in terms of god, 51 ff., 56, 63; and ethics, confusion of, with, 48 ff., 50, 55; confusion of words, 36 ff., 55, 56; distinction between terms "religion," "a religion," and "religious," 56 ff.; naturalistic approach, 61, 68; Flower's conception of, 18; Cook's, 28 ff.; Martineau's, 39; Hegel's, 39; Schleiermacher's, 40; Otto's, 41 ff.; 49; *a priorism*, 42; St. James's conception

of, 42; lodge conception of, 43; Kant's, 43; Troeltsch's, 45, Starbuck's, 44; Parson Thwackum's, 46; Ames's, 48; Haydon's, 48; Reinach's, 50; Soper's, 50; H. W. Wright's, 50; W. A. Brown's, 51; Wilkinson's, 52; James's, Wm., 53 ff., 113, 114; author's conception of, 56 ff.; author's formal definition of, 61 ff.; 65 ff.; 68 ff.

religions, 221; and ethics, 44; lodge, 43, 48; and theology and philosophy, 69 ff.; and social patterns, 66 ff., 71.

religious, expression, misinterpretations of, 6 ff.; not purely religious, 5 ff., 9-12, 14, 16, 18, 19, 23, 24 ff., 32, 33, 56 ff.; attitude and fear, 19 ff., 23 ff.; and wonder, 26 ff., 30, 47; *a priorism,* 42, 45, 46, 55, 105; *a priorism* of Troeltsch, 100 ff.; *a priorism* of Otto, 101 ff.; instinct, 44 ff., 55; philosophy and value, 127, 128, 140 ff.; appreciation, impediments against, 123; individual *vs.* professional pugilist, 63 ff.; genius, 67; realism, 115 ff., 291; experience, testimony to existence of God, 94 ff.; experience and the empirical assurance of personal immortality, 290 ff.; conservatism and immortality, 265; liberalism and immortality, 264, 266, 267. *See* humanism, religious; revelation; immortality; mysticism; knowledge; adjustment right, *see* perception, religious, religious meliorism.

religious cults, 189 ff., 265, 269, 283 ff.; and philosophical in Graeco-Roman world, 194 ff. *See* cults.

religious meliorism, *see* moral optimism.

Renaissance, the, 96.
Renouvier, Charles, 124.
repression, 160.
Republic, the, 277.
resurrection, 198, 205, 267 ff.; obscurity of ideas, 267; idea psychologically motivated, 264 ff.; of Jesus, 268 ff., 282; difficulties of, 268 ff. *See* apologetics; immortality.

retribution, 150.
revelation, 75, 77-79, 97, 107, 205.
revival, the Kentucky, 10 ff.
Ritschl, A., 51, 105 ff., 127; Ritschlianism, 108, 110, 117; and the value-argument for God, 104 ff.
Rivers, W. H. R., 13, 14.
Robinson, D. S., 59.
romanticism, literary, 239.
Ross, W. D., 193.
Royce, J., 57, 58, 104, 147, 226, 234; and freedom, 231 ff.; and personal immortality, 282.
Ruskin, 285.
Russell, B., 170.
Russellites, 265.

Sabbath Day, Puritan, 24 ff.
salvation, 178-179, 182, 189 ff., 194 ff., 200, 205.
Santayana, G., 119, 133, 170, 256, 257.
Satan, *see* Devil, the.
Schelling, 96.
Schleiermacher, F. E. D., 40-42, 51, 65, 105.
scholastics, 204; medieval scholasticism and re-discovery of Aristotle, 201-202.
schools of psychology, 212, 222, 260. *See* psychology.
Schopenhauer, A., 177, 180-182; his pessimism, 174 ff.
"science," 36; modern, 27 ff.; scientific thinking, 35, 116, 251, 252, 260; knowledge not wholly objective, 106, 127; attitude and concept of causation, 241 ff.; approach and personal immortality, 273 ff. *See* causation; determinism; mechanism.
seances and mediums, 284, 285 ff.
secondary qualities, *see* qualities.
self determinism, *see* determinism.
Sellars, R. W., 170.
Septuagint, the, 196.
Shakespeare, 294.
Sheldon, W. H., 294; on freedom and determinism, 244, 245.
Sheol, 152, 188.
Shinto, religion, 59.
Sic et Non, 180.

Sidgwick, H., 133, 285.
Simmons, M., 278-279.
sin, as anachronism, 159; and moral disease, 161; reinterpreted, 158 ff. *See* original sin; evil.
skepticism, 150, 254; James on, 113.
Sneath, E. H., 198.
Socrates, 35, 190, 292.
Soper, E. D., 46, 50.
soul, 260; in ancient and medieval thought, Chap. VIII; creation of, 205; defence of, 294; mind, and concepts of substance, 186 ff.; hierarchy of, 203; ghost, the origin of notion, 184 ff.; primitive conception of, 184 ff., 188, 189; variety of conceptions of, 185; in Hebrew thought, 188; Greek thought, 267; in Aristotle's thought, 191 ff.; in Plato's thought, 188 ff.; in Platonism, 193; in Stoic thought, 194 ff.; early Christian doctrines of, 197 ff.; Greek and Eastern religious cults, 189 ff.; Graeco-Roman, religious and philosophical cults, 194 ff.; St. Paul on, 197, 198, 267; in the Gospels, 197, 198; and Neo-Platonism, 199 ff.; according to Augustine, 200-201; according to Clement, 198, 199; according to Galen, 199; Aquinas on, 202 ff.; recent theories of, 194, 206; separation from body in modern thought, 205 ff. *See* dichotomy; trichotomy; spirit.
Spaulding, E. G., 135.
Spencer and Gillen, 52.
Spinoza, 146, 223.
spirit, 195; and soul, 188, 197, 198. *See* soul.
spiritualism, 265, 269, 275, 282; *pro* and *con*, 288-290; modern and immortality, 283 ff.
Starbuck, E. D., 44, 286.
Stirling, J. H., 104.
Stoicism, 75, 101, 194 ff., 197, 223.
Streeter, B. H., 160, 283.
subconscious, the, 160, 286, 287.
subjectivism, James's, 238, 239.
sublimation, 160.
sub specie aeternitates, 146.

substance, 193; concepts of, 186 ff.; considerations in favor of, 187; anti-substance philosophies of mind, 194.
substantive, *see* substance.
suffering, human, 175 ff., 179 ff., 182; Jewish-Christian attitude toward, 148 ff.; as punishment, 150, 153, 154; as sharing in God's nature, 151, 153 ff.; enigma of, 152; human and immortality, 280. *See* pain; evil.
"Suffering Servant of Yahweh," 151.
suggestion, social, 269, 286.
suicide, gradual, 225.
summum bonum, 89, 90, 92.
supernatural, 77 ff., 286, 289.
supralapsarianism, 224.
supra-theism, *see* theism, supra.
survival, *see* immortality, personal.
Swedenborg, E., 284; Swedenborgians, 265.
Sweet, W. W., 19, 23.
Swift, A. L., 49.

Taoism, 46.
teleological argument, 76, 79, 80, 83 ff., 124-126.
teleology, 83-85, 137 ff., 141, 163, 209, 211, 212, 243, 244; and thinking, 225.
telepathy, 286, 293.
Tennant, F. R., 158, 159.
Tennyson, 285.
tertiary qualities, *see* qualities.
Tertullian, 198.
theism, Chap. IV, V, 62, 75, 82, 85, 93, 95, 110, 114, 115, 126, 140, 141, 145, 147, 170, 171, 214, 221, 279; supra-, 52, 62, 125, 126; theistic arguments, 76 ff.; the three classical arguments and the Kantian criticisms, 79 ff. *See* ontological argument; cosmological; teleological; moral; God.
theodicy, Chap. VII, 145; contemporary considerations in relation to, 162 ff.; a, impossible, 174; of ancient Hebrews, 150; of the prophets, 150 ff.; of Wisdom literature, 151 ff.; of Job, 152; of Koheleth, 152-153; of Jesus, 153 ff.; of Augustine, 155 ff.; of Aquinas, 157-158; of

Leibniz, 161-162; of Palmer, G. H., 169; of Macintosh, 164 ff.; of Brightman, 164; 170 ff. *See* evil.

theology, as an empirical science, 125, 291. And religion, *see* religion.

theophagy, 16.

Theosophists, 265.

Thomism, 78. *See* Aquinas, Thomas.

Thouless, R. H., 160.

Timaeus, the, 82.

time, 232-235, 257, 259, 282. *See totum simul.*

timological theory of value, *see* value.

tobacco, 18.

Todas, the, 52; the Toda-Dairy priests, 13 ff.

totum simul, 231-235.

traducianist view, 157, 198.

Traherne, T., 96.

transcendentalism, 53.

transmutation, theory of, 162.

trichotomy, 188, 195, 197, 198.

Trinity, the, 31, 79.

Troeltsch, E., 45, 100-102.

tychism, 218. *See* chance.

Tylor, E. B., 184.

uncials, the, 149.

unconscious, the, 177 ff.

uniformity, 243, 244.

Upanishads, 96.

Urban, W. M., 133, 135, 142-144.

value, 227, 243, 245, 252; kinds, 129, 140-142; psychological classification of, historical classification of, 142; current theories of, Chap. VI; some contemporary theories of, 129 ff.; appreciative view, 129, 131; as indefinable, 131-133, 135, 143; elective theory, 130-133, 135, 136; as interest, 137 ff.; biocentric-psychocentric theory of, 131; relational theory, 130, 131, 137 ff., 146; as intrinsic and absolute, 133-136; timological view, 133-136; absolutistic theory, 142 ff.; relative, 130, 132, 133, 135, 136, 143; elective and timological theories evaluated, 135 ff.; positive and negative

interests, 139 ff.; objective, 142 ff.; objective and subjective, 138-141; pleasure and pain, 180 ff.; and metaphysics, 140, 141, 143, 144; and religious philosophy, 127, 128, 140 ff.; and existence, 143, 144; gradation of generic, 141 ff.; in terms of comparison, 131, 132, 141 ff.; and logic, 144; immortality of, 256, 257; argument for existence of God, 120; and immortality, 279 ff., 292; -judgments, the two of Ritschl, 106. *See* Ritschlianism.

variations in nature, 244, 245.

version, King James, authorized, 149.

Virgin, Blessed, the, 31, 47.

virtue, 89 ff.

vitalism, 211.

Von Hartmann, 180, 181, 183; his pessimism, 177 ff.

War, the World, 261, 279.

Ward, James, 126, 179, 182; on freedom, 240 ff.

watch-maker theory, 83 ff.

Watson, John, 104.

Watson, J. B., 170, 222.

Weigle, L. A., 240.

White, A. D., 49.

Whitefield, 25.

Whitehead, A. N., 125, 212.

whole, the, 230, 231.

Wieman, H. N., 125, 126, 148.

Wilkinson, W. R., 52.

will, a psychological account of, 208 ff.; -power, 209, 210; impotence of, 218, 219; and freedom according to Aquinas, 233 ff. *See* freedom.

"Will to Believe," the, 111 ff.

Willett, H. L., 149.

Willoughby, H. R., 16.

Winnebago, the, 16 ff.

Wisdom literature, 151 ff.

wishful thinking, *see* fallacy.

Wolff, C., 80.

wonder and religious attitude, *see* religious attitude and wonder.

Woodworth, R. S., 208, 212.

worlds, *see* best of possible.

Wright, H. W., 50.

Zoroastrianism, 46.